SIX FRENCH POETS

SIX FRENCH POETS

STUDIES IN CONTEMPORARY LITERATURE

BY

AMY LOWELL

Essay Index Reprint Series

BOOKS FOR LIBRARIES PRESS, INC.
FREEPORT, NEW YORK

First published 1915
Reprinted 1967

LIBRARY OF CONGRESS CATALOG CARD NUMBER:
67-28737

PRINTED IN THE UNITED STATES OF AMERICA

PREFACE

In the Spring of 1914, I was invited to deliver a series of lectures on modern French poetry in Boston during the following winter. This book consists of those lectures, rewritten and arranged for the press.

It is a strange thing that while so many Americans and English repair every year to France, so few of them, in either country, realized what a serious and self-sacrificing people the French were making of themselves, before the present war brought the fact to their notice. To students of French literature, this was no matter for surprise. They understood that the earnest and single-minded endeavour applied to the arts must have its counterpart in other branches of the national life. That this was the case, is now abundantly proved. We, in the English-speaking countries, are asking ourselves how we could have so misunderstood the French people. But to be misunderstood has been the lot of Frenchmen when dealing with Anglo-Saxons from time immemorial.

The bar of language has something to do with it, undoubtedly. Another reason is the unfortunate attitude of our schools and colleges, which always assume that everything worthy to be called literature, and therefore studied, ceased, in every country, a generation or two ago. This has prevented the mass of English-speaking people from realizing that France has just been passing through one of the great poetical epochs of her career — one of the great poetical epochs of the world.

It may be argued that during this period she has produced no poet of the first order. No poet to rank with Homer, or Shakespeare, or Dante. That would indeed seem to be true; but we speak of the time of Wordsworth, and Coleridge, and Shelley, and Keats, as being one of England's great poetic periods; and we speak of Germany in the same way, during the time of Goethe and Schiller. Beginning with Lamartine and Victor Hugo, France has been having a succession of remarkable poets for eighty years. The war will end this period, perforce. For whatever great poets may arise after the war will belong to a new era. So titanic an upheaval as the present war must snap the period which preceded it off short.

It seems a fitting moment, then, to stop and take our bearings; and it seems a fitting moment to introduce to those English-speaking readers not already familiar with them the last poets of an era just closing.

The poets I have chosen for this volume belong to the generation immediately succeeding that of Verlaine and Mallarmé. They are, with the exception of one, all alive to-day. But they are in no sense to be ranked with *les jeunes*. They are men of middle age and undisputed fame, and, were French taught as it ought to be, their names would be household words with us as they are in their native land.

So far, however, is this from being the case, that few libraries contain all their works, and of the mass of critical writings which has sprung up about them, only a scattered volume here and there is obtainable. These facts have been brought to my notice again and again, and it is because of them that the present volume has seemed to fill a need.

I am farther emboldened by the very kind reception which the lectures received, and by the fact that, to my knowledge, there is no other English book which covers the same ground. Mr. Edmund Gosse's "French Profiles" contains brief critical essays on Régnier, Verhaeren, Samain, and Fort, but with no biographic material, and does not include Gourmont or Jammes; and Mr. Vance Thompson's "French Portraits" was written fifteen years ago, before some of these poets had produced their best work, and makes no pretence at being more than a pleasant, anecdotic account of the writers he mentions.

In the following essays, I have pursued a slightly different arrangement from the one usual in such cases. Instead of first giving a biographical account of the man, and then a critical survey of his work, I have followed his career as he lived it, and taken the volumes in the order in which they were written. I have tried to give the reader the effect of having known the man and read his books as they were published, commenting upon them as they came along. The biographies are slight, as must always be the case while their subjects are still living, but they have been taken from reliable sources.

I have made no attempt at an exhaustive critical analysis of the various works of these authors. Rather, I have tried to suggest certain things which appear to the trained poet while reading them. The pages and pages of hair-splitting criticism turned out by erudite gentle-

men for their own amusement, has been no part of my
scheme. But I think the student, the poet seeking new
inspiration, the reader endeavouring to understand another
poetic idiom, will find what they need to set them on
their way.

I have given many quotations — as the best way to
study an author is to read him — and for the convenience
of those readers, well versed in French prose but not yet
fully at home in French poetry, translations of the poems
will be found in an appendix. The translations are in
prose. Verse translations must always depart somewhat
from the original, on account of the exigencies of rhyme
and metre. As my desire was not to make English poems
about a French original, but to make the French poems
in the text understandable, I have sacrificed the form
to the content. The translations are exact, and in every
case reproduce, as far as is possible in another language,
the "perfume" of the poem. By reading them, and then
turning to the original and reading it aloud in French,
those least versed in the tongue will get an idea of the
music of the poem, while at the same time understanding
it. In order not to tease those readers perfectly ac-
quainted with French, no figures nor asterisks appear in
the text, but each translation is accompanied by the
number of the page on which the original is to be found.

Another appendix contains bibliographies of the works
of each author and a bibliography of books upon the
subject, for the use of those who wish to pursue it farther.

In preparing this volume my thanks are due to M.
Alfred Vallette, editor of the *Mercure de France*, for
courteously permitting me to reproduce the portraits of

Émile Verhaeren, Albert Samain, Henri de Régnier, and Francis Jammes, and to quote freely from all books published by the *Mercure*; to MM. Remy de Gourmont * and Paul Fort, for sending me, one a drawing, and the other a photograph, for reproduction; to Mrs. Arthur Hutchinson (Mlle. Magdeleine Carret) for invaluable assistance and information, — to her intimate knowledge of her own language, unerring taste, and trained critical faculty, I owe all that I have been able to acquire of the French tongue; to Mlle. Jeanne Chéron, for valuable suggestions of technical detail; and to Mr. F. S. Flint, whose wide reading and critical articles on modern French poetry in " Poetry and Drama " have been of great service to me, for lists of books and expert knowledge.

AMY LOWELL.

June 24, 1915.

---

* It is with a profound sense of personal loss that I record the death of M. de Gourmont on September 28th. The news was received while this book was passing through the press, too late to be incorporated in the text. I wish here to express my great admiration for his work, and my gratitude for an encouragement which even under the heavy weight of illness he did not stint to give. By his death France loses one of the greatest and most sincere artists of his generation.

CONTENTS

	PAGE
ÉMILE VERHAEREN	1
ALBERT SAMAIN	49
REMY DE GOURMONT	105
HENRI DE RÉGNIER	147
FRANCIS JAMMES	211
PAUL FORT	269
APPENDIX A: TRANSLATIONS	327
APPENDIX B: BIBLIOGRAPHY	467

LIST OF ILLUSTRATIONS

ÉMILE VERHAEREN . . . . . *Frontispiece*

FACING PAGE

ALBERT SAMAIN 49

REMY DE GOURMONT 105

HENRI DE RÉGNIER 147

FRANCIS JAMMES 211

PAUL FORT 269

xiii

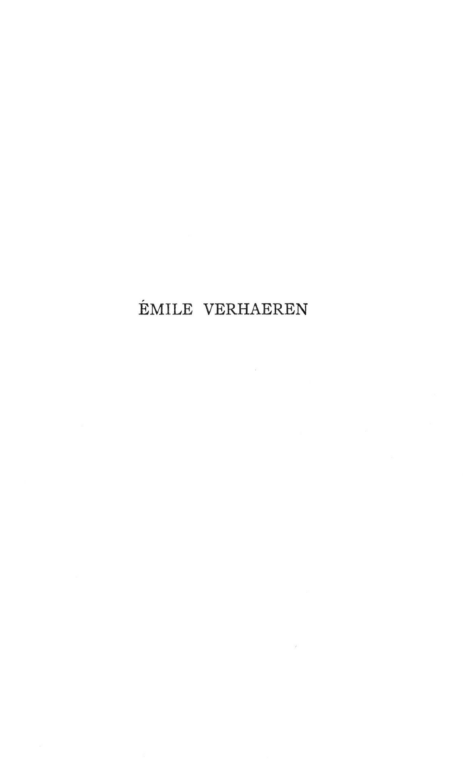

ÉMILE VERHAEREN

ÉMILE VERHAEREN

WHEN I planned this book, I realized that the name of Émile Verhaeren would be the best known of my group of six French poets. And I felt that I had a right to include him among French poets since he wrote in French. Now, the name of Émile Verhaeren is not only the best known name of my group, but a very well known name indeed. Newspapers and magazines are full of his fame, various publishers are issuing translations of his poems, and a translation of a German biography of him appeared a year ago. But the most important thing which time has effected in his regard is to divorce him forever from the stream of French literature. He ranks now, not only as the prophet of a new era, but as the authentic voice of a dead era. The Belgium he portrays has been devastated by war, and so completely crushed that at the moment it can hardly be said to exist. And even if in time the invaders are driven out, and Belgium is able to continue herself politically, it will be long before she will have leisure to devote her energies again to the arts. When that time does come, we may be very sure that it will be a different civilization with which the arts will have to deal. The pathetic splendour of circumstance, therefore, must always hang over Verhaeren's work, and enhance its natural greatness still farther. Future ages will not only study him as a great poet, but as an accurate portrayer of life in Belgium before the war. His artistic value, for many years at least, is bound to be overshadowed by his historic value. He stands out as the finest flower of a ruined country, and as such can never again be contemplated as merely walking step by step with the writers of any other country, no matter how great. At present, however, the war is still too new to be regarded in this perspective ; to us who are living not only to-day, but in such close relation to yesterday, it is enough to point out what must be Verhaeren's future position, and then return and consider him as he has hitherto appeared to our own generation.

To-day, Verhaeren is a man sixty years old, with twenty-three volumes of poems, three volumes of plays, and four volumes of prose to his credit. He has been writing for over thirty years, and has had a great influence upon young writers all over the world. It is in this connection which we shall consider him here. What future work he will do will belong to that after-the-war period which we can only dimly foresee. At the actual time of writing, Verhaeren has fled to England, where he has found an asylum and sympathetic friends. Vigorous as he is, the poems which he may write there will belong to a new epoch in his career, and with them future students of his work will have to deal. Our consideration of him ends with the war.

In understanding Verhaeren, one must first understand the conditions into which he was born. One of the great interests in his poetry is the effect it has had in changing and modifying those conditions. In 1868, Hippolyte Taine wrote — in his chapter on "The Painting in the Low Countries" in his "Philosophy of Art" — "to-day this literature hardly exists." Since then, Belgium has given us Verhaeren and Maeterlinck, in company with a host of lesser writers. Such fecundity is astonishing, and has called out a large number of volumes devoted to the study of so remarkable a phenomenon. And all since 1880, a period of little more than thirty years ! In his *Mouvement Littéraire Belge d'Expression Française*, M. Albert Heumann points out that "a fecund and independent literature commonly exists in a country of perfect material prosperity, and of an absolute political autonomy." That this is true, witness the ages of Pericles, the Emperor Augustus, and Louis XIV ; the period of the Renaissance in Italy ; or the England of Elizabeth, Queen Anne, or George IV ;

and we see the fact again in France at the present day.

Since 1831, when Belgium forced herself upon the Powers as a separate nation and elected a king to suit herself, she has enjoyed extraordinary prosperity. The enormous energy of the people has developed their unusual natural facilities to the fullest extent. There are the coal fields in the Boisinage district near Mons, and in the neighbourhood of Liége. There are iron mines, and iron and steel works, at Charleroi and Liége. There are quarries of marble, granite, and slate. Ghent is the capital of a vast textile industry; and lace is manufactured all over the country, Brussels point being famous throughout the world. But this is not all, Belgium carries on (or, alas! carried on) an enormous commerce. Antwerp is one of the largest and most important ports in the world. And again, this is not all, for Belgium is an agricultural country chiefly, and where everything is on so superlative a scale, "chiefly" means a great deal. In fact, it has about six and one-half millions of acres under cultivation. In this little bit of a country, less than half as big as the state of Maine, such an acreage is enormous.

But side by side with this booming modernism lives the other Belgium — mystic, superstitious — where moss-grown monasteries stand beside sluggish canals, and the angelus rings across flat, wind-blown fields. Belgium is a strange mixture of activities, races, and opinions. Roman Catholics and Socialists dispute for control of the government, and authors write and publish in German and French, some fanatics even insist on doing so in Flemish, and agitate to have Flemish taught in the schools, a desire with which the Celtic movement in Ireland has made us familiar.

In the little town of Saint-Amand in East Flanders, southwest of Antwerp and east of Ghent, on the river Escaut, Émile Verhaeren was born on the twenty-first of May, 1855. His father, Gustave Verhaeren, was the son of a cloth merchant of Brussels. His mother was a Mlle. Debock, a native of Saint-Amand, where her brother was proprietor of an oil plant. And presumably Gustave Verhaeren chose to live in Saint-Amand on account of his wife's connection in the country. The Verhaerens were probably of Dutch extraction, but the Debocks were certainly French (some centuries before, it is needless to say, as both families can be traced to different parts of Belgium in the eighteenth century). Curiously enough, only French was spoken in Gustave Verhaeren's household, and the servants all came from Liége. Émile Verhaeren has never known Flemish, although he took some lessons in it from the schoolmaster in the village, when he was seven years old.

Saint-Amand stands in a country of wide hori-

zons, where windmills stretch out their arms to the
sky, and broad clouds sweep over it, trailing their
shadows on the flat plain below. It is a grey,
northern country, of fogs and strong winds. All
these things impressed themselves upon the little
Verhaeren's brain, and became a natural part of his
consciousness, and the objects of his greatest love.
As the boy Constable is said to have grown familiar
with clouds, and to have acquired a love for them,
in tending his father's windmill, so the boy Verhaeren must have got his knowledge of weather and
skies while wandering along the level, paved roads
of East Flanders, buffeted by the wind and washed
by the sun, or while lying in bed listening to the
rain splash on tiled roofs, and patter against the
shutters. His poems are full of weather. They
are almost a "line-a-day" book of temperatures and
atmospheres. Take this of a violent wind, for instance :

> Un poing d'effroi tord les villages;
> Les hauts clochers, dans les lointains,
> Envoient l'écho de leurs tocsins
>   Bondir de plage en plage.

or this, of a gentle one :

> Le vent chante, le vent babille
> avec pinson, tarin, moineau,
> le vent siffle, brille et scintille
> à la pointe des longs roseaux,

le vent se noue et s'entrelace et se dénoue
et puis, soudain, s'enfuit jusqu'aux vergers luisants,
là-bas, où les pommiers, pareils à des paons blancs,
— nacre et soleil — lui font la roue.

Take this, of clouds :

Et Septembre, là-haut,
Avec son ciel de nacre et d'or voyage,
Et suspend sur les prés, les champs et les hameaux
Les blocs étincelants de ses plus beaux nuages.

Or this, of a little river :

L'entendez-vous, l'entendez-vous
Le menu flot sur les cailloux ?
Il passe et court et glisse,
Et doucement dédie aux branches,
Qui sur son cours se penchent,
Sa chanson lisse.

Gustave Verhaeren, his wife and little son, lived
in a cottage of their own, with a garden blazing full
of flowers. Behind it stretched the fields of yellow
wheat, and close beside it ran the slow river. In
one of his last books, Verhaeren has described his
childhood. He tells us how he played in the great
barns, and climbed steeples, and listened to the
maids singing old Flemish songs at their washing.
He describes himself sitting with the watchmaker
and marvelling at the little wheels of the watches,

and standing on the bank of the river and looking
at the heavy cargo boats sail by.

> Je me souviens du village près de l'Escaut,
> D'où l'on voyait les grands bateaux
> Passer ainsi qu'un rêve empanaché de vent
> Et merveilleux de voiles.
> Le soir en cortège sous les étoiles.

By and by, he was sent to school in Brussels for
two years, at the Institute Saint Louis; and when
he was thirteen or fourteen, he entered the Jesuit
College of Sainte-Barbe in Ghent. Here, a few
years later, came Maeterlinck also, but whether the
boys met there I have not been able to find out.

It had been decided in the family that Émile
should enter his uncle's oil works, and succeed to
the business. In the pleasant way of families from
time immemorial, this had apparently been arranged
without consulting Émile's wishes in the matter.
At twenty, the boy had finished his college course,
and he did come back to Saint-Amand and go into
the oil works for a year. But the life was most
distasteful to him; he needed to see the world, to
measure himself intellectually with other young
men, and there is no reason to suppose that he
showed the slightest taste or ability for business.
In order, however, to find some plausible reason for
his dislike of the work, he pleaded to be allowed to
study law. Whether he had tried writing at this

period and felt any desire to become a poet, I do not know. But to persuade a practical father and uncle to consent to his giving up a lucrative business in order to become a poet, would not be a simple task. And certainly in asking to become a lawyer, Émile stood more chance of having his wish granted.

It was granted. And young Verhaeren left home again to study law at the University of Louvain.

At Louvain, Verhaeren really did study law, strangely enough, and was graduated in 1881. But he did many other things also. He danced at *Kermesses,* drank beer, got drunk, and generally overdid things with the true Flemish ardour, whether for work or play. Among his fellow students there were various other tentative poets. Together they got up a little paper called *La Semaine,* and Verhaeren published several pieces in it, under the pseudonym of "Rodolph." That various of the traits which later distinguished the work of this new generation of Flemish writers were already in evidence, is apparent from the fact that the paper was suppressed by the University authorities in 1881, fifteen months after its foundation.

Here was Verhaeren, a full-fledged barrister, entering the office of Edmond Picard in Brussels. But his heart was not in the work, and he conducted the one or two quite unimportant cases he had to plead so half-heartedly, that Maître Picard, himself, advised him to give up the law.

During this time, an intellectual ferment had been going on in the young poet. Brought up as a Roman Catholic, educated in a Jesuit college, he had been ardent and devout. Yet, even then, the Jesuits had failed to persuade him to become a priest. Now, with every year, his zest for living grew, his mind expanded and dared, and Catholicism dropped away from him forever. The mystic side of the Flemish character was to show itself in quite a different form, and only much later.

In Brussels, Verhaeren found a set of young men, eager like himself, anxious to stamp themselves into literature. Zola's realistic novels were just beginning to be discussed in Belgium, and Camille Lemonnier was the interpreter of this new naturalism. And just as a whole generation of younger writers in France adopted Zola's theories, so did they attract the younger writers of Belgium. And really the protest was necessary to down that long set of sentimental hypocrisies known in England as "Victorian." For France and Belgium had their "Victorian" periods, too, although under different names.

In order to flaunt the banner of free, realistic art, with no taboos (as the current slang of the reviews calls it), a remarkable and intelligent young man, Max Waller, poet and writer of short stories, got up a review entitled *La Jeune Belgique*. In its effect on Belgian letters, this review has been compared to the *Mercure de France* and its place in

French literature. The early death of the founder of *La Jeune Belgique* kept it from becoming the world-famous periodical it might have been. While it existed, it gave an opening for many remarkable young men, among others, Verhaeren.

A pleasant anecdote is told of him at this time, how one rainy day he clumped into Lemonnier's lodgings (never having met Lemonnier, by the way), and blurted out, "Je veux vous lire des vers!" And what he read was the manuscript of his first book, *Les Flamandes*.

Lemonnier encouraged him, criticised him, and, shortly after, the book was published. Then the storm broke, and howled about Verhaeren. The book was strong, vivid, brutal. It was as violent, as coarse, as full of animal spirits, as the pictures of Breugel the Elder, Teniers, or Jan Steen. As one of the critics said, "M. Verhaeren pierced like an abscess." The critics were horrified, his own quite orthodox family was deeply shocked. The battle waged furiously. All those adherents of the old order of sentimental idealization fell upon the book, and in the columns of *L'Europe* Lemonnier strongly defended it.

And really it is a startling book, written with a sort of fury of colour. The red, fat flesh tints of Rubens have got into it, and the pages seem hot and smoky with perspiration. The desire to paint seems engrained in the Flemish character; M. Heu-

man declares that all Belgian writers, whether of
poetry or prose, are painters.   But, also, it must
not be forgotten that they are Flemish painters,
and their palettes are hot and highly coloured.   In
his poem, *Les Vieux Maîtres*, Verhaeren speaks of
these old masters as painting "les fureurs d'estomac,
de ventre et de débauche."   The description applies
equally well to his own poems in this book.   They
are marvellously done, blazing with colour and bla-
tant with energy.

Metrically, *Les Flamandes* is not particularly interesting, being written in the ordinary French
alexandrine.   The interest of the book lies in its
treatment of subjects.   Many of the most remarkable poems must be read in their context, but there
is a series of interiors, little Flemish *genre* pictures,
which show the vivid style in which the whole is
written.   This is one of them :

LA CUISINE

Le seuil de la cuisine était vieux et fendu.
Le foyer y brillait comme une rouge flaque,
Et ses flammes, mordant incessamment la plaque,
Y rongeaient un sujet obscène en fer fondu.

Le feu s'éjouissait sous le manteau tendu
Sur lui, comme l'auvent par-dessus la baraque,
Dont les clairs bibelots en bois, en cuivre, en laque,
Crépitaient moins aux yeux que le brasier tordu.

Les rayons s'échappaient comme un jet d'émeraudes,
Et, ci et là, partout donnaient des chiquenaudes
De clarté vive aux brocs de verre, aux plats d'émail.

A voir sur tout relief tomber des étincelles,
On eût dit — tant le feu s'émiettait par parcelles —
Qu'on vannait du soleil à travers un vitrail.

Notice how wonderfully bright and sparkling it all is, — "the snapping of light in the glasses" and the fire "crumbling itself into sparks." How excellently the word "crumbling" gives the up and down effect of firelight!

Les Flamandes appeared in 1883, and it was not until 1886 that Verhaeren's next book, *Les Moines*, published by quite a different firm, came out. Why Verhaeren changed his publisher, we do not know. Why he changed his whole manner of writing can be guessed.

I have said that the Flemish character is made up of two parts, one composed of violent and brutal animal spirits, the other of strange, unreasoning mysticism. This is shown by the fact that along the line of material prosperity the Belgians have advanced with leaps and bounds, while on the line of abstract ideas, of philosophical or scientific enlightenment, they have contributed almost nothing to the world. Their aspirations toward a broader point of view led them only to the Utopia of the materialistic socialist. Verhaeren himself, with all his effort and achievement, can never quite free himself from the trammels of the material. Because the idealistic side of the Belgian mind is feeble and poor, and cannot get along without the swaddling clothes of superstition, Belgian mysticism is charming, poetic, but — gets us nowhere.

Whether Verhaeren wrote *Les Moines* to satisfy the need of expression for this gentler side of his nature, whether his painter's eye was fascinated by the pictorial value of old monasteries and quiet monks, or whether he wished to prove to the world that he could do things that were not violent, it is impossible to say. None of his biographers has suggested the last reason. Presumably they would consider it beneath him, but I see no cause to suppose so great a man as Verhaeren to be in any way inhuman. And certainly to show the world that he has more than one string to his lute is a very natural desire in a young poet.

Les Moines is a sad book, a faded book. The monasteries are here, but bathed in the light of a pale sunset. As a boy, Verhaeren used often to go to the Bernhardine Monastery at Bornhem with his father. In order to renew his impressions of cloister life before writing this book, he passed three weeks at the monastery of Forges, near Chimay, and much of the book was written there.

There is nothing in *Les Moines* to detain us here.

It is a book of delicate etchings, pensive and melancholy, and again written in French alexandrines. In this book, more than in *Les Flamandes*, Verhaeren seems to be feeling his way.

Then Verhaeren broke down. He had travelled a great deal, had been to France, Germany, Spain, and England. That he had been overdoing, overthinking, is obvious. At any rate, he succumbed to what seems to have been a bad attack of nervous prostration, with gastric complications. Herr Zweig, in his exhaustive biography, spends a great deal of time in telling us how he had to have the door-bell taken off because he could not bear its ringing, and how the people in the house had to go about in felt slippers. Herr Zweig is delighted with *Les Soirs*, *Les Débâcles*, and *Les Flambeaux Noirs*, published respectively in 1887, 1888, and 1890, because he considers them so remarkable a portrayal of an unusual state of mind, and says they must be "priceless to pathologists and psychologists." I suspect that if Herr Zweig lived in America he would not be so interested in the description of what is to us quite a common occurrence. I do not suppose there is a person who will read these lines, who has not either been there himself or had a friend who has.

That Verhaeren should have written three books during his illness is not surprising. Writers always write, no matter how ill they are. With them it is so natural a function that it tires them less than to

c

do anything else. I could adduce a host of examples to prove this point, but two will do : Francis Parkman and Robert Louis Stevenson. I will quote two poems from *Les Soirs*, not because of their interest to the pathologist and psychologist, but because they are such remarkable pictures, and because they show that wedding of sound to sense which is to become one of Verhaeren's most characteristic powers.

LONDRES

Et ce Londres de fonte et de bronze, mon âme,
Où des plaques de fer claquent sous des hangars,
    Où des voiles s'en vont, sans Notre-Dame
Pour étoile, s'en vont, là-bas, vers les hasards.

Gares de suie et de fumée, où du gaz pleure
Ses spleens d'argent lointain vers des chemins d'éclair,
    Où des bêtes d'ennui bâillent à l'heure
Dolente immensément, qui tinte à Westminster.

Et ces quais infinis de lanternes fatales,
Parques dont les fuseaux plongent aux profondeurs,
    Et ces marins noyés, sous les pétales
Des fleurs de boue où la flamme met des lueurs.

Et ces châles et ces gestes de femmes soûles,
Et ces alcools de lettres d'or jusques aux toits,
    Et tout à coup la mort, parmi ces foules ;
O mon âme du soir, ce Londres noir qui traîne en toi !

See how long and slow the cadence is, and the heavy consonants make the poem knock and hum like the Westminster bells he mentions. It almost seems as though Big Ben must have been striking when he wrote the poem.

This intermixture of sound with pure painting is one of Verhaeren's most remarkable traits. In this next poem, *Le Moulin*, we have another sombre landscape, but the whole movement is different; from the first line we are conscious of sound, but it is no longer the insistent beating which underlies *Londres*; it is a sort of sliding, a faint, rushing noise. Any one reading the first stanza aloud cannot fail to be conscious of it. It is this presence of sounds in his verse, quite apart from the connotations of his words, which gives Verhaeren's work its strange, magic reality, and makes it practically impossible to translate.

LE MOULIN

Le moulin tourne au fond du soir, très lentement,
Sur un ciel de tristesse et de mélancolie,
Il tourne et tourne, et sa voile, couleur de lie,
Est triste et faible et lourde et lasse, infiniment.

Depuis l'aube, ses bras, comme des bras de plainte,
Se sont tendus et sont tombés ; et les voici
Qui retombent encor, là-bas, dans l'air noirci
Et le silence entier de la nature éteinte.

Un jour souffrant d'hiver sur les hameaux s'endort,
Les nuages sont las de leurs voyages sombres,
Et le long des taillis qui ramassent leurs ombres,
Les ornières s'en vont vers un horizon mort.

Autour d'un pâle étang, quelques huttes de hêtre
Très misérablement sont assises en rond ;
Une lampe de cuivre est pendue au plafond
Et patine de feu le mur et la fenêtre.

Et dans la plaine immense, au bord du flot dormeur,
Elles fixent — les très souffreteuses bicoques ! —
Avec les pauvres yeux de leurs carreaux en loques,
Le vieux moulin qui tourne et, las, qui tourne et meurt.

Before we leave these three books, I want to give
one more poem, *La Morte*, which is a sort of end
dedication to *Les Flambeaux Noirs*. Here, at last,
Verhaeren begins to use that extraordinary *vers libre*
for which he is afterwards to be so noted. Some
poets seem capable of expressing themselves perfectly in the classic alexandrine, some can use both
old and new forms according to the content of the
poem. Verhaeren's intimate friend, Henri de Régnier, is remarkable for this. But the alexandrine
has never seemed to fit Verhaeren. His tumultuous
nature seems cramped by its limitations. Figure
the "Siegfried Idyl" played by an orchestra of flutes,
and harps, and tambourines, and you will see what

I mean; or imagine Schumann's "Fantasie, Op.
17" spiritedly executed upon the harpsichord!
Verhaeren's *vers libre* is always rhymed. And in
a language so abounding in rhyme as the French,
that is no handicap to the free poet. Not only does
Verhaeren use end rhymes, he cannot resist the joy
of internal rhymes. But I am anticipating, for in
La Morte, as you will see, there are very few internal
rhymes, although his fondness for alliteration and
assonance begins to be noticeable. For the rest,
La Morte is a beautiful, foggy picture, sad, but with
a kind of sadness which is already beginning to
enjoy itself in a sombre sort of way. In other words,
Verhaeren is beginning to get well, but he is not
quite willing to admit it yet.

LA MORTE

En sa robe, couleur de fiel et de poison,
Le cadavre de ma raison
Traîne sur la Tamise.

Des ponts de bronze, où les wagons
Entrechoquent d'interminables bruits de gonds
Et des voiles de bateaux sombres
Laissent sur elle, choir leurs ombres.

Sans qu'une aiguille, à son cadran, ne bouge,
Un grand beffroi masqué de rouge
La regarde, comme quelqu'un
Immensément de triste et de défunt.

Elle est morte de trop savoir,
De trop vouloir sculpter la cause,
Dans le socle de granit noir,
De chaque être et de chaque chose,
Elle est morte, atrocement,
D'un savant empoisonnement,
Elle est morte aussi d'un délire
Vers un absurde et rouge empire.
Ses nerfs ont éclaté,
Tel soir illuminé de fête,
Qu'elle sentait déjà le triomphe flotter
Comme des aigles, sur sa tête.
Elle est morte n'en pouvant plus,
L'ardeur et les vouloirs moulus,
Et c'est elle qui s'est tuée,
Infiniment exténuée.

Au long des funèbres murailles,
Au long des usines de fer
Dont les marteaux tonnent l'éclair,
Elle se traîne aux funérailles.

Ce sont des quais et des casernes,
Des quais toujours et leurs lanternes,
Immobiles et lentes filandières
Des ors obscurs de leurs lumières :
Ce sont des tristesses de pierres,
Maison de briques, donjon en noir
Dont les vitres, mornes paupières,
S'ouvrent dans le brouillard du soir ;

Ce sont de grands chantiers d'affolement,
Pleins de barques démantelées
Et de vergues écartelées
Sur un ciel de crucifiement.

En sa robe de joyaux morts, que solennise
L'heure de pourpre à l'horizon,
Le cadavre de ma raison
Traîne sur la Tamise.

Elle s'en va vers les hasards
Au fond de l'ombre et des brouillards,
Au long bruit sourd des tocsins lourds,
Cassant leur aile, au coin des tours.
Derrière elle, laissant inassouvie
La ville immense de la vie ;
Elle s'en va vers l'inconnu noir
Dormir en des tombeaux de soir,
Là-bas, où les vagues lentes et fortes ;
Ouvrant leurs trous illimités,
Engloutissent à toute éternité :
Les mortes.

In one line of this poem Verhaeren has given us
the real cause of his illness. His reason has died,
he says, " from knowing too much." Or, to paraphrase this, his sanity has fled before the vision of
a more extended knowledge. The mystic and the
modern man have been struggling within him. It is
this struggle which has forced so many French poets
back to the Catholic Church. But Verhaeren was
made of more resisting stuff. The struggle downed

him, but did not betray him. He fell back into no
open arms; by sheer effort he pushed himself up
on his feet.

I should have said that for some reason or other,
Verhaeren spent most of these years of illness in
London. His biographers imagine that the fog and
gloom, what one of them calls the "melancholy
scenery of industrial cities," was in harmony with
his mood. Perhaps this is true, and if so I think
we are right in believing that his state of mind had
more to do with his illness than the poor digestion
to which it is usually attributed. However that
may be, Verhaeren got better. He came out of his
illness, as is usually the case with strong people, a
sane, more self-reliant man. He left the obscurity
of London side streets to plunge into the stream of
active life in the cities of his native Belgium.

In 1891, Verhaeren published two volumes of
poems, with two different publishers. One, *Les
Bords de la Route*, is a collection of poems written
at the time of *Les Flamandes* and *Les Moines*; the
other, *Apparus dans Mes Chemins*, marks the beginning of a new epoch. Verhaeren is feeling the zest
of life again, but it is a more spiritual zest than
before, if one can use the term for such a very
materialistic spirituality. Verhaeren is waking up,
as it were, like a man stretching his arms, not yet
fully awake. *Saint Georges* is probably the best
known poem of the volume; it begins charmingly:

Ouverte en large éclair, parmi les brumes,
Une avenue ;
Et Saint Georges, fermentant d'ors,
Avec des plumes et des écumes,
Au poitrail blanc de son cheval, sans mors,
Descend.

L'équipage diamentaire
Fait de sa chute, un triomphal chemin
De la pitié du ciel, vers notre terre.

But it has too few of Verhaeren's peculiar excellencies to be worth quoting in full. As my purpose in this book is to show and study each poet's individual characteristics, I shall only quote those poems which most evidently illustrate them.

And now we have come to Verhaeren's great period ; to the books which have made him the greatest poet of Belgium, and one of the greatest poets of the world. *Les Campagnes Hallucinées* appeared in 1893, *Les Villages Illusoires* in 1895, and also in 1895, *Les Villes Tentaculaires.* In these three books we have all Verhaeren's excellencies in rich profusion. Here are the towns, with their smoking factories, crowded streets, noisy theatres, and busy wharves ; here are the broad, level plains of Flanders starred with windmills, the little villages and farms, and the slow river where fishermen come. And here are painted a whole gallery of trades : cabinet-makers, blacksmiths, millers, rope-walkers. We see the

peasants selling everything they possess to follow
the long, white roads to the city — white tentacles
for the swallowing city. And weather! In these
volumes, Verhaeren first shows that remarkable
series of weather pieces to which I referred in the
beginning of this essay. Verhaeren had found himself. At a time when France was in the midst of
Symbolisme; when nature, divorced from the pathetic fallacy, made little general appeal; when
every-day life was considered dull, and not to be
thought about if possible; — Verhaeren wrote of
nature, of daily happenings, and of modern inven-
tions. He not only wrote, he not only sang; he
shrieked, and cut capers, and pounded on a drum.

Writing in French, Verhaeren has never been able
to restrain himself within the canons of French
taste. His effervescing nature found the French
clarity and precision, that happy medium so
cherished by the Gallic mind, as hampering as he
would have found Greek artistic ideals had he lived
several centuries earlier. He *must* put three rhymes
one after the other if he felt like it; he *must* have a
couple of assonances in a line, or go on alliterating
down half a page. There was nothing in his nature
to make the ideas of the *Symbolistes* attractive to
him; he would none of them. The mysticism of
which I have spoken modified itself into a great
humanitarian realization. He believed in mankind,
in the future. Not precisely (nothing is precise

with Verhaeren), but vaguely, magnificently, with all the faith his ancestors had placed in the Church.

A Frenchman would have felt constrained to put some definiteness into these hopes. To give some form to what certainly amounted to a religion. Verhaeren was troubled by no such teasing difficulty. He simply burned with a nebulous ardour, and was happy and fecund. This is one of the reasons why Verhaeren's poetry is so much better understood and appreciated by Englishmen and Americans — Anglo-Saxons in short — and by Germans, than any other French poetry. There is a certain Teutonic grandeur of mind in Verhaeren which is extremely sympathetic to all Anglo-Saxons and Germans. Where the French intellect seems coldly analytic and calm, Verhaeren charms by his fiery activity.

One of the devices which Verhaeren employs with consummate skill, is onomatopœia, or using words which sound like the things described. (This is at once wedded to, and apart from, the sort of sound I have mentioned above.) He carries this effect through whole poems, and it is one of the reasons for the vividness of his poems on nature.

An excellent example of this is *La Pluie* from *Les Villages Illusoires*.

LA PLUIE

Longue comme des fils sans fin, la longue pluie
Interminablement, à travers le jour gris,
Ligne les carreaux verts avec ses longs fils gris,
Infiniment, la pluie,
La longue pluie,
La pluie.

Elle s'effile ainsi, depuis hier soir,
Des haillons mous qui pendent,
Au ciel maussade et noir.
Elle s'étire, patiente et lente,
Sur les chemins, depuis hier soir,
Sur les chemins et les venelles,
Continuelle.

Au long des lieues,
Qui vont des champs, vers les banlieues,
Par les routes interminablement courbées,
Passent, peinant, suant, fumant,
En un profil d'enterrement,
Les attelages, bâches bombées ;
Dans les ornières régulières
Parallèles si longuement
Qu'elles semblent, la nuit, se joindre au firmament,
L'eau dégoutte, pendant des heures ;
Et les arbres pleurent et les demeures,
Mouillés qu'ils sont de longue pluie,
Tenacement, indéfinie.

Les rivières, à travers leurs digues pourries,
Se dégonflent sur les prairies,
Où flotte au loin du foin noyé ;
Le vent gifle aulnes et noyers ;
Sinistrement, dans l'eau jusqu'à mi-corps,
De grands bœufs noirs beuglent vers les cieux tors ;
Le soir approche, avec ses ombres,
Dont les plaines et les taillis s'encombrent,
Et c'est toujours la pluie
La longue pluie
Fine et dense, comme la suie.

La longue pluie,
La pluie — et ses fils identiques
Et ses ongles systématiques
Tissent le vêtement,
Maille à maille, de dénûment,
Pour les maisons et les enclos
Des villages gris et vieillots :
Linges et chapelets de loques
Qui s'effiloquent,
Au long de bâtons droits ;
Bleus colombiers collés au toit ;
Carreaux, avec, sur leur vitre sinistre,
Un emplâtre de papier bistre ;
Logis dont les gouttières régulières
Forment des croix sur des pignons de pierre ;
Moulins plantés uniformes et mornes,
Sur leur butte, comme des cornes ;
Clochers et chapelles voisines,

La pluie,
La longue pluie,
Pendant l'hiver, les assassine.

La pluie,
La longue pluie, avec ses longs fils gris,
Avec ses cheveux d'eau, avec ses rides,
La longue pluie
Des vieux pays,
Éternelle et torpide!

The long sweeping *l's* of the first stanza give the effect of the interminable lines of rain in an extraordinary manner, and the repetition of

> . . . la pluie,
> La longue pluie,
> La pluie.

adds a continuous drawing out, a falling — falling — falling — as it were.   Even apart from the beauty and surprise of the rhymes, the movement of this poem, and its pictorial quality, make it one of Verhaeren's masterpieces.

He has done this same thing in a number of other poems in this volume, such as *La Neige, Le Silence, Le Vent.*   I only wish I had space to give them all.

Two other poems in this book I cannot pass by. They are pictures of village life, full of feeling and understanding, and rich in that pictorial sense which never deserts Verhaeren.   The first one, *Le Meunier,* is made up of the beauty of terror — terror worked up, little by little, from the first line to the last. Verhaeren is no mere descriptive poet. Neither is he a surface realist. His realism contains the psychologic as well as the physiologic. Spadeful by spadeful, the earth rattles down on the coffin, and with each spadeful the grave-digger's terror grows, with the silence of the night, and the gradual pervading, haunting, of the personality of the dead miller, all about, till "the wind passes by as though it were someone," and the grave-digger throws down his spade and flees. After that, "total silence comes." It is all, and it is enough.

LE MEUNIER

Le vieux meunier du moulin noir,
On l'enterra, l'hiver, un soir
De froid rugueux, de bise aiguë
En un terrain de cendre et de ciguës.

Le jour dardait sa clarté fausse
Sur la bêche du fossoyeur ;
Un chien errait près de la fosse,
L'aboi tendu vers la lueur.

La bêche, à chacune des pelletées,
Telle un miroir se déplaçait,
Luisait, mordait et s'enfonçait,
Sous les terres violentées.
Le soleil chut sous les ombres suspectes.

Sur fond de ciel, le fossoyeur,
Comme un énorme insecte,
Semblait lutter avec la peur ;
La bêche entre ses mains tremblait,
Le sol se crevassait
Et quoi qu'il fît, rien ne comblait
Le trou qui, devant lui,
Comme la nuit, s'élargissait.

Au village là-bas,
Personne au mort n'avait prêté deux draps.

Au village là-bas,
Nul n'avait dit une prière.

Au village là-bas,
Personne au mort n'avait sonné le glas.

Au village là-bas,
Aucun n'avait voulu clouer la bière.

Et les maisons et les chaumières
Qui regardaient le cimetière,
Pour ne point voir, étaient là toutes,
Volets fermés, le long des routes.

Le fossoyeur se sentit seul
Devant ce défunt sans linceul
Dont tous avaient gardé la haine
Et la crainte, dans les veines.

Sur sa butte morne de soir,
Le vieux meunier du moulin noir,
Jadis, avait vécu d'accord
Avec l'espace et l'étendue
Et le vol fou des tempêtes pendues
Aux crins battants des vents du Nord ;
Son cœur avait longuement écouté
Ce que les bouches d'ombre et d'or
Des étoiles dévoilent
Aux attentifs d'éternité ;
Le désert gris des bruyères austères
L'avait cerné de ce mystère
Où les choses pour les âmes s'éveillent
Et leur parlent et les conseillent ;
Les grands courants qui traversent tout ce qui vit
Étaient, avec leur force, entrés dans son esprit,
Si bien que par son âme isolée et profonde
Ce simple avait senti passer et fermenter le monde.

Les plus anciens ne savaient pas
Depuis quels jours, loin du village,
Il perdurait, là-bas,
Guettant l'envol et les voyages
Et les signes des feux dans les nuages.

Il effrayait par le silence
Dont il avait, sans bruit,
Tissé son existence ;
Il effrayait encor
Par les yeux d'or
De son moulin tout à coup clairs, la nuit.

D

Et personne n'aurait connu
Son agonie et puis sa mort,
N'étaient que les quatre ailes
Qu'il agitait vers l'inconnu,
Comme des suppliques éternelles,
Ne s'étaient, un matin,
Définitivement fixées,
Noires et immobilisées,
Telle une croix sur un destin.

Le fossoyeur voyait l'ombre et ses houles
Grandir comme des foules
Et le village et ses closes fenêtres
Se fondre au loin et disparaître.

L'universelle inquiétude
Peuplait de cris la solitude ;
En voiles noirs et bruns,
Le vent passait comme quelqu'un ;
Tout le vague des horizons hostiles
Se précisait en frôlements fébriles
Jusqu'au moment où, les yeux fous,
Jetant sa bêche n'importe où,
Avec les bras multiples de la nuit
En menaces, derrière lui,
Comme un larron, il s'encourut.

　　　　　　　　　　　　Alors,
Le silence se fit, total, par l'étendue,
Le trou parut géant dans la terre fendue
Et rien ne bougea plus ;

Et seules les plaines inassouvies
Absorbèrent, en leur immensité
D'ombre et de Nord,
Ce mort
Dont leur mystère avait illimité
Et exalté jusques dans l'infini, la vie.

Very different is *Les Meules Qui Brûlent*. A splendid impressionist picture, with the burning hay-ricks starting up, one after the other, out of the blackness.

LES MEULES QUI BRÛLENT

La plaine, au fond des soirs, s'est allumée,
Et les tocsins cassent leurs bonds de sons,
Aux quatre murs de l'horizon.

— Une meule qui brûle ! —

Par les sillages des chemins, la foule,
Par les sillages des villages, la foule houle
Et dans les cours, les chiens de garde ululent.

— Une meule qui brûle ! —

La flamme ronfle et casse et broie,
S'arrache des haillons qu'elle déploie,
Ou sinueuse et virgulante
S'enroule en chevelure ardente ou lente

Puis s'apaise soudain et se détache
Et ruse et se dérobe — ou rebondit encor :
Et voici, clairs, de la boue et de l'or,
Dans le ciel noir qui s'empanache.

— Quand brusquement une autre meule au loin s'allume ! —

Elle est immense — et comme un trousseau rouge
Qu'on agite de sulfureux serpents,
Les feux — ils sont passants sur les arpents
Et les fermes et les hameaux, où bouge,
De vitre à vitre, un caillot rouge.

— Une meule qui brûle ! —

Les champs ? ils s'illimitent en frayeurs ;
Des frondaisons de bois se lèvent en lueurs,
Sur les marais et les labours ;
Des étalons cabrés, vers la terreur hennissent ;
D'énormes vols d'oiseaux s'appesantissent
Et choient, dans les brasiers — et des cris sourds
Sortent du sol ; et c'est la mort,
Toute la mort brandie
Et ressurgie, aux poings en l'air de l'incendie.

Et le silence après la peur — quand, tout à coup, là-bas
Formidable, dans le soir las,
Un feu nouveau remplit les fonds du crépuscule ?

— Une meule qui brûle ! —

Aux carrefours, des gens hagards
Font des gestes hallucinés,
Les enfants crient et les vieillards
Lèvent leurs bras déracinés
Vers les flammes en étendards.
Tandis qu'au loin, obstinément silencieux,
Des fous, avec de la stupeur aux yeux — regardent.

— Une meule qui brûle ! —

L'air est rouge, le firmament
On le dirait défunt, sinistrement,
Sous les yeux clos de ses étoiles.
Le vent chasse des cailloux d'or,
Dans un déchirement de voiles.
Le feu devient clameur hurlée en flamme
Vers les échos, vers les là-bas,
Sur l'autre bord, où brusquement les au-delà
Du fleuve s'éclairent comme un songe :
Toute la plaine ? elle est de braise, de mensonge,
De sang et d'or — et la tourmente
Emporte avec un tel élan,
La mort passagère du firmament,
Que vers les fins de l'épouvante,
Le ciel entier semble partir.

One strange thing about Verhaeren is his true greatness. No matter how onomatopœic he becomes, no matter how much he alliterates, or whatever other devices he makes use of, he never becomes claptrap. Every young poet knows how dangerous the methods I am speaking of are, with what terrible ease they give a poem a meretricious turn, and immediately a certain vaudevillian flavour has crept in. No matter what Verhaeren does, his work remains great, and full of what Matthew Arnold calls " high seriousness." The purists may rail, that only shows how narrow the purists are. A great genius will disobey all rules and yet produce works of art, perforce.

Verhaeren's message has become so much a part of our modern temper that we hardly realize how new and original it was in poetry twenty years ago. Jules Romain in *La Vie Unanime* has gone Verhaeren one better, but would he have been there at all if Verhaeren had not preceded him? Remy de Gourmont, over-subtilized French intellect that he is, thinks that Verhaeren hates the groaning towns, the lonely villages. Which only proves that even remarkable minds have their limitations. A brooding Northerner, Verhaeren sees the sorrow, the travail, the sordidness, going on all about him, and loves the world just the same, and wildly believes in a future in which it shall somehow grind itself back to beauty. *Les Villes Tentaculaires* is full of this sordidness, a sordidness overlaid with grandeur, as iridescent colour plays over the skin of a dying fish. But it is also full of the constant, inevitable pushing on, the movement, one might call it, of change.

One poem from *Les Villes Tentaculaires* will serve
as illustration :

LA BOURSE

La rue énorme et ses maisons quadrangulaires
Bordent la foule et l'endiguent de leur granit
Œillé de fenêtres et de porches, où luit
L'adieu, dans les carreaux, des soirs auréolaires.

Comme un torse de pierre et de métal debout,
Avec, en son mystère immonde,
Le cœur battant et haletant du monde,
Le monument de l'or, dans les ténèbres, bout.

Autour de lui, les banques noires
Dressent des lourds frontons que soutiennent, des bras,
Les Hercules d'airain dont les gros muscles las
Semblent lever des coffres-forts vers la victoire.

Le carrefour, d'où il érige sa bataille,
Suce la fièvre et le tumulte
De chaque ardeur vers son aimant occulte ;
Le carrefour et ses squares et ses murailles
Et ses grappes de gaz sans nombre,
Qui font bouger des paquets d'ombre
Et de lueurs, sur les trottoirs.

Tant de rêves, tels des feux roux,
Entremêlent leur flamme et leurs remous,
De haut en bas, du palais fou !
Le gain coupable et monstrueux

S'y resserre, comme des nœuds,
Et son désir se dissémine et se propage
Partant chauffer de seuil à seuil,
Dans la ville, les contigus orgueils.
Les comptoirs lourds grondent comme un orage,
Les luxes gros se jalousent et ragent
Et les faillites en tempêtes,
Soudainement, à coups brutaux,
Battent et chavirent les têtes
Des grands bourgeois monumentaux.

L'après-midi, à tel moment,
La fièvre encore augmente
Et pénètre le monument
Et dans les murs fermente.
On croit la voir se raviver aux lampes
Immobiles, comme des hampes,
Et se couler, de rampe en rampe,
Et s'ameuter et éclater
Et crépiter, sur les paliers
Et les marbres des escaliers.

Une fureur réenflammée
Au mirage d'un pâle espoir,
Monte parfois de l'entonnoir
De bruit et de fumée,
Où l'on se bat, à coups de vols, en bas.
Langues sèches, regards aigus, gestes inverses,
Et cervelles, qu'en tourbillons les millions traversent,
Échangent là, leur peur et leur terreur.
La hâte y simule l'audace

Et les audaces se dépassent ;
Des doigts grattent, sur des ardoises,
L'affolement de leurs angoisses ;
Cyniquement, tel escompte l'éclair
Qui casse un peuple au bout du monde ;
Les chimères sont volantes au clair ;
Les chances fuient ou surabondent ;
Marchés conclus, marchés rompus
Luttent et s'entrebutent en disputes ;
L'air brûle — et les chiffres paradoxaux,
En paquets pleins, en lourds trousseaux,
Sont rejetés et cahotés et ballottés
Et s'effarent en ces bagarres,
Jusqu'à ce que leurs sommes lasses,
Masses contre masses,
Se cassent.

Tels jours, quand les débâcles se décident,
La mort les paraphe de suicides
Et les chutes s'effritent en ruines
Qui s'illuminent
En obsèques exaltatives.
Mais, le soir même, aux heures blêmes,
Les volontés, dans la fièvre, revivent ;
L'acharnement sournois
Reprend, comme autrefois.

On se trahit, on se sourit et l'on se mord
Et l'on travaille à d'autres morts.
La haine ronfle, ainsi qu'une machine,
Autour de ceux qu'elle assassine.

On vole, avec autorité, les gens
Dont les avoirs sont indigents.
On mêle avec l'honneur l'escroquerie,
Pour amorcer jusqu'aux patries
Et ameuter vers l'or torride et infamant,
L'universel affolement.

Oh l'or! là-bas, comme des tours dans les nuages,
Comme des tours, sur l'étagère des mirages,
L'or énorme! comme des tours, là-bas,
Avec des millions de bras vers lui,
Et des gestes et des appels la nuit
Et la prière unanime qui gronde,
De l'un à l'autre bout des horizons du monde!

Là-bas! des cubes d'or sur des triangles d'or
Et tout autour les fortunes célèbres
S'échafaudant sur des algèbres.

De l'or! — boire et manger de l'or!
Et, plus féroce encor que la rage de l'or,
La foi au jeu mystérieux
Et ses hasards hagards et ténébreux
Et ses arbitraires vouloirs certains
Qui restaurent le vieux destin;
Le jeu, axe terrible, où tournera autour de l'aventure,
Par seul plaisir d'anomalie,
Par seul besoin de rut et de folie,
Là-bas, où se croisent les lois d'effroi
Et les suprêmes désarrois,
Éperdûment, la passion future.

Comme un torse de pierre et de métal debout,
Avec, en son mystère immonde,
Le cœur battant et haletant du monde,
Le monument de l'or dans les ténèbres bout.

The dramatic intensity of this poem equals that of *Le Meunier*. And this is Verhaeren's third great gift: the dramatic. I have already spoken of his visualizing gift, of his power of reproducing sound in words; the third side of his greatness is the sense of drama. In spite of the decoration in *La Bourse*, in spite of such lines, beautiful in themselves, as

Là-bas! des cubes d'or sur des triangles d'or,
Et tout autour les fortunes célèbres
S'échafaudant sur des algèbres.

— beautiful, but painfully prone to stick out of a poem like knobs on an embossed wall-paper — the poet has managed to keep them in their place, so that they do not interfere, but rather add to the drama of the whole.

Verhaeren is not a didactic poet. He does not suggest a way out. He states, and hopes, and firmly believes; that is all. And always remember, in thinking of Verhaeren's work in the light of his philosophy, that he is first of all an artist, a painter, and he must always take a painter's delight in pure painting. For those people who prefer a more clear, more classic style of poetry, Verhaeren has no charm.

He is nebulous and redundant. His colours are bright and vague like flash-lights thrown on a fog. But his force is incontestable, and he hurls along upon it in a whirlwind of extraordinary poetry. Of Verhaeren's life from now on, there is little to say. He is a poet, and a poet's life is in creating poems. On his return to Belgium, he threw himself into active life and was immediately seduced by the Socialist doctrines then just being felt in Belgium. He seconded M. Vandevelde and others in starting a democratic movement, and went so far as to become a member of the "Comité de la Maison du Peuple." How long he kept up this active life in Belgium I have not been able to find out, nor why he abandoned it; but now he spends his Winters at Saint Cloud, returning to Belgium for the Summers. Of course, I mean that was what he did before the war.

That Verhaeren must have married sometime before 1896 is clear, because *Les Heures Claires*, published in that year, is the first of a series of love poems, of which *Les Heures de l'Après-midi*, published in 1905, and *Les Heures du Soir*, published in 1911, are the other volumes.

Verhaeren's love story has evidently been tranquil and happy. The poems are very sweet and graceful, but it must be confessed not of extreme importance. They are all written in regular metre, which seems almost typical of their calm and unoriginal flow. Verhaeren does not belong to the type of man to whom love is a divine adventure. He has regarded it as a beneficent haven in which to repair himself for new departures. No biographer mentions who Madame Verhaeren was, or anything about her, except to pay her the tribute of understanding and cherishing a great man. That she has been a helpmeet to him in every way these poems prove.

We have reached the last stage of Verhaeren's career. The stage of powers ripening, growing, solidifying. His part is taken; he has learnt his peculiar medium, and formulated his ideas. His final volumes, many though they are, merely show him writing still remarkable poems along the lines he has chosen. There is no diminution of his genius, and his fecundity is extraordinary. In 1899, appeared *Les Visages de la Vie*; in 1902, *Les Forces Tumultueuses*; in 1906, *La Multiple Splendeur*; in 1910, *Les Rhythmes Souverains*; and in 1913, *Les Blés Mouvants*. Four volumes of poems entitled *Toute la Flandre*, appeared at intervals from 1901 to 1909. And there are one or two other small volumes. Remember, Verhaeren has written twenty-three volumes of poems, and to speak of them all in detail would require an entire volume.

I only wish it were possible to give something from each of these books. But I must content myself with one more quotation from his last book, *Les Blés Mouvants*. It will show that Verhaeren has lost nothing of his great vigour, and that the rage for justice which made him a socialist still burns in him.

ALLEZ-VOUS-EN

Allez-vous-en, allez-vous-en
L'auberge entière est aux passants.

— Elle est à nous, elle est à nous,
Depuis bientôt trois cents années.
Elle est à nous, elle est à nous,
Depuis la porte aux longs verrous
Jusqu'aux faîtes des cheminées.

— Allez-vous-en, allez-vous-en,
L'auberge entière est aux passants.

— Nous en savons, nous en savons,
Les ruines et les lézardes,
Mais c'est nous seuls qui prétendons
En remplacer les vieux moellons
Des bords du seuil jusqu'aux mansardes.

— Allez-vous-en, allez-vous-en,
L'auberge entière est aux passants.

— Nous vénérons ceux qui sont morts
Au fond de leurs cercueils de chêne,
Nous envions ceux qui sont morts
Sans se douter des cris de haine
Qui bondissent de plaine en plaine.

— Allez-vous-en, allez-vous-en,
L'auberge entière est aux passants.

— C'est notre droit, c'est notre droit,
D'orner notre enseigne d'un Aigle ;
C'est notre droit, c'est notre droit,
De posséder selon les lois
Plus qu'il ne faut d'orge et de seigle.

— Allez-vous-en, allez-vous-en,
Gestes et mots ne sont plus rien.
Allez-vous-en, allez-vous-en,
      Et sachez bien
Que notre droit, c'est notre faim.

What Verhaeren has done for poetry is this. He has made it realize the modern world. He has shown the grandeur of everyday life, and made us understand that science and art are never at variance. He has shown that civic consciousness is not necessarily dry and sterile, but can be as romantic as an individual. And he has done all this without once saying it directly, by force of the greatest and most complete art.

Albert Samain

ALBERT SAMAIN

ALBERT SAMAIN

THIS chapter will be very different from the last one. Then we were engaged with a great poet. A man of large and exuberant nature, whose work was remarkable for its originality, force, dramatic power, and fecundity. Now we are going to consider a minor poet of delicate and graceful talent, whose entire poetical output is contained in three volumes. It is chamber-music, as tenuous and plaintive as that played by old eighteenth century orchestras, with their *viole da gamba* and *hautbois d'amour*. Albert Samain would seem to lack his century, were it not that one cannot help feeling that in no century would the shy, solitary, diffident man have been at home. Centuries are strangely alike for those living them, they only change their values when their outlines are blurred by distance. The qualities which make a man great are the same in all ages. Samain would have been a minor poet in the ninth century as he was in the nineteenth.

In the biography of the poet by Léon Bocquet, there is a preface by Francis Jammes. He says: "Albert

Samain's forehead wrinkled like my mother's —
from the bottom up. His arm had the elegant gesture of a stork which moves its foot backward. His
face and body were slender. At times his blue
eyes, behind his glasses, became heavenly, that is
to say they looked up and whitened. . . . Albert
Samain was a swan. I am hardly expressing myself
figuratively here. He had the harmonious stiffness
and the gaze of a swan. Not the sharp, furious,
wounded gaze of the bird of prey, but the impassive
gaze of the sacred bird which flies, in high relief, on
the frieze of some temple, the gaze which only reflects the appearance of things floating away beneath
it in the water of the stream. He had the cold and
sad attitude of the swan too. Swan, the friend of
shade. I see him, sailing, spread out, over the lake
in *Le Jardin de l'Infante*. . . . He does not
listen to the whispers of this splendour which he
himself has created, nor to the rising sea of his
fame. He only listens to the bells of a church which
ring in the distance — I do not know where, in a
country which is not mine, in a country where the
things are which one does not see. He only hears
the chimes of this Flemish church, of this church in
which an old woman is praying." Whether by this
old woman Francis Jammes means Samain's mother,
to whom the poet gave a lifelong devotion, or
whether it is merely figurative, I cannot say. But
the whole description, fanciful though it is, gives a

better picture of the man than pages of biography and straightforward analysis could do.

Samain is said to have looked like a Spaniard, and certainly his photographs might be those of some Spanish grandee; there is the haughty, spare figure of the Spaniard, and the sad, proud face of slender lines. We must not forget that Flanders was for some time owned by Spain, and that Lille only became a part of France in 1667, when Louis XIV besieged it and forced it to surrender. Now, Albert-Victor Samain was born in Lille on the third of April, 1858.

His family were Flemish, and from time immemorial had lived in the town or its suburbs, so that Samain's Spanish appearance was probably no mere accident, but the result of a remote heredity. His family belonged to the large class of the minor *bourgeoisie*. At the time of his birth, his father, Jean-Baptiste Samain, and his mother, Elisa-Henriette Mouquet, conducted a business in "wines and spirits" at 75 rue de Paris. Some distant ancestral strain seems to have had more effect upon Samain than his immediate surroundings; certainly, the ancestor who gave him his figure and colouring seems to have given him his character also, for no trace of the influences which usually mould the small shopkeeper's son to fit his father's routine are visible in him.

This is the more surprising, as all the ease and

assurance which he might have derived from his father's owning his own business were promptly swept away by the death of his father when he was fourteen. At this time, Samain was in the third class in the *Lycée* at Lille. His father's death found him the eldest of three children, with a widowed mother whom he must help to support the family. *Noblesse oblige*, whether another trait of his Spanish ancestor or merely derived from the fine thriftiness of the French *bourgeoisie*, was always strong in Samain. He left school and entered the office of a banker, where he seems to have held the position of errand-boy. From there he went into the business of sugar-broking, in what capacity is not stated, but it would seem to have been at the bottom of the ladder, as was natural at his age. That the work was very hard is evident, for Samain says : "I was very miserable there for many years, working from half-past eight in the morning until eight at night, and on Sundays until two."

It was at this time that Samain began to lead the life of a solitary, which after that he never succeeded in shaking off. In spite of his twelve hours of work there were off times — the twelve other hours, only some of which could be spent in sleep ; and the Sunday afternoons. A provincial town offers very little in the way of amusement to an intelligent young man. Samain was hardly the sort of fellow to enjoy cock-fights, or find pleasure in lounging in cafés ogling the passers-by. There was the Museum, but museums do not last forever as an inspiring relaxation, and for a young fellow of eighteen or thereabouts wandering round a museum is usually a lonely joy. The boys with whom he had gone to school had passed on to the University; and besides, what could they have to do with an under-clerk in a business house! Samain was too proud to push against cold shoulders. He simply withdrew more and more into himself, and laid the foundation for that sadness from which he could never afterwards entirely free himself.

If circumstances separated him from his old schoolfellows, his tastes (and also his taste) removed him from his fellow clerks. A single friend he made, however — a M. Victor Lemoigne. This man not only was his friend, he believed in him, a precious necessity to a young writer. For Samain at last confided to him that he wrote verses. It must have been the greatest comfort to tell somebody, for Samain had been writing in silence and solitude for some time. But he had not only been writing, he had been training himself for a writer, and in that best of all methods, studying foreign tongues.

If there were no amusements in Lille, there was at least a library. And in the absence of any other distractions Samain spent long hours there. Perhaps it was lucky that nothing else exerted a strong enough pull to make his going there in the least difficult. He studied, and endeavoured to complete his arrested education. Of course, he read rather vaguely, as people do without a teacher, but he succeeded in perfecting himself in Greek and English so that he could read them both fluently. He delighted in English, and afterwards liked to give his poems English titles, and put English words into the middle of them. Edgar Allan Poe was one of his greatest admirations and inspirations. Years after he wrote: "I have been reading Poe this week. Decidedly, he must be classed among the greatest. The power of his conceptions, the magnificence of his hypotheses, the marvellous force of his imagination, always contained and held in check by an extraordinary will, make him an almost unique figure in art. . . . If the word perfection can ever be used, it is in such a case."

Fortunately for Samain, and for us, Lemoigne was sympathetic and enthusiastic. He liked the poems which Samain showed him, and at once decided that the young man was sure of a glorious future.

There is no doubt that these over-confident and admiring friends do a young writer as much good as harm. Adverse or carping criticism often discourages to the point of sterilization, while even ill-judged praise gives confidence and the strength to go on. In a man of Samain's diffident temperament, such full-blooded encouragement must have been of the greatest value. But, as the desire to learn, to talk, to mix in an intellectual life, grew upon him, more and more did Samain find the life of a little clerk in the provinces insupportable. It is truer of France than of any other country that its capital is the centre of its entire intellectual life. Samain had paid a flying visit to Paris in 1878, to see the Exposition. Even more than at ordinary times, the Paris of an Exposition year dazzles, and snaps, and glows. After his return to the wearisome dulness of Lille, Samain thought of it as the Mecca of all his dreams. It lured like the Pot of Gold at the end of the Rainbow. As luck would have it, in July, 1880, his firm decided to send him to its Paris house. He was to be only a transient addition, but he intended to stay if he could, and on expressing this wish to his superiors it was acceded to, and his salary raised to 2400 francs a year.

It might seem now as though things were at last coming Samain's way. Here he was, transplanted to Paris, and with the exciting possibility of having some famous literary celebrity living just round the corner. But in cities like Paris, "round the corner" might just as well be across the Channel. Albert Samain was living in Paris, which, as a thought, must have given him considerable satisfaction; but the satisfaction began and ended in the realms of the idea.

He knew nobody; he had no introductions; and his hours were longer than in Lille. Now, he was at his office from nine in the morning until after midnight. Only once or twice a week did he even have some hours of freedom in the evening. And then there was no energy left to do any good work. So Samain lived in Paris more solitarily than he had done in Lille, for there was no M. Lemoigne there. And he could not work so well because he had less time. They were not cheerful letters which he sent back to M. Lemoigne. They were bitter, discouraged letters. He *must* change his business, there was no other way; but to what?

The faithful Lemoigne was instant in suggestion. His friend must try journalism; and, succeeding in that, have leisure for greater literary effort. It must have been a constant strain for Lemoigne to push his friend along, and his patience and effort were remarkable. Samain always held back, and was discouraged before he began. But Lemoigne firmly insisted. Poor Samain hastily wrote a paper on Offenbach and took it to the *Figaro*. It was not liked. Then he wrote to the editors of *Gil Blas*, and the *Beaumarchais*. His letters were not answered. So that seemed to be an end to journalism in Paris.

Samain was willing to give it up. Lemoigne was not. If Paris would not see his friend's genius, Lille should. Really Lemoigne's unswerving faith is very beautiful, and it is a satisfaction to realize how abundantly it was justified.

There was at this time in Lille a weekly called *Le Bonhomme Flamand.* It amounted to very little, as, of course, Lemoigne knew, but Samain must be printed. And two little stories of Samain's did appear in it signed *Gry-Pearl,* for Samain was afraid of the amusement of his friends if he signed his own name. The quasi-English flavour of the pseudonym is interesting. Shortly afterwards, *Le Bonhomme Flamand* died a natural death. The editor of another Lille paper annoyed Samain by chopping up one of the latter's articles to suit himself, so Samain refused to send any more, and forced M. Lemoigne to approve. Here ended Samain's attempt to push open the doors of journalism, if we except two articles in an unknown gazette, and a little piece in *L'Illustration.* Samain slipped back to his old solitary life, writing for himself alone.

In July, 1881, Mme. Samain joined her son in Paris. And from this time on they were never separated. Even among Frenchmen, whose affection for their mothers has become a proverb, Samain's love for, and care of, his is extraordinary. For her sake he never married ; his salary was not enough to support two women.

Later, his youngest brother Paul joined them ; Alice, his sister, remaining behind in Lille where she had married. It was a quiet, family life they lived in the little apartment, rue des Petits-Champs. It was a safe, excellent life for a rising young clerk, sure of stepping up in his business from position to higher position, and finally attaining to a business of his own. But for a poet, how petty, how exacting! How painful to weary the brain all day with figures so that at night it cannot find words! Weak in many ways though Samain was, he never wavered in his firm resolution to write. If he could only gain enough to keep his mother he would be satisfied; for himself he only demanded a less fatiguing work, with more leisure. He watched, and watched, until he found something. And what he found was a small clerkship in the third bureau of the Department of Instruction, with a salary of 1800 francs a year. In spite of suggestions and offers from his firm, he took it without a moment's hesitation. And it speaks excellently for Mme. Samain that she apparently bore him no ill-will for so materially cutting down their income.

The change was undoubtedly a good thing for Samain. He was only obliged to be at his desk for seven hours a day, his colleagues were men of better education than those in the sugar house, and finding a copy of Boileau open upon the table of his chief gave him the feeling of being in a sympathetic atmosphere. But still, taking everything by and large, Samain could not feel very successful. He had left Lille, true; he had got rid of the detested

sugar-broking; he was definitely settled in Paris.
And there was an end to his achievements. In a
letter written much later, he says: "At twenty-five
years old, without the slightest exaggeration, I had
not a single literary friend or acquaintance. My
only relations were with young men belonging to the
business world."

He had made three wild dashes into the world of
letters. The momentary, hazarding exploits of a
very young man. From his boyhood he had fed
upon the Romantics; Lamartine, Hugo, and Musset
had been his gods. Two of these giants being unhappily dead and the third a very old man, he wor-
shipped their belated shadows: Théodore de Banville
and Jean Richepin. He sent a letter with an enthusiastic ode to Banville, but the visit which Banville
invited him to make in return was unfortunate in
the extreme. Banville carped and criticised, and
Samain took flight never to go back again. Twice
more, Samain was so ill-judged as to tempt Fate in
this way. He sent letters to both Jean Richepin and
Octave Feuillet. Both asked him to call, possibly
the visits were repeated more than once, but they
had no result. Samain was tasting the bitter lesson,
that fecund intimacies fall from the lap of the gods,
and are never the result of painstaking endeavour.

Samain gave up seeking access to celebrities and
went back to his writing, still worshipping the dead
authors who had not snubbed him, and writing *dans*

le goût d'avant-hier. But, though Samain, alone in the quiet lamplit evenings, still bowed before the old shrines, other young men were more adventurous. Various hot bloods got up a society, or rather they organized a group, and called it *Nous Autres.* They met at a *cabaret* in Montmartre, and drank *bocks*, and disputed theories of art and letters, and undoubtedly damned every one who was not themselves, after the manner of young artists. By and by, they changed *cabarets*, going to *Le Chat Noir*, and made it famous by their presence. A kind of vaudeville show was given there, and a series of silhouette plays, in a little puppet theatre, by Henri Rivière had a great vogue. On occasions, at the end of an evening, the young writers read their poems aloud and had their angles rubbed off by one another's criticism. A friend took Samain to one of these gatherings, and he soon became an *habitué.* He read a part of his poem, *Les Monts*, there. He also read *Tsilla*, and Laurent Tailhade and Jean Lorrain applauded him.

Le Chat Noir had a little paper, and in the copy of it for December, 1884, *Tsilla* appeared on the front page. *Tsilla* was apparently liked and praised by the frequenters of *Le Chat Noir*, and Samain wrote a satisfied and happy letter to M. Lemoigne on the strength of it. Rather pathetically he tells how he has been praised for the healthy quality of his verses, and hopes that he will be able to avoid the *maladive* contagion of the period.

To my mind, *Tsilla* is one of the dullest poems that ever was written, and gives no hint of the charm of some of his later work. It is the story of a young girl of antiquity (that charming and convenient antiquity so beloved of poets, which never existed anywhere, at any time), who loves an Angel. In a crisis of adventurousness, she urges the Angel to fly up in the sky, taking her with him, which he does, and they go so near to the rising sun that her black hair is turned to gold. Owing to which accident, she is the first woman in the world who ever had blond hair. The verses are no more interesting nor original than the story.

If praise of such an insignificant poem had been all that Samain got out of his *cénacle* of young poets, his frequenting it would have been a mere waste of time. But it was not all. He got a complete upheaval of ideas. He learnt that Lamartine and Victor Hugo were *vieux jeu*, that François Coppée was not the last word in poetry to these young iconoclasts. He learnt that Verlaine and Mallarmé were the proper objects of worship for an up-to-date poet. Any one who has listened to a set of young writers tearing down the generation which has preceded them, showing up all the faults it never knew it had, and sneering at the good points it undoubtedly has, can reproduce these evenings perfectly. But Samain was a young provincial. All this talk disturbed him. This familiar scoffing

at names he considered the greatest in the world
unsettled him.   What should he do?   Whom should
he follow?   For Samain must follow, he was as
incapable of leadership as a man could well be.
He did follow a little way, but only a little way —
gingerly, like one stepping over a slippery bridge
and clinging tightly to a hand-rail.

It is easy to be an iconoclast in French poetry.
The classic metres are so exceedingly prescribed and
confined that the least little change lands one in
nonconformity.   But for us, living more than thirty
years after the period I am speaking of, for us who
are accustomed to the innovations of the *vers libristes*,
Samain's tentative efforts at modernity of form have
become almost invisible.   We can find them if we
hunt, but to the naked perception they are lost in
the general effect of conformity to metrical rules.
Yet, to Samain, his not always putting the cæsura
in the middle of the line, or failing to alternate mas-
culine and feminine endings, or occasionally rhyming
plurals with singulars (all unalterable rules of
French classic metre), must have seemed violent
innovations indeed.

The meetings at *Le Chat Noir* did not only affect
Samain's technical habit, they affected his ideas
about everything, even, and most, his religion.
Brought up a Catholic, he had hitherto never
doubted his faith; now it tumbled off him like a
shrivelled leaf.   Scepticism, a state of mind pecul-

iarly unsuited to his temperament, swept over him. The realization that he had lost the support of religion, that its consolations could no longer comfort him, was agony. The idea, the resultant void, preoccupied him. He could no longer write, he could only worry and mourn. This was particularly unfortunate as he was at the moment composing the poems which afterwards made up *Au Jardin de l'Infante*, his first volume, which was not published until six years later. The sapping of his vitality by doubt naturally lasted longer with a man of Samain's gentle and resigned disposition than it does with people of bolder characters.

In his state of mind, the hilarious and not over-refined pleasures of the literary *cabarets* were most distasteful. He was too straightforward and simple himself not to see through the poses and childish debauches of his coterie. He withdrew from it, and retired once more within himself. But he was lonely, bitterly lonely. His brother Paul had been called to his military service, and once more he and his mother lived alone. His modest income of 1800 francs was not sufficient to enable him to think of marriage while he still had his mother to support. Whether Samain ever had a definite love story is not known. It seems hardly possible for him to have escaped such a usual happening ; but, at any rate, whether it was a particular woman whom he gave up, or whether he merely resigned himself to bachelorhood in the ab-

F

stract, certain it is that Samain felt his life bordered and arranged, and that he looked forward to no bright happening to change it. Mme. Samain adored him and was proud of him, but from his reticence about his work at home, she does not appear to have been fitted, either by education or natural ability, to be much of a help to him in it.

Only seven hours a day at the Hôtel de Ville, and the rest of the time his own! That "rest of the time," which was to have been filled with the work he could not do. It hung heavy on his hands, and to distract himself he took to taking long walks about Paris. He would stroll along the Seine, turning over the leaves of the books in the *bouquiniste's* boxes on the parapets of the *quais*, amusing himself with the old engravings in the ten centimes boxes, breathing in the sharp scent of the river and the perfume of old, passed centuries; he would wander in the once fashionable quarters of the town, now fallen from grace, and imagine the days when they were full of sedan chairs and elegant ladies. His love for the faded, the graceful, vanished past, grew and solaced him. How many of his poems seem to be merely efforts to reproduce it, and so dwell in it for a few minutes!

Side by side with these imaginative pleasures were others. He began to see nature, real nature, as it is even to-day. His walks in the suburbs gave him many a picture which he turned to account later in *Aux Flancs du Vase.* The splendid, differing sunsets gave him infinite pleasure ; sometimes he would get into one of the *bateaux mouches* which go up and down the river, and watch the yellows and reds of the sunset repeat themselves in the water. He had none of that modern spirit which enables one to see beauties in tram-cars and smoking chimneys, so he eliminated them from his thought. In love with beauty as he conceived it, he took the changing colours which all sorts of weather threw over Paris, and, eternal as they are, lit his pictures of other centuries with them. He speaks of "la suavité suprême de Paris d'Automne;" the frail gold of Autumn always pleased him. He describes dark gardens where the fountains "font un bruit maigre, frileux et comme désolé dans l'abandon du crépuscule." He loved rainy days, and deserted streets, the "mélancolie vieillotte des rues où quelque chose est en train de mourir." Once he says : "Il me semblait voir, sous mes yeux, 1830 — le 1830 de Lamartine et de Hugo — toute mon adolescence ivre d'enfant lyrique s'en aller là dans cette solitude morne, silencieuse, provinciale."

A gentle soul; when he was particularly depressed he used to put a bunch of tuberoses, or a single pale rose, in a glass on his desk. "Quand je me sens devenir pessimiste, je regarde une rose," he used to say. Flowers were the only luxury he permitted

himself. Except (and this is the great "except")
his imagination.

His room was as bare as a cell in a monastery,
neither painting nor engraving hung on the walls.
But listen to the room he would have had if —
evoking it to amuse himself on an Autumn evening: "My room. Hung with velvet of steel-
coloured grey, with blue lights in it. The rose-
tinted ceiling fades off into mauve and has a large
decorative design — Renaissance — in old silver,
embossed at the corners. Hangings hide the door.
No windows; the room only being used by artificial
light. Near the floor, forming a base-board, a
band of old silver openwork *appliquéd* on the same
velvet as the hangings, a flower design, with knots of
pink pearl tassels at intervals. A carpet with a
silver nap; against one side of the wall, a divan of
steel-grey velvet. No movable furniture. In one
corner, directly under the bosses of the ceiling, an
ebony table with silver lion's claws for feet; the
table is covered with a cloth of steel-grey velvet,
with a great silver tulip with rose-coloured leaves
embroidered in the corner. An Etruscan armchair,
made entirely of ebony, with silver nails. Negli-
gently thrown over the armchair to soften the
sharpness of the angles and the hardness of the
wood, a grey bear skin. A lamp of old silver, mas-
sive and slender, with a long neck of a clear shape,
and without ornament. Shade of faded moss-rose

colour. Blotting pad of steel-grey morocco, with a heraldic device; a penholder of old gold. Books: Corbière, Mallarmé, *Fleurs du Mal*, in small folios, bound in white pigskin and tied with cords of rose-colour and silver, edges of old gold, titles printed in Roman letters, crude red on the top and on the left side. A fireplace with a historical plaque over it — Renaissance, and andirons of wrought steel terminating in couched chimeras. Three sides of the room are empty. In the corner opposite the table, on the wall, two metres from the ground, a console covered with steel-grey velvet supported by a Renaissance chimera in iron. . . . Upon the console, a great horn of crystal, very tapering, in which are two roses, one rose a sulphur yellow, one wine-coloured. In an alcove hidden by a curtain is a deep niche, bathed in the half-light of a gold altar lamp hanging by a little chain. The globe of the lamp is made of pieces of many-coloured glass cut in facets so that they shine like great stones: ruby, sapphire, emerald. In the niche, which is hung with crimson velvet, on a column with a Doric capital, stands the Young Faun of Praxiteles. . . ."

Lacking this room, why bother with engravings! Yet Samain never complained of the ugliness and meagreness of actual life. He only played his games on windy nights in his bare room.

It would be unjust to Samain to represent him as passing all his evenings wrapped in sugary dreams. He studied science, history, philosophy. It is a curious fact, that he was one of the first men in France to recognize the genius of Nietzsche.

In compensation for the many bitternesses of his life, beginning in 1884 came the happiness of two friendships. Samain made the acquaintance, and quickly became the intimate friend, of Paul Morisse and Raymond Bonheur. Paul Morisse was a constant traveller, and with him Samain made his first considerable journey. The two friends went to Germany. They saw the Rhine, Bingen, Mayence, etc. Samain was charmed with all he saw. He possessed the gift of wonder; an inestimable possession, by the way. Unfortunately it was hard to find money for these excursions. Samain called the lack of money "the defective side" of his life. When the French Academy crowned his first book, he gave himself the present of a month at Lake Annecy.

So at last we reach his first book, privately printed in 1893, when the poet had passed his thirty-fifth birthday.

At this time the *Mercure de France* had just come into existence, and Samain was one of its founders. It was in the pages of the *Mercure* that most of his poems appeared. Samain never seems to have seriously considered collecting them into a book. Over-diffident and self-critical, he worked at them, changed them, polished them. At rare intervals one was printed. Samain was in love with perfection, and very little that he did ever seemed to him worthy to leave his hands. This excessive scrupulousness works both ways. A poem so treated gains in beauty, but frequently loses in vitality. There is great danger of its becoming a thing of mummied splendour. That Samain's poems absolutely lost vigour by this polishing, I cannot fairly say. The poems I have seen in several states do seem to have gained technically in their final one, and to have parted with practically none of their original *élan*. *Élan* is too strong a word. Samain's poems are never dashing with life. Let us say rather, not that his poems lost by his treatment of them, but that the kind of man who could so treat them was of a slightly depressed, unvital temper. How considerable a course of discipline he put them through can be imagined when I mention that, in the four versions extant of a poem of twenty-eight lines, only four which were in the first version appear in the last.

But to return to that first volume. At the instance of M. Bonheur, Samain consented to print it. Not publish it, observe. It was issued in a charming, privately printed edition. This was in October, 1893. And in the *Journal* for the 15th of March, 1894, appeared a review of it by no less a person than François Coppée. How the volume came into

Coppée's hands I do not know, but he instantly recognized its value and said so frankly. Five months of reviewing and praise in the young reviews had not been able to do for Samain what the hundred lines from François Coppée did at once. It was celebrity, almost fame. The little, privately printed edition was quickly exhausted. Another was called for, and at last the book, *Au Jardin de l'Infante*, was published. Still Samain was diffident, and when a third edition was needed, he hesitated again; but the third edition came out three years after the first. The edition I have is marked "twenty-fifth," so it appears that Samain was unnecessarily timid. The book was given a prize by the French Academy, and Samain was one of the poets of the hour.

There was nothing very new in *Au Jardin de l'Infante*, it is true. The metre was the classic alexandrine, for the most part, varied by lighter, gayer rhythms equally well sanctioned. But the book was full of the shy, delicate personality of the poet. Here were his sumptuous imaginings, and the haunting sadness which never quite left him. Here was his tenderness for lovely, fragile things; his preoccupation with the past. Finally here was his love for English — the volume bore this motto from Edgar Allan Poe:

> Was it not Fate, that, on this July midnight —
> Was it not Fate (whose name is also Sorrow)

That bade me pause before that garden-gate
To breathe the incense of those slumbering roses?

*   *   *   *   *   *

(Ah! bear in mind this garden was enchanted!)

The following poem is printed in italics as a sort
of dedication to the book :

Mon âme est une infante en robe de parade,
Dont l'exil se reflète, éternel et royal,
Aux grands miroirs déserts d'un vieil Escurial,
Ainsi qu'une galère oubliée en la rade.

Aux pieds de son fauteuil, allongés noblement,
Deux lévriers d'Écosse aux yeux mélancoliques
Chassent, quand il lui plaît, les bêtes symboliques
Dans la forêt du Rêve et de l'Enchantement.

Son page favori, qui s'appelle Naguère,
Lui lit d'ensorcelants poèmes à mi-voix,
Cependant qu'immobile, une tulipe aux doigts,
Elle écoute mourir en elle leur mystère . . .

Le parc alentour d'elle étend ses frondaisons,
Ses marbres, ses bassins, ses rampes à balustres ;
Et, grave, elle s'enivre à ces songes illustres
Que recèlent pour nous les nobles horizons.

Elle est là résignée, et douce, et sans surprise,
Sachant trop pour lutter comme tout est fatal,
Et se sentant, malgré quelque dédain natal,
Sensible à la pitié comme l'onde à la brise.

Elle est là résignée, et douce en ses sanglots,
Plus sombre seulement quand elle évoque en songe
Quelque Armada sombrée à l'éternel mensonge,
Et tant de beaux espoirs endormis sous les flots.

Des soirs trop lourds de pourpre où sa fierté soupire,
Les portraits de Van Dyck aux beaux doigts longs et purs,
Pâles en velours noir sur l'or vieilli des murs,
En leurs grands airs défunts la font rêver d'empire.

Les vieux mirages d'or ont dissipé son deuil,
Et dans les visions où son ennui s'échappe,
Soudain — gloire ou soleil — un rayon qui la frappe
Allume en elle tous les rubis de l'orgueil.

Mais d'un sourire triste elle apaise ces fièvres ;
Et, redoutant la foule aux tumultes de fer,
Elle écoute la vie — au loin — comme la mer . . .
Et le secret se fait plus profond sur ses lèvres.

Rien n'émeut d'un frisson l'eau pâle de ses yeux,
Où s'est assis l'Esprit voilé des Villes mortes ;
Et par les salles, où sans bruit tournent les portes,
Elle va, s'enchantant de mots mystérieux.

L'eau vaine des jets d'eau là-bas tombe en cascade,
Et, pâle à la croisée, une tulipe aux doigts,
Elle est là, reflétée aux miroirs d'autrefois,
Ainsi qu'une galère oubliée en la rade.

Mon Ame est une infante en robe de parade.

Who, after reading that poem, could approach the book in other than a sympathetic mood?

Is it by chance that he figures his soul under the guise of a Spanish Infanta; or does he feel in himself something exotic, un-French, something which is descended to him from those possible Spanish ancestors? This poem seems almost a complete epitome of Samain's soul. An old, magnificent splendour is here, all about his seated, quiescent Infanta, "immobile, une tulipe aux doigts." And again,

> Elle est là, reflétée aux miroirs d'autrefois,
> Ainsi qu'une galère oubliée en la rade.

Yes, Samain has paraphrased himself in this poem — the haughty, noble, anachronistic self, hidden under the appearance of an insignificant government employee.

This introduction is followed by a second motto from Mallarmé: "D'une essence ravie aux vieillesses des roses," and then we come to the book itself. This is the first poem:

HEURES D'ÉTÉ

I

> Apporte les cristaux dorés,
> Et les verres couleur de songe;
> Et que notre amour se prolonge
> Dans les parfums exaspérés.

Des roses! Des roses encor!
Je les adore à la souffrance.
Elles ont la sombre attirance
Des choses qui donnent la mort.

L'été d'or croule dans les coupes;
Le jus des pêches que tu coupes
Éclabousse ton sein neigeux.

Le parc est sombre comme un gouffre . . .
Et c'est dans mon cœur orageux
Comme un mal de douceur qui souffre.

These poems are as fragile as the golden crystals
he speaks of. What do they give us? It is impossible to say. A nuance, a colour, a vague magnificence. Here is an evocation of that eighteenth
century, by which he was haunted:

MUSIQUE SUR L'EAU

Oh! Écoute la symphonie;
Rien n'est doux comme une agonie
Dans la musique indéfinie
Qu'exhale un lointain vaporeux;

D'une langueur la nuit s'enivre,
Et notre cœur qu'elle délivre
Du monotone effort de vivre
Se meurt d'un trépas langoureux.

Glissons entre le ciel et l'onde,
Glissons sous la lune profonde ;
Toute mon âme, loin du monde,
S'est réfugiée en tes yeux,

Et je regarde tes prunelles
Se pâmer sous les chanterelles,
Comme deux fleurs surnaturelles
Sous un rayon mélodieux.

Oh ! écoute la symphonie ;
Rien n'est doux comme l'agonie
De la lèvre à la lèvre unie
Dans la musique indéfinie . . .

The insistence of Autumn evenings with their
suggestion of melancholy is in *Octobre*:

OCTOBRE

Octobre est doux. — L'hiver pèlerin s'achemine
Au ciel où la dernière hirondelle s'étonne.
Rêvons . . . le feu s'allume et la bise chantonne.
Rêvons . . . le feu s'endort sous sa cendre d'hermine.

L'abat-jour transparent de rose s'illumine.
La vitre est noire sous l'averse monotone.
Oh ! le doux "remember" en la chambre d'automne,
Où des trumeaux défunts l'âme se dissémine.

La ville est loin. Plus rien qu'un bruit sourd de voitures
Qui meurt, mélancolique, aux plis lourds des tentures . . .
Formons des rêves fins sur des miniatures.

Vers de mauves lointains d'une douceur fanée
Mon âme s'est perdue ; et l'Heure enrubannée
Sonne cent ans à la pendule surannée . . .

And here is a splendid one of a fête — eighteenth century, of course — in the Palazzo Lanzoli at Bergamo, and all done with a touch :

NOCTURNE

Nuit d'été. — Sous le ciel de lapis-lazuli,
Le parc enchanté baigne en des ténèbres molles.
Les fleurs rêvent, l'amour se parfume aux corolles.
Tiède, la lune monte au firmament pâli.

Ce soir, fête à Bergame au palais Lanzoli !
Les couples enlacés descendent des gondoles.
Le bal s'ouvre, étoilé de roses girandoles.
Flûtes et cordes, l'orchestre est conduit par Lulli.

Les madrigaux parmi les robes essaimées
Offrent, la lèvre en cœur, leurs fadeurs sublimées ;
Et, sur le glacis d'or des parquets transparents,

Les caillettes Régence, exquisement vieillotes,
Détaillent la langueur savante des gavottes
Au rhythme parfumé des éventails mourants.

Notice how deftly the poet places his picture by speaking of Bergamo and the Lanzoli Palace. And bringing in Lulli as a rhyme, is a delightful thing.

But perhaps the prettiest one of that kind is *L'Ile Fortunée*, undoubtedly suggested by Watteau's picture, *Le Départ pour Cythère.* Not Verlaine himself has done a more beautiful eighteenth century picture, nor one which sings more gracefully.

L'ILE FORTUNÉE

Dites, la Bande Jolie,
J'ai l'âme en mélancolie,
Dites-moi, je vous supplie,
    Où c'est.
Est-ce à Venise, à Florence?
Est-ce au pays d'Espérance?
Est-ce dans l'Ile-de-France?
    Qui sait?

Viens, tu verras des bergères,
Des marquises bocagères,
Des moutons blancs d'étagères,
    Et puis
Des oiseaux et des oiselles,
Des Lindors et des Angèles,
Et des roses aux margelles
    Des puits.

Viens, tu verras des Lucindes,
Des Agnès, des Rosalindes,
Avec des perles des Indes,
    Gardant

Sur l'index une perruche,
Le col serré dans la ruche,
Le grand éventail d'autruche
    Pendant.

Les Iris, et les Estelles
En chaperons de dentelles
Rêvent près des cascatelles
    En pleurs,
Et fermant leurs grandes ailes
Les papillons épris d'elles
En deviennent infidèles
    Aux fleurs.

Unis d'une double étreinte
Les Amants rôdent, sans crainte,
Aux détours du labyrinthe
    Secret.
Sur le jardin diaphane
Un demi-silence plane,
Où toute rumeur profane
    Mourrait.

C'est la Divine Journée,
Par le songe promenée
Sur l'herbe comme fanée
    Un peu.
Avec des amours sans fraude,
Des yeux d'ambre et d'émeraude
Et de lents propos que brode
    L'aveu.

Le soir tombe . . . L'heure douce
Qui s'éloigne sans secousse
Pose à peine sur la mousse
    Ses pieds ;
Un jour indécis persiste,
Et le Crépuscule triste
Ouvre ses yeux d'améthyste
    Mouillés.

Des cygnes voguent par troupes . . .
On goûte sur l'herbe en groupes ;
Le dessert choque les coupes
    D'or fin.
Les assiettes sont de Sèvres ;
Et les madrigaux, si mièvres,
Caramélisent les lèvres
    Sans fin.

L'après-midi qui renie
L'ivresse du jour bannie
Expire en une infinie
    Langueur . . .
Le toit des chaumières fume,
Et dans le ciel qui s'embrume
L'argent des astres s'allume,
    Songeur.

Les amants disent leurs flammes,
Les yeux fidèles des femmes
Sont si purs qu'on voit leurs âmes
    Au fond ;

G

Et, deux à deux, angéliques,
Les Baisers mélancoliques
Au bleu pays des reliques
    S'en vont.

Au son des musiques lentes,
Les Amoureuses dolentes
Ralentissent, nonchalantes,
    Le pas . . .
Du ciel flotte sur la terre ;
Et, dans le soir solitaire,
L'angélus tinte à Cythère,
    Là-bas . . .

The whole volume is full of delicate, almost artificial, light and shade ; bells ring over still lakes, roses in cut glass vases mirror themselves in the marble tops of tables, silken skirts brush over polished floors, but — in the distance, everything is in the distance. The poet himself, kind, patient, sad, is always by our side assuring us that it is only his soul, "en robe de parade." Still, there are sterner poems in this collection, such as *Silence* and *Douleur*. No one understands better than Samain how to give the emotion, the grandeur, or the tragedy, of an epoch, in the confines of a sonnet.

VILLE MORTE

Vague, perdue au fond des sables monotones,
La ville d'autrefois, sans tours et sans remparts,

Dort le sommeil dernier des vieilles Babylones,
Sous le suaire blanc de ses marbres épars.

Jadis elle régnait ; sur ses murailles fortes
La Victoire étendait ses deux ailes de fer.
Tous les peuples d'Asie assiégeaient ses cent portes ;
Et ses grands escaliers descendaient vers la mer . . .

Vide à présent, et pour jamais silencieuse,
Pierre à pierre, elle meurt, sous la lune pieuse,
Auprès de son vieux fleuve ainsi qu'elle épuisé

Et, seul, un éléphant de bronze, en ces désastres,
Droit encore au sommet d'un portique brisé,
Lève tragiquement sa trompe vers les astres.

Or this, which seems, in its fourteen lines, to give
both sides of Napoleon's character so that no more
need be said. Napoleon, sending to Corsica for his
old nurse, so that she might be present at his Coro-
nation, is one of those strange beauties which start
up along his career.

LE SACRE

Notre-Dame annonçait l'apothéose prête
Avec la voix d'airain de ses beffrois jumeaux ;
Au loin les grands canons grondaient, et les drapeaux
Se gonflaient, frissonnants, sous l'orgueil de la fête.

L'Empereur s'inclina, les mains jointes, nu-tête,
Et le Pape apparut, dans l'éclat des flambeaux,
Tenant entre ses doigts étincelants d'anneaux
La couronne portant la croix latine au faîte.

Mon fils ! dit le pontife . . . alors l'orgue se tut.
Sur tous les fronts baissés un seul frisson courut,
Comme le battement soudain d'une aile immense ;

Et l'on n'entendit plus, ô César triomphant,
Dans la nef où planait un auguste silence,
Qu'une vieille à genoux qui pleurait son enfant.

There are still two more poems which I must
quote. They tell more about his poetry than any
words of mine can do. The first is *Dilection*, and
enumerates the subjects he prefers :

DILECTION

J'adore l'indécis, les sons, les couleurs frêles,
Tout ce qui tremble, ondule, et frissonne, et chatoie,
Les cheveux et les yeux, l'eau, les feuilles, la soie,
Et la spiritualité des formes grêles ;

Les rimes se frôlant comme des tourterelles,
La fumée où le songe en spirales tournoie,
La chambre au crépuscule, où Son profil se noie,
Et la caresse de Ses mains surnaturelles ;

L'heure de ciel au long des lèvres câlinée,
L'âme comme d'un poids de délice inclinée,
L'âme qui meurt ainsi qu'une rose fanée,

Et tel cœur d'ombre chaste, embaumé de mystère,
Où veille, comme le rubis d'un lampadaire,
Nuit et jour, un amour mystique et solitaire.

The second poem starts off without any title and speaks of the technique he strives to attain :

Je rêve de vers doux et d'intimes ramages,
De vers à frôler l'âme ainsi que des plumages,

De vers blonds où le sens fluide se délie,
Comme sous l'eau la chevelure d'Ophélie,

De vers silencieux, et sans rythme et sans trame,
Où la rime sans bruit glisse comme une rame,

De vers d'une ancienne étoffe, exténuée,
Impalpable comme le son et la nuée,

De vers de soirs d'automne ensorcelant les heures
Au rite féminin des syllabes mineures,

De vers de soirs d'amour énervés de verveine,
Où l'âme sente, exquise, une caresse à peine,

Et qui au long des nerfs baignés d'ondes câlines
Meurent à l'infini en pâmoisons félines,
Comme un parfum dissous parmi des tiédeurs closes,

Violes d'or, et *pianissim'amorose* . . .

Je rêve de vers doux mourant comme des roses.

These two poems together are an excellent analysis
of his work.

Good fortune did not change Samain. He was
gentle, unaffected, painstaking, as before. He did
not rush into print as the result of his success; on
the contrary, it was not until 1898 that his next
book, *Aux Flancs du Vase*, was published.

In the meantime, Samain and Raymond Bonheur
had been to Provençe in September, 1897, and
stopped at Orthez to see Francis Jammes. Between
this simple and great poet and Samain, two days
were enough to cement a friendship which lasted
for the rest of Samain's life. They only saw each
other for these few days, and once, later, when
Jammes came to Paris for a short stay, and wandered
about the park of Versailles with Samain, but the
memory of his friend has never left Jammes. One
of his most beautiful *Élégies* is to Samain.

These little journeys, including one to Italy, gave
Samain great pleasure, and showed him more kinds
of natural scenery than he had ever seen before.

The poems in his posthumous volume, *Le Chariot
d'Or*: *Forêts*, *Les Monts*, *Le Fleuve*, are probably
the result of those journeys.

About this time, Samain's health began to give
way. He complains of discomfort. This is the
moment to follow up his success. M. Brunetière
makes advances to him for the *Revue des Deux
Mondes*, and twice his poems are printed in it. But
he is indifferent. His health is failing. He is writing
Aux Flancs du Vase, and says that the idea of it
"me hante comme un cauchemar," and that he cannot sleep for thinking of it.

Unhappily, the moment passes, and when the book
comes out in 1898, it goes almost unnoticed. Too
long a time had elapsed, Coppée was ill, and there
was no fashionable critic to do for this volume what
he had done for the other.

Yet *Aux Flancs du Vase* is not a whit behind
Au Jardin de l'Infante in beauty of purpose or
technique. Twenty-five little poems, of a singularly advised simplicity and charm. The scenes
are set in a conventional antiquity by means of
Greek names being given to the characters, and
the whole reminds one of a set of engravings by
Boucher, or Fragonard, or Watteau. Not paintings,
but engravings, each set in an oval, and faintly
coloured.

It is a little boy struggling with a goat; or a mother
and child threading and bargaining their way through

a market; or a girl chasing and catching a frog.
But here are three of these little pieces:

LE REPAS PRÉPARÉ

Ma fille, laisse là ton aiguille et ta laine;
Le maître va rentrer; sur la table de chêne
Avec la nappe neuve aux plis étincelants
Mets la faïence claire et les verres brillants.
Dans la coupe arrondie à l'anse en col de cygne
Pose les fruits choisis sur des feuilles de vigne:
Les pêches que recouvre un velours vierge encor,
Et les lourds raisins bleus mêlés aux raisins d'or.
Que le pain bien coupé remplisse les corbeilles,
Et puis ferme la porte et chasse les abeilles . . .
Dehors le soleil brûle, et la muraille cuit.
Rapprochons les volets, faisons presque la nuit.
Afin qu'ainsi la salle, aux ténèbres plongée,
S'embaume toute aux fruits dont la table est chargée.
Maintenant, va puiser l'eau fraîche dans la cour;
Et veille que surtout la cruche, à ton retour,
Garde longtemps, glacée et lentement fondue,
Une vapeur légère à ses flancs suspendue.

LA BULLE

Bathylle, dans la cour où glousse la volaille,
Sur l'écuelle penché, souffle dans une paille;
L'eau savonneuse mousse et bouillonne à grand bruit,
Et déborde.   L'enfant qui s'épuise sans fruit
Sent venir à sa bouche une âcreté saline.
Plus heureuse, une bulle à la fin se dessine,

Et, conduite avec art, s'allonge, se distend
Et s'arrondit enfin en un globe éclatant.
L'enfant souffle toujours ; elle s'accroît encore :
Elle a les cent couleurs du prisme et de l'aurore,
Et reflète aux parois de son mince cristal
Les arbres, la maison, la route et le cheval.
Prête à se détacher, merveilleuse, elle brille !
L'enfant retient son souffle, et voici qu'elle oscille,
Et monte doucement, vert pâle et rose clair,
Comme un frêle prodige étincelant dans l'air !
Elle monte . . . Et soudain, l'âme encore éblouie,
Bathylle cherche en vain sa gloire évanouie . . .

PANNYRE AUX TALONS D'OR

Dans la salle en rumeur un silence a passé . . .
Pannyre aux talons d'or s'avance pour danser.
Un voile aux mille plis la cache tout entière.
D'un long trille d'argent la flûte la première
L'invite ; elle s'élance, entre-croise ses pas,
Et, du lent mouvement imprimé par ses bras,
Donne un rythme bizarre à l'étoffe nombreuse,
Qui s'élargit, ondule, et se gonfle et se creuse,
Et se déploie enfin en large tourbillon . . .
Et Pannyre devient fleur, flamme, papillon !
Tous se taisent ; les yeux la suivent en extase.
Peu à peu la fureur de la danse l'embrase.
Elle tourne toujours ; vite ! plus vite encore !
La flamme éperdument vacille aux flambeaux d'or ! . . .
Puis, brusque, elle s'arrête au milieu de la salle ;
Et le voile qui tourne autour d'elle en spirale,

Suspendu dans sa course, apaise ses longs plis,
Et, se collant aux seins aigus, aux flancs polis,
Comme au travers d'une eau soyeuse et continue,
Dans un divin éclair, montre Pannyre nue.

Little dramas, they are, sufficient each one to itself with a perfect finality. And the delicacy with which they are done defies analysis. They are transparent, hardly printing themselves upon the atmosphere, like egg-shell china held to the light. And yet what movement they have! One can almost hear the soft snap with which the soap-bubble bursts, and Pannyre's dance makes one giddy with its whirl; and by what means he has given the folding of the draperies to stillness — to such utter, drooping heaviness — I do not know. But there it is.

While Samain was preparing this book for the press, his mother was taken ill. Sick himself, Samain nursed his mother and hung over her, fearing the event he dared not realize. It came in December, 1898, and Samain was alone.

His grief was desolating. His health, already extremely feeble, became worse. Consumption declared itself. He must be got away from Paris and the five flights of stairs to his apartment. M. Raymond Bonheur took him to Villefranche, but the winds were too strong and he moved to Vence.

In the Spring he is back in Paris, but no better. Still he starts to work again, and writes the little play in verse, *Polyphème* — attractive, insignificant —

which was published in the second edition of *Aux Flancs du Vase*, in 1901.

The Winter was disastrous, his letters are full of his suffering. In the Spring, he paid a visit to his sister in Lille, but it rained all the time and he could not leave the house. Paris again, and the five flights almost impossible to negotiate. Then M. Bonheur, generous and devoted as always, took him to his own house at Magny-les-Hammeaux in the department of Seine-et-Oise. But Samain feared to be a burden on his friend, and after a few weeks as his guest insisted upon hiring a house on the other side of the road and moving into it, believing, with the invincible optimism of the consumptive, that he should get well, and that they would go to Italy together in the Autumn. Albert Samain died on the 18th of August, 1900, and was buried in his native town of Lille.

In 1901, appeared his last volume of poems, *Le Chariot d'Or*, and in 1903, a volume of prose stories, entitled *Contes*, both collections due to the care and affection of his friends.

Le Chariot d'Or is, if anything, superior to both *Au Jardin de l'Infante* and *Aux Flancs du Vase*. Not so polished as the latter probably, nor so artificially captivating as the former. But many of the poems seem to have a larger humanity. The eighteenth century pieces are here, but more tenderly, more regretfully done. This one, called *Watteau*,

might serve as a companion piece to *L'Ile Fortunée*,
but how differently executed :

WATTEAU

Au-dessus des grands bois profonds
L'étoile du berger s'allume . . .
Groupes sur l'herbe dans la brume . . .
Pizzicati des violons . . .
Entre les mains, les mains s'attardent,
Le ciel où les amants regardent
Laisse un reflet rose dans l'eau ;
Et dans la clairière indécise,
Que la nuit proche idéalise,
Passe entre Estelle et Cydalise
L'ombre amoureuse de Watteau.

Watteau, peintre idéal de la *Fête jolie*,
Ton art léger fut tendre et doux comme un soupir,
Et tu donnas une âme inconnue au Désir
En l'asseyant aux pieds de la Mélancolie.

Tes bergers fins avaient la canne d'or au doigt ;
Tes bergères, non sans quelques façons hautaines,
Promenaient, sous l'ombrage où chantaient les fontaines,
Leurs robes qu'effilait derrière un grand pli droit . . .

Dans l'air bleuâtre et tiède agonisaient les roses ;
Les cœurs s'ouvraient dans l'ombre au jardin apaisé,
Et les lèvres, prenant aux lèvres le baiser,
Fiançaient l'amour triste à la douceur des choses.

Les Pèlerins s'en vont au Pays idéal . . .
La galère dorée abandonne la rive ;
Et l'amante à la proue écoute au loin, pensive,
Une flûte mourir, dans le soir de cristal . . .

Oh ! partir avec eux par un soir de mystère,
O maître, vivre un soir dans ton rêve enchanté !
La mer est rose. . . . Il souffle une brise d'été,
Et quand la nef aborde au rivage argenté

La lune doucement se lève sur Cythère.

L'éventail balancé sans trêve
Au rythme intime des aveux
Fait, chaque fois qu'il se soulève,
S'envoler au front des cheveux,
L'ombre est suave . . . Tout repose.
Agnès sourit ; Léandre pose
Sa viole sur son manteau ;
Et sur les robes parfumées,
Et sur les mains des Bien-Aimées,
Flotte, au long des molles ramées,
L'âme divine de Watteau.

Take these four sonnets on Versailles. Again,
the artificiality has gone. The melancholy wears
its natural complexion as it were, unpainted, and
in No. II is a fine irony, gentle, — the author is
Samain — but healthy and keen.

VERSAILLES

I

O Versailles, par cette après-midi fanée,
Pourquoi ton souvenir m'obsède-t-il ainsi?
Les ardeurs de l'été s'éloignent, et voici
Que s'incline vers nous la saison surannée.

Je veux revoir au long d'une calme journée
Tes eaux glauques que jonche un feuillage roussi,
Et respirer encore, un soir d'or adouci,
Ta beauté plus touchante au déclin de l'année.

Voici tes ifs en cône et tes tritons joufflus,
Tes jardins composés où Louis ne vient plus,
Et ta pompe arborant les plumes et les casques.

Comme un grand lys tu meurs, noble et triste, sans bruit;
Et ton onde épuisée au bord moisi des vasques
S'écoule, douce ainsi qu'un sanglot dans la nuit.

II

Grand air.   Urbanité des façons anciennes.
Haut cérémonial.   Révérences sans fin.
Créqui, Fronsac, beaux noms chatoyants de satin.
Mains ducales dans les vieilles valenciennes,

Mains royales sur les épinettes.   Antiennes
Des évêques devant Monseigneur le Dauphin.

Gestes de menuet et cœurs de biscuit fin ;
Et ces grâces que l'on disait Autrichiennes . . .

Princesses de sang bleu, dont l'âme d'apparat,
Des siècles, au plus pur des castes macéra.
Grands seigneurs pailletés d'esprit.   Marquis de sèvres.

Tout un monde galant, vif, brave, exquis et fou,
Avec sa fine épée en verrouil, et surtout
Ce mépris de la mort, comme une fleur, aux lèvres !

III

Mes pas ont suscité les prestiges enfuis.
O psyché de vieux saxe où le Passé se mire . . .
C'est ici que la reine, en écoutant Zémire,
Rêveuse, s'éventait dans la tiédeur des nuits.

O visions : paniers, poudre et mouches ; et puis,
Léger comme un parfum, joli comme un sourire
C'est cet air vieille France ici que tout respire ;
Et toujours cette odeur pénétrante des buis . . .

Mais ce qui prend mon cœur d'une étreinte infinie,
Aux rayons d'un long soir dorant son agonie,
C'est ce Grand-Trianon solitaire et royal,

Et son perron désert où l'automne, si douce,
Laisse pendre, en rêvant, sa chevelure rousse
Sur l'eau divinement triste du grand canal.

IV

Le bosquet de Vertumne est délaissé des Grâces.
Cette ombre, qui, de marbre en marbre gémissant,
Se traîne et se retient d'un beau bras languissant,
Hélas, c'est le Génie en deuil des vieilles races.

O Palais, horizon suprême des terrasses,
Un peu de vos beautés coule dans notre sang ;
Et c'est ce qui vous donne un indicible accent,
Quand un couchant sublime illumine vos glaces !

Gloires dont tant de jours vous fûtes le décor,
Ames étincelant sous les lustres. Soirs d'or.
Versailles . . . Mais déjà s'amasse la nuit sombre.

Et mon cœur tout à coup se serre, car j'entends,
Comme un bélier sinistre aux murailles du temps,
Toujours, le grand bruit sourd de ces flots noirs dans l'ombre.

A new vigour, utterly foreign to the other volumes,
is here. Occasionally, something almost like humour
and animal spirits creeps in. Here are two little
sonnets called *Paysages*, in which Samain shows the
Flemish love of painting :

PAYSAGES

I

L'air est trois fois léger. Sous le ciel trois fois pur,
Le vieux bourg qui s'effrite en ses noires murailles
Ce clair matin d'hiver sourit sous ses pierrailles
A ses monts familiers qui rêvent dans l'azur . . .

Une dalle encastrée, en son latin obscur,
Parle après deux mille ans d'antiques funérailles.
César passait ici pour gagner ses batailles,
Un oiseau du printemps chante sur le vieux mur . . .

Bruissante sous l'ombre en dentelle d'un arbre,
La fontaine sculptée en sa vasque de marbre
Fait briller au soleil quatre filets d'argent.

Et pendant qu'à travers la marmaille accourue
La diligence jaune entre dans la grand'rue,
La tour du Signador jette l'heure en songeant.

II

L'horloger, pâle et fin, travaille avec douceur ;
Vagues, le seuil béant, somnolent les boutiques ;
Et d'un trottoir à l'autre ainsi qu'aux temps antiques
Les saluts du matin échangent leur candeur.

Panonceaux du notaire et plaque du docteur . . .
A la fontaine un gars fait boire ses bourriques ;
Et vers le catéchisme en files symétriques
Des petits enfants vont, conduits par une sœur.

Un rayon de soleil dardé comme une flèche
Fait tout à coup chanter une voix claire et fraîche
Dans la ruelle obscure ainsi qu'un corridor.

De la montagne il sort des ruisselets en foule,
Et partout c'est un bruit d'eau vive qui s'écoule
De l'aube au front d'argent jusqu'au soir aux yeux d'or.

H

There is certainly humour in the yellow diligence, and in the door-plates of the doctor and notary. *La Cuisine* is the most Flemish thing that Samain ever did. It is a whole palette of shouting colours, and as realistic as Zola's still life pictures in *Le Ventre de Paris.*

LA CUISINE

Dans la cuisine où flotte une senteur de thym,
Au retour du marché, comme un soir de butin,
S'entassent pêle-mêle avec les lourdes viandes
Les poireaux, les radis, les oignons en guirlandes,
Les grands choux violets, le rouge potiron,
La tomate vernie et le pâle citron.
Comme un grand cerf-volant la raie énorme et plate
Gît fouillée au couteau, d'une plaie écarlate.
Un lièvre au poil rougi traîne sur les pavés
Avec des yeux pareils à des raisins crevés.
D'un tas d'huîtres vidé d'un panier couvert d'algues
Monte l'odeur du large et la fraîcheur des vagues.
Les cailles, les perdreaux au doux ventre ardoisé
Laissent, du sang au bec, pendre leur cou brisé;
C'est un étal vibrant de fruits verts, de légumes,
De nacre, d'argent clair, d'écailles et de plumes.
Un tronçon de saumon saigne et, vivant encor,
Un grand homard de bronze, acheté sur le port,
Parmi la victuaille au hasard entassée,
Agite, agonisant, une antenne cassée.

One more quotation and I have done. It is a poem with the title *Nocturne Provincial*, and it is

modern — yes, modern, as we to-day understand
the term — in subject, in treatment, even in its
changing rhythms.

NOCTURNE PROVINCIAL

La petite ville sans bruit
Dort profondément dans la nuit.

Aux vieux réverbères à branches
Agonise un gaz indigent ;
Mais soudain la lune émergeant
Fait tout au long des maisons blanches
Resplendir des vitres d'argent.

La nuit tiède s'évente au long des marronniers . . .
La nuit tardive, où flotte encor de la lumière.
Tout est noir et désert aux anciens quartiers ;
Mon âme, accoude-toi sur le vieux pont de pierre,
Et respire la bonne odeur de la rivière.

Le silence est si grand que mon cœur en frissonne.
Seul, le bruit de mes pas sur le pavé résonne.
Le silence tressaille au cœur, et minuit sonne !

Au long des grands murs d'un couvent
Des feuilles bruissent au vent.
Pensionnaires . . . Orphelines . . .
Rubans bleus sur les pèlerines . . .
C'est le jardin des Ursulines.

Une brise à travers les grilles
Passe aussi douce qu'un soupir.
Et cette étoile aux feux tranquilles,
Là-bas, semble, au fond des charmilles,
Une veilleuse de saphir.

Oh ! sous les toits d'ardoise à la lune pâlis,
Les vierges et leur pur sommeil aux chambres claires,
Et leurs petits cous ronds noués de scapulaires,
Et leurs corps sans péché dans la blancheur des lits ! . . .

D'une heure égale ici l'heure égale est suivie,
Et l'Innocence en paix dort au bord de la vie . . .

Triste et déserte infiniment
Sous le clair de lune électrique,
Voici que la place historique
Aligne solennellement
Ses vieux hôtels du Parlement.

A l'angle, une fenêtre est éclairée encor.
Une lampe est là-haut, qui veille quand tout dort !
Sous le frêle tissu, qui tamise sa flamme,
Furtive, par instants, glisse une ombre de femme.

La fenêtre s'entr'ouvre un peu ;
Et la femme, poignant aveu,
Tord ses beaux bras nus dans l'air bleu . . .

O secrètes ardeurs des nuits provinciales !
Cœurs qui brûlent ! Cheveux en désordre épandus !
Beaux seins lourds de désirs, pétris par des mains pâles !
Grands appels suppliants, et jamais entendus !

Je vous évoque, ô vous, amantes ignorées,
Dont la chair se consume ainsi qu'un vain flambeau,
Et qui sur vos beaux corps pleurez, désespérées,
Et faites pour l'amour, et d'amour dévorées,
Vous coucherez, un soir, vierges dans le tombeau !

Et mon âme pensive, à l'angle de la place,
Fixe toujours là-bas la vitre où l'ombre passe.

Le rideau frêle au vent frissonne . . .
La lampe meurt . . . Une heure sonne.
Personne, personne, personne.

There are other parts to the book. Parts not so
interesting, not so different. We know that many
of the poems in the volume date from the time of
Au Jardin de l'Infante. Which ones are they? I
wonder. Were the ones we think more modern
really written later, or did Samain, at one time in
his career, confuse art with artificiality, and elimi-
nate these poems as less good than others? Here
they are, beautiful works of art for us to speculate
upon, and proofs of the power of the modern world,
which imposes itself upon us whether we will or not.

In closing, I cannot help asking myself the question: Have I evoked a man for you? Have I shown him as he was: a genius, graceful, timid, proud, passionate, and reserved? Let me end by two quotations, descriptions, by men who knew him. The first one is in a letter from the poet Robert de Montesquiou; he says: "I had occasion to meet the author of *Au Jardin de l'Infante* at the house of a mutual friend..... The simplicity of his attitude and manners, the dignity of his life, could only add to the predilection his works had inspired. But his life was shut like his soul, fastened as well. One could only, one would wish only, to distract it for brief moments. The rest resolves itself into the pure, tender, penetrating songs which are his books. I had the pleasure of meeting Albert Samain many times. . . . He always showed himself reserved without affectation, the result of his distinguished and discreet nature."

The other quotation is Francis Jammes' elegy on Albert Samain:

ÉLÉGIE PREMIÈRE

A ALBERT SAMAIN

Mon cher Samain, c'est à toi que j'écris encore.
C'est la première fois que j'envoie à la mort
ces lignes que t'apportera, demain, au ciel,
quelque vieux serviteur d'un hameau éternel.
Souris-moi pour que je ne pleure pas. Dis-moi:
"Je ne suis pas si malade que tu le crois."

Ouvre ma porte encore, ami. Passe mon seuil
et dis-moi en entrant : "Pourquoi es-tu en deuil?"
Viens encore. C'est Orthez où tu es. Bonheur est là.
Pose donc ton chapeau sur la chaise qui est là.
Tu as soif? Voici de l'eau de puits bleue et du vin.
Ma mère va descendre et te dire : "Samain . . ."
et ma chienne appuyer son museau sur ta main.

Je parle. Tu souris d'un sérieux sourire.
Le temps n'existe pas. Et tu me laisses dire.
Le soir vient. Nous marchons dans la lumière jaune
qui fait les fins du jour ressembler à l'Automne.
Et nous longeons le gave. Une colombe rauque
gémit tout doucement dans un peuplier glauque.
Je bavarde. Tu souris encore. Bonheur se tait.
Voici la route obscure au déclin de l'Eté,
voici l'ombre à genoux près des belles-de-nuit
qui ornent les seuils noirs où la fumée bleuit.

Ta mort ne change rien. L'ombre que tu aimais,
où tu vivais, où tu souffrais, où tu chantais,
c'est nous qui la quittons et c'est toi qui la gardes.
Ta lumière naquit de cette obscurité
qui nous pousse à genoux par ces beaux soirs d'Été
où, flairant Dieu qui passe et fait vivre les blés,
sous les liserons noirs aboient les chiens de garde.

Je ne regrette pas ta mort. D'autres mettront
le laurier qui convient aux rides de ton front.
Moi, j'aurais peur de te blesser, te connaissant.
Il ne faut pas cacher aux enfants de seize ans
qui suivront ton cercueil en pleurant sur ta lyre,
la gloire de ceux-là qui meurent le front libre.

Je ne regrette pas ta mort.   Ta vie est là.
Comme la voix du vent qui berce les lilas
ne meurt point, mais revient après bien des années
dans les mêmes lilas qu'on avait cru fanés,
tes chants, mon cher Samain, reviendront pour bercer
les enfants que déjà mûrissent nos pensées.

Sur ta tombe, pareil à quelque pâtre antique
dont pleure le troupeau sur la pauvre colline,
je chercherais en vain ce que je peux porter.
Le sel serait mangé par l'agneau des ravines
et le vin serait bu par ceux qui t'ont pillé.

Je songe à toi.   Le jour baisse comme ce jour
où je te vis dans mon vieux salon de campagne.
Je songe à toi.   Je songe aux montagnes natales.
Je songe à ce Versailles où tu me promenas,
où nous disions des vers, tristes et pas à pas.
Je songe à ton ami et je songe à ta mère.
Je songe à ces moutons qui, au bord du lac bleu,
en attendant la mort bêlaient sur leurs clarines.

Je songe à toi.   Je songe au vide pur des cieux.
Je songe à l'eau sans fin, à la clarté des feux.
Je songe à la rosée qui brille sur les vignes.
Je songe à toi.   Je songe à moi.   Je songe à Dieu.

It is all in that one line: "Knowing you, I feared
to wound you."

Remy de Gourmont

REMY DE GOURMONT

REMY DE GOURMONT

Of the six poets whom I have chosen for the subjects of these essays, it is certain that the one for whom Anglo-Saxon readers must feel the least sympathy is Remy de Gourmont. He is also the one who, considered strictly as poet, must be acknowledged to be the least considerable. Out of the forty-one, or so, volumes which he has published, his poetry is easily contained in one volume and some thirty pages of another. And nowhere among his poems is there one which can be considered a masterpiece. As a masterpiece of pure poetry, I should say, for of masterpieces of cunning verbal *nuances* there are several.

Why then, it may very well be asked, include him among my six poets? Because no one of the later period of French literature has been more prominent than he, and no one has had a greater influence upon the generation of writers that have followed his. He has had this influence directly, through his poems; and indirectly, by his critical writings and philological studies.

As it used to be said that Meredith was the
writer's writer, I might say that Gourmont is the
poet for poets. He is the great teacher of certain
effects, the instructor in verbal shades. No one
has studied more carefully than he the sounds of
vowels and consonants. Not even from his great
teacher, Mallarmé, can more be learnt. As a
producer of colour in words, he cedes to no one;
his knowledge of the technique of poetry is un-
surpassed.

"Poet, critic, dramatist, *savant*, biologist, philosopher, novelist, philologian and grammarian," is
the way the editors of *Poètes d'Aujourd'hui* style
him. And really, the extent of his literary activity
take one's breath away. Of course, the danger to
such a man is in the almost inevitable Jack-of-all-
Trades result which such a multitude of avocations
trails along with it. It is heresy to whisper such a
thing, but it cannot really be denied that in only
one of these branches has Gourmont made himself
supreme. But in that he has no equal. The
æsthetic of the French language (to borrow one
of his own titles); there he is on absolutely indis-
putable ground.

Yet it would not be fair to give you the idea that
he has done merely well along his other lines. Can
a man so conversant with the art of writing ever
write merely well? Gourmont's novels and tales
are among the best of the last twenty years, only

others have surpassed him; the same is true of his poems. But the way he has written, no one can surpass him there; and we, who try to write, mull over his pages for hours at a time, and endeavour to learn the lesson which he has analyzed and illustrated for us. Along with that is another lesson, written as clearly in his pages, of what not to do, of the necessity for singleness of purpose, of the terrible pitfall looming always before the man who is at once an artist and an insatiably curious person.

Great, excessively great, people can do it. Leonardo da Vinci did it. He pulled the two characters along side by side, to the profit of both. But Remy de Gourmont has not quite done it, and it is natural to suppose that the literary masterpieces he might have made have wasted away while he dabbled in science. *Physique de l'Amour* is a most interesting volume on the sexual instinct in animals. But there are many books on the subject by others more competent for the task. And I cannot help thinking it a little odd that this should be the only purely scientific essay he has written. Interesting though it is, contemplated in its place among Gourmont's work as a whole, should we not consider it as another evidence of that preoccupation with sex which has robbed his books of the large view they might have had? It cannot be denied that a man who plays perpetually upon an instrument of one string is confining himself within a very small musical compass.

Is Gourmont's work so diversified after all? Yes,
and no. But let us work up to these considera-
tions gradually, and examine them in their proper
place.

Remy de Gourmont was born in the Château of
La Motte at Bazoches-en-Houlme, in Normandy,
on the fourth of April, 1858. He is the descendant
of a remarkable family of painters, engravers, and
printers, of the fifteenth and sixteenth centuries.
One of the family, Gilles de Gourmont, was the first
person in Paris to use Greek and Hebrew types in
printing. On his mother's side, Gourmont is directly
descended from the family of François de Malherbe
— the great Malherbe, of whom Boileau said, "He
was the master of our great classic writers."

Of the youth of Remy de Gourmont I know nothing, as the only real biography of him I have been
unable to get. But, in 1883, he came up to Paris,
like all energetic young Frenchmen with intellectual
tendencies, and obtained a position in the Bibliothèque Nationale. Here he remained until 1891,
when an article of his called *Le Joujou Patriotisme*
was too much for the authorities, and he lost his
position.

His first book, a novel called *Merlette*, appeared
in 1886, and very little of his real originality appeared in it, although it contained pleasant descriptions of Normandy. His next book, *Sixtine*,
came out in 1890. Its second title was *Roman*

de la Vie Cérébrale, and that might stand as subtitle for all his work. Oh, the delightful book that *Sixtine* is! I remember reading it in a sort of breathless interest. The hero is a writer, and everything that happens to him he translates almost bodily into his work. Two stories are carried on at the same time, the real one and the one he is writing. The chapters follow each other with no regular order, the reader only knows which story is which by the context, and the incidents of the written story are sometimes all he learns of the real story, which is taken up again later at a point farther on. But what a childish way to tell of a book so full of startling revolutionism! *Sixtine* is indeed a novel of the life of the brain. Gourmont wishes to prove that the world is only a simulacrum, and the perception of it hallucinatory. *Sixtine* is metaphysics masking as a story, and Hubert d'Entrague is the Gourmont of the period, with his knowledge, his curiosity, and, too, his sensual side. But, inconceivable undercurrent though it has, it has an appearance of firm ground. Paris is there, with its *quais,* its Luxembourg, its boulevards, its Museum, its Bibliothèque Nationale; and Normandy is there, with its fields and apple orchards. And here is that wonderful writing, that gift of words. I will quote two passages from it, both in prose. (A poem which is also in the book I wish to keep until we reach his poetry.) The first of these passages is about a sort of ghostly apparition which appears in a mirror. Notice the colours, and the way the figure is gradually drawn out of the glass :

> J'ai vu le portrait. La lune pâle et verte planait dans ma chambre ; je venais de me réveiller et d'obscures et ophidiennes visions me hantaient encore. L'œil fiévreux, je regardais autour de moi avec défiance. . . . Étais-je dans ma chambre et dans mon lit ? . . . Peut-être. Voilà qu'au-dessus de la cheminée la glace lentement change de teinte : son vert lunaire, son vert d'eau transparente sous des saules s'avive et se dore. On dirait qu'au centre de la lueur, comme sur la face même de la lune, des ombres se projettent avec des apparences de traits humains, tandis qu'autour de la vague figure une ondulation lumineuse serpente comme des cheveux blonds dénoués et flottants.

Vert lunaire — those words in *ère* are favourites with Gourmont, we shall meet them many times. Also, the green light of the moon is nice, and, incidentally, true.

The other is the description of a Madonna over the door of a church in Naples. In the names of the unusual stones, we see an evidence of Gourmont's wide knowledge :

> Une église de fuyants contreforts, écrasée et lourde, attirait d'abord le regard inexperimenté et par la splendeur de sa Madone enrubannée le fixait. Quand le soleil déclinant allait au fond de la niche ogivale la baigner de rayons, les rubis et les péridots de sa tiare, les lépidolithes et les topazes, auréole étoilée, réverbéraient l'éclat d'autant d'astres et la figure aux yeux diamantés extasiait.

Not only do we get the brilliance of the sunset lighting up the church and its Madonna, the sound is not sacrificed to the picture, extraordinarily vivid though that is. Listen to the different vowel sounds before the *l's* in *auréole étoilée*; and the *s's*, and *ai* sound, in the last line.

Properly speaking, these are not poems. They are written as prose and intended to be prose, but Gourmont himself has said, "beautiful prose should have a rhythm which makes one doubt if it be prose. Buffon wrote only poems, and Bossuet and Chateaubriand and Flaubert."

In an interview accorded to a representative of the *Écho de Paris*, shortly after the publication of *Sixtine*, Gourmont says, "They tell me that in my recently published novel, *Sixtine*, I have produced *Symbolisme*. Now behold my innocence. I never guessed it. Nevertheless, I learned it without great astonishment : unconsciousness plays so large a part in intellectual operations. I even believe it plays the greatest of all." Certainly, Remy de Gourmont had "produced *Symbolisme*," as unconsciously as most of the *Symbolistes* produced it at first. "*Symbolisme* is an attitude of mind, not a school," as Tancrède de Visan very well says, in his *L'Attitude du Lyrisme Contemporain*, "a lyric ideal in conformity with other tendencies of modern life." To understand what this lyric ideal was, and how it came about, we must go back a little. No study of

I

Remy de Gourmont can be complete without taking him in connection with the *Symboliste* movement.

Poetry, like all art, is organic. It is endowed with a life of its own, and must naturally carry within it the seeds of evolution and change. Every true artistic movement is a necessary movement toward maturity. It is as silly to attempt to stop the artistic clock, as it was for King Canute to forbid the advance of the waves. It is the eternal penance of the artist to be in advance of the people. Writing to be read (otherwise why write!), the true artist can seldom write to suit the taste of the actual public. If he lives to a reasonable age, the public may come round to him, but his beginnings will always be looked upon with suspicion.

Every artist knows this, and yet every artist rails against the besotted ignorance of the public, as if he were the only person who had ever experienced the phenomenon, and his time the only one in which it had appeared.

Remy de Gourmont, and the men of his age, came along at the heels of the Romantic Movement. Musset and Hugo were dead, so was Baudelaire, who might be called the last of the Romantics. As a protest against the somewhat turgid manner into which Romanticism had fallen, a small group of men, notably Théophile Gautier, Leconte de Lisle, and José-Maria de Heredia, took to writing poems of severe, plastic beauty, deprived of over-rich ornament, and delighting by their sharp and beautiful contours. Their verses were so cold as to be almost frozen into immobility, but instead of Hugo's moral preoccupations, they propounded the theory of "art for art's sake," then a new and vigorous battle-cry. These men form the Parnassian School. Theirs was a protest against fantasticality. And extraordinarily different though it appears to be, this movement was prompted by the same protest which in prose produced first Flaubert, then De Maupassant and Zola: the Realistic School of Fiction.

The poetry of the Parnassian School is very beautiful, but it hardly lends itself to the expression of all the phases of our complex modern life. Mallarmé, in love with pure sound, could not content himself within an art which was almost entirely sculpture. Verlaine, choking with emotions, filled with lyric despairs, found no relief in carving beautiful cameos. These men broke away from the Parnassian School, and each in his way attempted to widen the scope of French poetry.

Mallarmé is the great master of the later *Symbolistes*. His was an original contribution to French poetry. And original contributions, as we shall see in a moment, were the foundation stones of the *Symboliste* movement. Mallarmé formed a theory that poetry lies more in the sound of words than in their sense. He did not break away from the classic alexandrine, but made it more undulating and tuneful. Verlaine had no particular theory except to express himself (also a thoroughly Symbolistic point of view); but he found this impossible in the shining ice of the alexandrine. He fell back to the old ballad metres, and Ronsard. He, too, was preoccupied with sound. "De la musique avant toute chose," he has said.

With Mallarmé and Verlaine the *Symboliste* movement may be said to be fairly started. But Mallarmé and Verlaine were not called *Symbolistes*, at first, they were called *Décadents*, partly because Mallarmé was known to have studied and been influenced by the Latin writers of the Decadence, partly because these lines appeared in Verlaine's first book:

Je suis l'Empire à la fin de la décadence.

That did it, and the unfortunate and unfair appellation was lanced. It was after hearing this line recited in a café in the *Quartier Latin*, that Paul Adam founded a little paper and bravely called it *La Décadence*, and other young men followed with another little sheet called *Le Décadent*.

It was a silly name. One of the greatest periods of French poetry was the result of these so-called *Décadents*. Never has there been a more fertile moment in any literature. Talents rose to the surface every day. And the great Parisian public went about its business quite unconscious, fêted its Coppées, and Octave Feuillets; and if it thought of these new men at all, thought of them only to scoff. 'Twas ever thus, and we need not be surprised that Paris, clever though she be, is not entirely apart from the stream of common humanity.

Naturally, their writings were not welcomed in the regular reviews, and the poets were reduced to printing little sheets of their own. One of these, and one which Gourmont calls the most singular of all, was named *La Cravache*. It was a ridiculous little paper, where finance alternated with literature, and the printer cared very little what went into it, provided that the first three pages were filled. Georges Lecomte discovered this small journal, and with Adolph Retté made it one of the most curious literary gazettes which it is possible to imagine. The contributors were Huysmans, Moréas, Henri de Régnier, Kahn, Vielé-Griffin, Paul Adam, Hennique, Charles Morice, Fénéon, — and finally, Verlaine. It was in the obscure *Cravache* that the first version of his volume, *Parallèlement*, appeared. Verlaine had already published *Sagesse*, but still no other journal in Paris was open to his poems. In the *Cravache* also, Huysmans' study on *La Bièvre* was printed, and Vielé-Griffin's translations of Walt Whitman's poems.

Gourmont remarks, with what seems to us, aware of the conditions both here and in England, a strange optimism : "I believe that only in France is such a thing possible. Ten writers and poets of talent, of whom one is Verlaine and another Huysmans, to whom all the serious newspapers are closed, and practically all the reviews."

La Cravache was not the only little review ; there were a great many others, among them *La Vogue, La Pléiade,* and *Le Scapin,* this last edited by a young man named Alfred Vallette. Toward the end of 1889, some one approached Gourmont and asked him to collaborate in a little review to be called *Le Mercure de France* and edited by this same Alfred Vallette. He consented, and in so doing became one of the founders of that now famous publication, together with Samain, Régnier, and all the others of their group. Of course, there was no money, and to meet this difficulty so-called "Founders' Shares" were issued, at sixty francs a share. The founders seem to have been able to compass that, the richest man among them, Jules Renard, buying four.

The *Mercure de France* instantl, leapt into fame, because of a series of satirical ballad. by Laurent Tailhade, *Poil de Carotte* by Jules Renard, and the delicate verses of Albert Samain. Saint-Pol-Roux, who called himself an "*idéo-réaliste,*" contributed a series of short poems in rhythmic prose, notably

Le Pèlerinage de St. Anne. The *Mercure* also became famous for its critics, not the least of these being Remy de Gourmont himself. It is interesting to note that, until 1914, no number had come out without something from his pen, either poetry, novel, tale, or criticism.

Since 1895, the *Mercure* has become the official organ of the *Symboliste* School. But what is the *Symboliste* School? We have seen what the *Décadents* were, and how they started. What changed them into *Symbolistes*?

Let me quote Gourmont himself, in the "Preface" to the first *Livre des Masques*: "What does *Symbolisme* mean? If one keeps to its narrow and etymological sense, almost nothing; if one goes beyond that, it means: individualism in literature, liberty of art, abandonment of existing forms, a tending toward what is new, strange, and even bizarre; it also may mean idealism, disdain of the social anecdote, anti-naturalism, a tendency to take only the characteristic detail out of life, to pay attention only to the act by which a man distinguishes himself from another man, and to desire only to realize results, essentials; finally, for poets, *Symbolisme* seems associated with *vers libre*." And farther on in the same "Preface," contradicting Nordau, who believes that only when conforming to existing standards is art sane, Gourmont says: "We differ violently from this opinion. The capital crime for a writer is conformity, imitation, the submission to rules and teaching. The work of a writer should be, not merely the reflection, but the enlarged reflection, of his personality.

"The sole excuse which a man can have for writing is to write down himself, to unveil for others the sort of world which mirrors itself in his individual glass ; his only excuse is to be original ; he should say things not yet said, and say them in a form not yet formulated. He should create his own æsthetics — and we should admit as many æsthetics as there are original minds, and judge them for what they are and not what they are not. Admit then that *Symbolisme* is, even though excessive, even though tempestuous, even though pretentious, the expression of individualism in art." As the organ of "the expression of individualism in art," the *Mercure* is as up to date to-day as it was the year it was founded.

Remy de Gourmont is one of the foremost *Symbolistes* then, from every point of view. He has aided the movement and flaunted its banner, first unconsciously, as we have seen, later consciously. Individualism, not only in art, but in everything else, has been his creed. He has welcomed young men of talent, and been their encourager and adviser. For himself, his novels are all "romans de la vie cérébrale," they are pictures of the intimate life of his own brain and personality. He is an intellectual; and his novels, and tales, and poems, are intellectual *tours de force.* Let us stop for a moment and consider this personality, so strangely diverse, and yet so unified.

In an article in the "Weekly Critical Review," M. Louis Dumur says of Remy de Gourmont: "With him there is nothing which tells of the particularity of a province. . . . He is neither Southern, nor Breton; nor is he Parisian. He is a Frenchman of France, and even of old France. He belongs a little, if you like, to the North, that North which was the cradle of the *Langue d'Oïl,* the section which experienced most intimately that fusion of Roman, Celt, and Frank, from which has come the history, the language, and the spirit, of this country (France).

"One must be lettered to fully appreciate M. de Gourmont. His work does not impress itself immediately upon the simple and ignorant public. Nobody, certainly, is more modern than he; but his modernity presupposes the past. . . . He is of the great literary line; he takes his place naturally there, in his own time — traditionalist, because his race sparkles in him; innovator, because there is no pleasure in, nor reason for, existing, except in the evolution of ideas, of trend, of temperament. If one wished to draw the genealogical tree of M. de Gourmont, it would not be an absolutely vain amusement. To my mind, there would be, in their legitimate order of ascent, Renan, Balzac, Stendhal, Chateaubriand, Voltaire, Fénelon, Montaigne; one could even put, in spite of his probable protestations, Boileau and Vaugelas. This tree would plunge its roots on all sides of the Middle Ages, the tap-root would be anchored upon scholasticism and theology; the deep soil of Latin antiquity would bear it; . . . the light foreign infiltration would be represented first by Italy, and next by the Germany of Nietzsche; on the margin one could add the title to debatable quarterings: Villiers de l'Isle Adam, Gérard de Nerval, Chamfort . . . and perhaps the Marquis de Sade."

I have quoted M. Dumur at length because I thought he presented the many sides of this brilliant personality better than I could do.

Sixtine was followed, in 1892, by *Le Latin Mystique*, with a preface by J.-K. Huysmans. This book is a study of the Latin writers of the Middle Ages, who greatly attracted Gourmont, as they had Mallarmé and Huysmans. In the poem which appeared in *Sixtine*, and which I did not quote when we were considering that book, the influence of the Latin mediæval writers is very evident. It is even written in one of their favourite forms called a Sequence. It is an extraordinary thing in its virtuosity. Notice the prevalence of the *ère* sound so beloved by him, and the alliterations:

FIGURE DE RÊVE

SÉQUENCE

La très chère aux yeux clairs apparaît sous la lune,
Sous la lune éphémère et mère des beaux rêves.
La lumière bleuie par les brumes cendrait
D'une poussière aérienne
Son front fleuri d'étoiles, et sa légère chevelure
Flottait dans l'air derrière ses pas légers :
La chimère dormait au fond de ses prunelles.
Sur la chair nue et frêle de son cou
Les stellaires sourires d'un rosaire de perles
Étageaient les reflets de leurs pâles éclairs. Ses poignets
Avaient des bracelets tout pareils ; et sa tête,
La couronne incrustée des sept pierres mystiques
Dont les flammes transpercent le cœur comme des glaives,
Sous la lune éphémère et mère des beaux rêves.

Perhaps it was his stay at the Bibliothèque Nationale, perhaps it was his fondness for things beautiful and *recherché* inherited from those old engravers and printers of the sixteenth century, at any rate Gourmont published many of his early books in limited editions in extremely small format, and with special paper and type. His poems, *Fleurs de Jadis* and *Hiéroglyphes*, came out in that way, and also some of his prose books. *Fleurs de Jadis* is called an *édition elzévirienne*, and the forty-seven copies on Holland paper were each numbered and signed by the author. *Le Château Singulier*, a prose tale, is "ornamented with thirty-two vignettes in red and blue;" a third, *L'Ymagier*, in "grand quarto" with "nearly three hundred engravings, reproductions of ancient woodcuts of the fifteenth and sixteenth centuries, great coloured pictures, pages of old books, miniatures, lithographs, woodcuts, drawings, etc. by Whistler, Gauguin," etc., etc., etc. It will be seen that Gourmont was something of a bibliographical dandy. And it is a sort of literary dandyism which principally appears in these early poems. They are extremely interesting, but, it must be admitted, a bit precious. At the same time that he was publishing these special editions, in the early nineties, various others of his books were being issued in the ordinary way. Among them, the strangest and most successful of his poems, *Litanies de la Rose.*

A strange thing with Latin writers, and one which we, here in America, can never quite accustom ourselves to, is the great hold which Catholicism has on them. When they are believers, professing allegiance to the Church, we can understand it. But when they have ceased to believe, we expect them to cease to think of the Church at all. On the contrary, all the French sceptic writers I have read scream their scepticism from the house tops, and "go and bang it against the front door." They delight in what I am forced to consider a very childish form of sacrilege. For Gourmont to call his poem a "litany" evidently gave him a piquant thrill. We see the same thing in the half-shivering delight which Huysmans takes in describing the Black Mass in *Là-Bas*. But Huysmans ended by tumbling back into the arms of the Church, so it is evident that its hold upon him had never really been lost. With Gourmont, profound believer in natural science that he was then, and that he has gone on being in a constantly increasing ratio ever since, this pleasure in being audaciously impertinent to holy things is a little hard to explain. To commit the crime of lese-majesty there must be a "Majesty" first. To profane a holy thing, you must first admit it to be holy ; if you deny the holiness, where is the sacrilege? And without the sacrilege, where is the fun? The truth seems to be that, to most Frenchmen, Catholicism is more of a superstition than a religion. I hardly believe religion, as we conceive the term, to be possible to the Latin mind. They throw off the superstition violently and flauntingly, but, like small boys and their proud denial of the existence of the bogey-man, there is always the underlying fear that this thing you do not believe in may put out a huge claw, some dark night, and scrape you in. Gourmont has his little sacrilegious pleasures quite frequently, notably in the poem, *Oraisons Mauvaises*, and in various of the stories.

But I only paused here to note a curious trait in the Latin character, and one which is often misunderstood, and always thoroughly disliked, by Anglo-Saxons. It appears so often in Gourmont and others of the *Symbolistes*, particularly the prose writers, that it seemed necessary to take cognizance of it, and put it where it belonged. I wish I could quote the whole of *Litanies de la Rose.* Here the author has given roses of fifty-seven colours. Nowhere else is his wonderful manipulation of words so apparent, and his gift for perceiving and describing colours so displayed. The poem is an astounding profusion of sounds, of pictures, of colours, of smells. It is a mixture of artifice and spontaneity, "of Heaven and Hell," as a critic has said. Each rose is supposed to be a woman, and the kind of women can best be shown by the two lines with which the poem begins:

> Fleur hypocrite,
> Fleur du silence.

That Gourmont has not much opinion of women, this poem would seem to prove. But that need not matter to us. Some poems are beautiful because of what they say, some because of the way they say it. Gourmont describes these unpleasant women, compounded of lies and deceits, in a way to make one weep with the beauty of the presentation. We have:

> Rose aux yeux noirs, miroir de ton néant, rose aux yeux noirs, fais-nous croire au mystère, fleur hypocrite, fleur du silence. . .

Rose couleur d'argent, encensoir de nos rêves, rose couleur
d'argent, prends notre cœur et fais-en de la fumée, fleur hypocrite, fleur du silence. . .

Rose vineuse, fleur des tonnelles et des caves, rose vineuse,
les alcools fous gambadent dans ton haleine : souffle-nous
l'horreur de l'amour, fleur hypocrite, fleur du silence.

We have : "Rose en papier de soie," "Rose
couleur de l'aurore, couleur du temps, couleur de
rien," "Rose incarnate," "Rose au cœur virginal,"
"Rose couleur du soir," "Rose bleue, rose iridine,"
"Rose escarboucle, rose fleurie au front noir du
dragon," and this whole stanza again :

Rose hyaline, couleur des sources claires jaillies d'entre les
herbes, rose hyaline, Hylas est mort d'avoir aimé tes yeux, fleur
hypocrite, fleur du silence.

The poem ends with this stanza :

Rose papale, rose arrosée des mains qui bénissent le monde,
rose papale, ton cœur d'or est en cuivre, et les larmes qui perlent
sur ta vaine corolle, ce sont les pleurs du Christ, fleur hypocrite,
fleur du silence.
Fleur hypocrite,
Fleur du silence.

A strange ending for a poem which sets out to be
audacious and sacrilegious. An odd pitiful tenderness is here, and an irony as fine and sad as mist.
Fleurs de Jadis and *Le Dit des Arbres*, are the two
other poems in this pattern. Again they are women,
but the bitter jabbing is not here. *Fleurs de Jadis*

is built round this beautiful, melancholy beginning:
"Je vous préfère aux cœurs les plus galants, cœurs
trépassés, cœurs de jadis." Here again Gourmont
shows his erudition, his observation, and his love
for nature. His flowers are beautiful, believable:
"Jonquilles, dont on fit les cils purs de tant de
blondes filles;" "Aconit, fleur casquée de poison,
guerrière à plume de corbeau;" "Campanules,
amoureuses clochettes que le printemps tintinna-
bule" (that last has a touch of Heine); "Belle-de-
nuit qui frappas à ma porte, il était minuit, j'ai
ouvert ma porte à la Belle-de-nuit et ses yeux
fleurissaient dans l'ombre;" "Lavande, petite séri-
euse, odeur de la vertu, . . . chemise à la douzaine
dans des armoires de chêne, lavande pas bien mé-
chante, et si tendre;" "Alysson, dont la belle âme
s'en va toute en chansons." Delicate, lovely, is it
not?

It is the same with the trees: "Bouleau, frisson
de la baigneuse dans l'océan des herbes folles, pendant que le vent se joue de vos pâles chevelures;"
"Sorbier, parasol des pendeloques, grains de corail
au cou doré des gitanes;" "Mélèze, dame aux
tristes pensées, parabole accoudée sur la ruine d'un
mur, les araignées d'argent ont tissé leurs toiles à
tes oreilles;" "Maronnier, dame de cour en paniers,
dame en robe brodée de trèfles et de panaches, dame
inutile et belle."

Undoubtedly these three are Gourmont's finest

poems. They, and particularly *Litanies de la Rose*, are the ones to which Gourmont's admirers chiefly refer. I am an admirer of Gourmont's myself, and I prefer these poems to his others. They contain more of his original and peculiar qualities. But Gourmont has left them out of a collection of his poems called *Divertissements*, which was published in 1914. He has underscored this volume *Poèmes en Vers*, which I suppose means poems in regular metres. This is what he says about it in the "Preface:" "In this collection there are very few purely verbal poems, those dominated by the pleasure of managing the obliging flock of words; it can easily be understood that forcing such obedience has discouraged me in the exact measure that I assured myself of their excessive docility. Perhaps it will be found that I have ended by conceiving the poem under a too despoiled form, but that was perhaps permitted to the author of *Litanies de la Rose*, which poem has been rejected for a collection that I wished representative of a life of sentiment rather than a life of art." The rest of the sentence we need not quote, it is very sad, and shows Gourmont at fifty-seven considering himself an old man, and rightly so I fear, with waning powers.

What does that mean? That *vers libre*, which he himself considers as one of the most indigenous qualities of the *Symboliste* poet, as we saw in his

K

Preface to the *Livre des Masques*, has been with
him not a conviction, but an experiment? Or that
this extremely French Frenchman finds himself, now
that his energies are weakening, atavistically returning to the traditions of his race? We can only say
that whatever his theories, *vers libre* has never seemed
an irresistible form with him.

But I am suffering the common lot of biographers
and writers about Remy de Gourmont, I am getting side-tracked by first one phase of his genius
and then another. It is impossible to follow him
coherently. His life has been a congestion of intellectual activities.

Let us come back to 1893, or thereabouts. In
1894, appeared *Histoires Magiques*, prose stories, and
in 1894 also, *Hiéroglyphes*, a collection of poems. In
this book appears the *Séquence* from *Sixtine* I read
you a little while ago, and this poem, *Ascension*:

ASCENSION

Un soir, dans la bruyère délaissée,
Avec l'amie souriante et lassée . . .
O soleil, fleur cueillie, ton lourd corymbe
Agonise et descend tout pâle vers les limbes.
Ah! si j'étais avec l'amie lassée,
Un soir, dans la bruyère délaissée!

Les rainettes, parmi les reines des prés
Et les roseaux, criaient énamourées.

Les scarabées grimpent le long des prêles,
Les geais bleus font fléchir les branches frêles.
On entendait les cris énamourés
Des rainettes, parmi les reines des prés.

Un chien, au seuil d'une porte entr'ouverte,
Là-haut, pleure à la lune naissante et verte
Qui rend un peu de joie au ciel aveugle ;
La vache qu'on va traire s'agite et meugle,
Un chien pleure à la lune naissante et verte,
Là-haut, au seuil d'une porte entr'ouverte.

Pendant que nous montons, l'âme inquiète
Et souriante, vers la courbe du faîte,
Le Rêve, demeuré à mi-chemin,
S'assied pensif, la tête dans sa main,
Et nous montons vers la courbe du faîte,
Nous montons souriants, l'âme inquiète.

The following years saw the publication of a number of books, all in prose, and his first volume of contemporary criticism, *Le Livre des Masques*. That Gourmont is a poet in his prose, this description of Maeterlinck's plays will abundantly prove :

Il y a une île quelque part dans les brouillards, et dans l'île il y a un château, et dans le château il y a une grande salle éclairée d'une petite lampe, et dans la grande salle il y a des gens qui attendent. Ils attendent quoi ? Ils ne savent pas. Ils attendent que l'on frappe à la porte, ils attendent que la lampe s'éteigne, ils attendent la Peur, ils attendent la Mort. Ils

parlent; oui, ils disent des mots qui troublent un instant le silence, puis ils écoutent encore, laissant leurs phrases inachevées et
leurs gestes interrompus. Ils écoutent, ils attendent. Elle ne
viendra peut-être pas? Oh! elle viendra. Elle vient toujours.
Il est tard, elle ne viendra peut-être que demain. Et les gens
assemblés dans la grande salle sous la petite lampe se mettent à
sourire et ils vont espérer. On frappe. Et c'est tout; c'est
toute une vie, c'est toute la vie.

More novels and tales, a second *Livre des Masques*,
and in 1899, another book of poems, *Les Saintes
du Paradis*. Gourmont has succeeded in throwing
off the superstition. *Les Saintes du Paradis* might
have been written by a believer, or by an artist
using Catholicism merely as decoration. Gourmont has assured us that with him this latter
is the case. With simplicity, with charm, these
saints pass before us. Here are nineteen saints
stepped out of some old missal, each with her legend
carefully detailed, and each painted in the beautiful,
bright colours so dear to the mediæval illuminator.
In the following "Dedication," they file past us in
some country of clear pinks and greens, painted by
Fra Angelico.

DÉDICACE

O pérégrines qui cheminez songeuses,
Songeant peut-être à des roses lointaines,
Pendant que la poussière et le soleil des plaines
Ont brûlé vos bras nus et votre âme incertaine,

O pérégrines qui cheminez songeuses,
Songeant peut-être à des roses lointaines !

Voici la route qui mène à la montagne,
Voici la claire fontaine où fleurissent les baumes,
Voici le bois plein d'ombre et d'anémones,
Voici les pins, voici la paix, voici les dômes,
Voici la route qui mène à la montagne,
Voici la claire fontaine où fleurissent les baumes !

O pérégrines qui cheminez songeuses,
Suivez la voix qui vous appelle au ciel :
Les arbres ont des feuillages aussi doux que le miel
Et les femmes au cœur pur y deviennent plus belles.
O pérégrines qui cheminez songeuses,
Suivez la voix qui vous appelle au ciel.

Here are the poems on Saint Agatha, martyred
for her chastity, for refusing the proposals of the
Sicilian Governor, Quintarius ; on Saint Collette,
foundress of seventeen convents of the strict obser-
vance, and terrible sufferer from her own rigours ;
on Jeanne d'Arc ; and on Saint Ursula, the English
saint and teacher, who preferred death at the hands
of the Hun to violation :

AGATHE

Joyau trouvé parmi les pierres de la Sicile,
Agathe, vierge vendue aux revendeuses d'amour,
Agathe, victorieuse des colliers et des bagues,

Des sept rubis magiques et des trois pierres de lune,
Agathe, réjouie par le feu des fers rouges,
Comme un amandier par les douces pluies d'automne,
Agathe, embaumée par un jeune ange vêtu de pourpre,
Agathe, pierre et fer, Agathe, or et argent,
Agathe, chevalière de Malte,
Sainte Agathe, mettez du feu dans notre sang.

COLETTE

Douloureuse beauté cachée dans la prière,
Colette, dure à son cœur et plus dure à sa chair,
Colette prisonnière dans les cloîtres amers
Où les colliers d'amour sont des chaînes de fer,
Colette qui pour mourir se coucha sur la terre,
Colette après sa mort restée fraîche comme une pierre,
Sainte Colette, que nos cœurs deviennent durs comme des pierres.

JEANNE

Bergère née en Lorraine,
Jeanne qui avez gardé les moutons en robe de futaine,
Et qui avez pleuré aux misères du peuple de France,
Et qui avez conduit le Roi à Reims parmi les lances,
Jeanne qui étiez un arc, une croix, un glaive, un cœur, une lance,
Jeanne que les gens aimaient comme leur père et leur mère,
Jeanne blessée et prise, mise au cachot par les Anglais,
Jeanne brûlée à Rouen par les Anglais,
Jeanne qui ressemblez à un ange en colère,
Jeanne d'Arc, mettez beaucoup de colère dans nos cœurs.

URSULE

Griffon du nord, bête sacrée venue
Dans la lumière bleue d'un rêve boréal,
Ursule, flocon de neige bu par les lèvres de Jésus.
Ursule, étoile rouge vers la tulipe de pourpre,
Ursule, sœur de tant de cœurs innocents,
Et dont la tête sanglante dort comme une escarboucle
Dans la bague des arceaux,
Ursule, nef, voile, rame et tempête,
Ursule, envolée sur le dos de l'oiseau blanc,
Sainte Ursule, emportez nos âmes vers les neiges.

In 1890, appeared the first of Gourmont's philological works, *Esthétique de la Langue Française*, followed, in 1900, by another, *La Culture des Idées*. Between them was another novel, *Le Songe d'une Femme*, and in 1900, the last of his poems came out. It is entitled, *Simone, Poème Champêtre*. There is nothing very astounding about *Simone*, but there is a great deal that is very delightful. Gourmont is doing something more than play with words. Here he makes his words subordinate themselves to feeling, to sentiment. We no longer have the artificial and learned *vers libre* of *Litanies de la Rose* and *Fleurs de Jadis*, nor the long, quiet, uneven lines of *Les Saintes du Paradis* — eleven, thirteen, sometimes nineteen syllables in length. For the first time, Gourmont tries more tripping metres, metres of a sharp, light rhythm. It seems as though a greater interior calm had left him room for simpler, gayer-hearted joys.

I have chosen a great many poems from *Simone* to print. They almost say themselves, and as you read you can see the clouds sailing over the trees under which we are sitting, and hear "the shepherd's clapping shears," as Leigh Hunt has it. Notice, in *Les Cheveux*, how, under the guise of a love poem, Gourmont has given us all the flora of his countryside, and with the same matter-of-fact, and yet somehow bewitching, statement, which is a peculiarity of the old herbals:

LES CHEVEUX

Simone, il y a un grand mystère
Dans la forêt de tes cheveux.

Tu sens le foin, tu sens la pierre
Où des bêtes se sont posées ;
Tu sens le cuir, tu sens le blé,
Quand il vient d'être vanné ;
Tu sens le bois, tu sens le pain
Qu'on apporte le matin ;
Tu sens les fleurs qui ont poussé
Le long d'un mur abandonné ;
Tu sens la ronce, tu sens le lierre
Qui a été lavé par la pluie ;
Tu sens le jonc et la fougère
Qu'on fauche à la tombée de la nuit ;

Tu sens le houx, tu sens la mousse,
Tu sens l'herbe mourante et rousse
Qui s'égrène à l'ombre des haies ;
Tu sens l'ortie et le genêt,
Tu sens le trèfle, tu sens le lait ;
Tu sens le fenouil et l'anis ;
Tu sens les noix, tu sens les fruits
Qui sont bien mûrs et que l'on cueille ;
Tu sens le saule et le tilleul
Quand ils ont des fleurs pleins les feuilles ;
Tu sens le miel, tu sens la vie
Qui se promène dans les prairies ;
Tu sens la terre et la rivière ;
Tu sens l'amour, tu sens le feu.

Simone, il y a un grand mystère
Dans la forêt de tes cheveux.

It is the same in this next poem, only here the presence of Simone has become more a part of the beauty. In spite of the quite usual temper of the poem, where only April, first throwing down the violets and then thrusting them under the brambles, is in the least new, it has a feeling of complete freshness :

LE HOUX

Simone, le soleil rit sur les feuilles de houx :
Avril est revenu pour jouer avec nous.

Il porte des corbeilles de fleurs sur ses épaules,
Il les donne aux épines, aux marronniers, aux saules ;

Il les sème une à une parmi l'herbe des prés,
Sur le bord des ruisseaux, des mares et des fossés ;

Il garde les jonquilles pour l'eau, et les pervenches
Pour les bois, aux endroits où s'allongent les branches ;

Il jette les violettes à l'ombre, sous les ronces
Où son pied nu, sans peur, les cache et les enfonce ;

A toutes les prairies il donne des pâquerettes
Et des primevères qui ont un collier de clochettes ;

Il laisse les muguets tomber dans les forêts
Avec les anémones, le long des sentiers frais ;

Il plante des iris sur le toit des maisons,
Et dans notre jardin, Simone, où il fait bon,

Il répandra des ancolies et des pensées,
Des jacinthes et la bonne odeur des giroflées.

Le Brouillard is a pure lyric. It is not highly
original in either thought or expression. But its
simplicity is so sincere that its lack of originality
makes really no difference. Here are the first two
verses :

LE BROUILLARD

Simone, mets ton manteau et tes gros sabots noirs,
Nous irons comme en barque à travers le brouillard.

Nous irons vers les îles de beauté où les femmes
Sont belles comme des arbres et nues comme des âmes ;
Nous irons vers les îles où les hommes sont doux
Comme des lions, avec des cheveux longs et roux.
Viens, le monde incréé attend de notre rêve
Ses lois, ses joies, les dieux qui font fleurir la sève
Et le vent qui fait luire et bruire les feuilles.
Viens, le monde innocent va sortir d'un cercueil.

Simone, mets ton manteau et tes gros sabots noirs,
Nous irons comme en barque à travers le brouillard.

Nous irons vers les îles où il y a des montagnes
D'où l'on voit l'étendue paisible des campagnes,
Avec des animaux heureux de brouter l'herbe,
Des bergers qui ressemblent à des saules, et des gerbes
Qu'on monte avec des fourches sur le dos des charrettes :
Il fait encore soleil et les moutons s'arrêtent
Près de l'étable, devant la porte du jardin,
Qui sent la pimprenelle, l'estragon et le thym.

Simone, mets ton manteau et tes gros sabots noirs,
Nous irons comme en barque à travers le brouillard.

Much more unusual, much more important, is *Les Feuilles Mortes*, with its wistful refrain. How beautiful is the line of the dead leaves which "font un bruit d'ailes ou de robes de femme !"

LES FEUILLES MORTES

Simone, allons au bois : les feuilles sont tombées ;
Elles recouvrent la mousse, les pierres et les sentiers.

Simone, aimes-tu le bruit des pas sur les feuilles mortes ?

Elles ont des couleurs si douces, des tons si graves,
Elles sont sur la terre de si frêles épaves !

Simone, aimes-tu le bruit des pas sur les feuilles mortes ?

Elles on l'air si dolent à l'heure du crépuscule,
Elles crient si tendrement, quand le vent les bouscule !

Simone, aimes-tu le bruit des pas sur les feuilles mortes ?

Quand le pied les écrase, elles pleurent comme des âmes,
Elles font un bruit d'ailes ou de robes de femme.

Simone, aimes-tu le bruit des pas sur les feuilles mortes ?

Viens : nous serons un jour de pauvres feuilles mortes.
Viens : déjà la nuit tombe et le vent nous emporte.

Simone, aimes-tu le bruit des pas sur les feuilles mortes ?

Truly, in reading these poems, we go from one pleasant country scene to another, and step from season to season of the bucolic year. Not the least interesting part of them is the new side they show

us of Gourmont's complex character. Here is the
river, which sings "un air ingénu." One can almost
hear its clear rippling over a pebble bottom, so flowing is the movement of the poem; and what a
youthful, happy line he has given us in "Et moi, je
verrai dans l'eau claire ton pied nu."

LA RIVIÈRE

Simone, la rivière chante un air ingénu,
Viens, nous irons parmi les joncs et la ciguë;
Il est midi : les hommes ont quitté leur charrue,
Et moi, je verrai dans l'eau claire ton pied nu.

La rivière est la mère des poissons et des fleurs,
Des arbres, des oiseaux, des parfums, des couleurs;

Elle abreuve les oiseaux qui ont mangé leur grain
Et qui vont s'envoler pour un pays lointain;

Elle abreuve les mouches bleues dont le ventre est vert
Et les araignées d'eau qui rament comme aux galères.

La rivière est la mère des poissons : elle leur donne
Des vermisseaux, de l'herbe, de l'air et de l'ozone;

Elle leur donne l'amour; elle leur donne les ailes
Pour suivre au bout du monde l'ombre de leur femelles.

La rivière est la mère des fleurs, des arcs-en-ciel,
De tout ce qui est fait d'eau et d'un peu de soleil :

Elle nourrit le sainfoin et le foin, et les reines
Des prés qui ont l'odeur du miel, et les molènes

Qui ont des feuilles douces comme un duvet d'oiseaux ;
Elle nourrit le blé, le trèfle et les roseaux ;

Elle nourrit le chanvre ; elle nourrit le lin ;
Elle nourrit l'avoine, l'orge et le sarrasin ;

Elle nourrit le seigle, l'osier et les pommiers ;
Elle nourrit les saules et les grands peupliers.

La rivière est la mère des forêts : les beaux chênes
Ont puisé dans son lit l'eau pure de leurs veines.

La rivière féconde le ciel : quand la pluie tombe,
C'est la rivière qui monte au ciel et qui retombe ;

La rivière est une mère très puissante et très pure,
La rivière est la mère de toute la nature.

Simone, la rivière chante un air ingénu,
Viens, nous irons parmi les joncs et la ciguë,
Il est midi : les hommes ont quitté leur charrue,
Et moi, je verrai dans l'eau claire ton pied nu.

But of all of these poems, I prefer *Le Verger*. The metre is irresistible, and lilts along like a gay tune. One can hardly resist the pleasure of reading it aloud, and then — reading it again. The tune gets

into one's head, and one goes about for half a day,
murmuring :

> Allons au verger, Simone,
> Allons au verger.

Yes, Remy de Gourmont is a many-sided man
indeed !

LE VERGER

> Simone, allons au verger
> Avec un panier d'osier.
> Nous dirons à nos pommiers,
> En entrant dans le verger :
> Voici la saison des pommes,
> Allons au verger, Simone,
> Allons au verger.
>
> Les pommiers sont pleins de guêpes,
> Car les pommes sont très mûres :
> Il se fait un grand murmure
> Autour du vieux doux-aux-vêpes.
> Les pommiers sont pleins de pommes,
> Allons au verger, Simone,
> Allons au verger.
>
> Nous cueillerons la calville,
> Le pigeonnet et la reinette,
> Et aussi des pommes à cidre
> Dont la chair est un peu doucette.
> Voici la saison des pommes,
> Allons au verger, Simone,
> Allons au verger.

Tu auras l'odeur des pommes
Sur ta robe et sur tes mains,
Et tes cheveux seront pleins
Du parfum doux de l'automne.
Les pommiers sont pleins de pommes,
Allons au verger, Simone,
Allons au verger.

Simone, tu seras mon verger
Et mon pommier de doux-aux-vêpes;
Simone, écarte les guêpes
De ton cœur et de mon verger.
Voici la saison des pommes,
Allons au verger, Simone,
Allons au verger.

Following *Simone* in *Divertissements*, is a group of
poems called *Paysages Spirituels*. The one I am
going to quote bears the date 1898, and although it
therefore precedes the publication of *Simone*, it does
not really precede it, for *Simone* was written in 1892.

CHANSON DE L'AUTOMNE

Viens, mon amie, viens, c'est l'automne,
L'automne humide et monotone,
Mais les feuilles des cerisiers
Et les fruits mûrs des églantiers
Sont rouges comme des baisers,
Viens, mon amie, viens, c'est l'automne.

Viens, mon amie, le rude automne
Serre son manteau et frissonne
Mais le soleil a des douceurs ;
Dans l'air léger comme ton cœur,
La brume berce sa langueur,
Viens, mon amie, viens, c'est l'automne.

Viens, mon amie, le vent d'automne
Sanglote comme une personne.
Et dans les buissons entr'ouverts
La ronce tord ses bras pervers,
Mais les chênes sont toujours verts,
Viens, mon amie, viens, c'est l'automne.

Viens, mon amie, le vent d'automne
Durement gronde et nous sermonne,
Des mots sifflent par les sentiers,
Mais on entend dans les halliers
Le doux bruit d'ailes des ramiers,
Viens, mon amie, viens, c'est l'automne.

Viens, mon amie, le triste automne
Aux bras de l'hiver s'abandonne,
Mais l'herbe de l'été repousse,
La dernière bruyère est douce,
Et on croit voir fleurir la mousse,
Viens, mon amie, viens, c'est l'automne.

Viens, mon amie, viens, c'est l'automne,
Tout nus les peupliers frissonnent,

L

Mais leur feuillage n'est pas mort;
Gonflant sa robe couleur d'or,
Il danse, il danse, il danse encor,
Viens, mon amie, viens, c'est l'automne.

Almost a return to the old ballad form, you see. So he works out his destiny, at once modern and rooted to the past. After *Simone* came more philology. *Le Chemin de Velours*, and *Le Problème du Style.* Then his one scientific essay, *Physique de l'Amour*, in which if there were space I could show that he is always a poet, as well in science as in criticism. Then follow the four volumes of literary essays, *Promenades Littéraires*, and the three volumes of *Promenades Philosophiques.* Four volumes of *Épilogues*, which are reflections on current topics, and two more novels, *Une Nuit au Luxembourg* and *Un Cœur Virginal.*

What can one say of such a man? How classify him? How measure the extent of his accomplishment, of his influence? In one short chapter it is impossible. I have only considered him as a poet. And in spite of his tales, his novels, his plays, his criticisms, and his essays, I believe him to be first of all a poet. He has said somewhere, "I write to clarify my ideas." The artist has been crowded out by the thinker, the seeker after truth. Has that been a misfortune? Who knows.

Henri de Régnier

HENRI DE RÉGNIER

HENRI DE RÉGNIER

HENRI DE RÉGNIER is universally considered the greatest of the *Symboliste* poets. And if we exclude Émile Verhaeren from the list, as having stepped beyond the school and into a newer age, and exclude Jammes and Fort, as belonging to a younger generation, there is no doubt about it. Who are the other *Symbolistes*, strictly speaking? Verlaine and Mallarmé were the starters, the masters; but who were the men who looked up to them, and followed them, and became the *Symboliste* School, so-called? They are Vielé-Griffin, Stuart Merrill (both, amusingly enough, Americans), Gustave Kahn, Albert Samain, Remy de Gourmont, Jean Moréas, Saint-Pol-Roux, etc., etc. Clearly, Henri de Régnier is far above them all. But he is even more than that, he is one of the great poets of France; no greater than his master, Mallarmé, be it granted, but as great. Only, and here comes in the strangest thing about him, he is an even greater novelist. Such a novelist as there can be only a dozen or so in any nation's history. Hugo, Stendhal, Balzac, Flaubert, Zola,

Anatole France, is he inferior to any of these? Perhaps we are too near him to be able to tell definitely, but the general opinion of critics would seem to be that he is their equal.

Yet, so far as I know, none of his books have been translated into English. Is this because of a certain Rabelaisian gusto in some of them, and a thoroughly Gallic quality in all? Perhaps. The educated public can read them in French; the uneducated public, possibly, would not understand them in any language. But the "Gallicisms" are no more in number, and hardly more audacious, than those of Anatole France. Still, Anatole France is known to everybody, while Régnier's name is only vaguely familiar. Yet this man is one of the Immortals, having been elected to the Academy in 1911, and is an acknowledged master of French prose, receiving the mantle slowly dropping from the shoulders of Anatole France!

Henri de Régnier is still a comparatively young man; although perhaps I should qualify that, as poetry seems to be, for some strange reason, a young man's job, and say that he is only on the edge of middle age, having just passed his fifty-first birthday. For Henri-François-Joseph de Régnier was born at Honfleur on the twenty-eighth of December, 1864.

The Régniers are an old aristocratic family, and Henri de Régnier is the product of a race, if ever a man was. The lives and exploits of his ancestors seem like a page out of one of his own seventeenth century novels. And the polish and reserve which characterize all his books have as certainly descended to him, as has his cold and somewhat haughty expression, and his exceedingly delicate features. In 1585, a certain Crespin de Régnier was a *Seigneur* of Vigneux in Thiérache, and as captain of a company of fifty men-at-arms, he served under the Duc de Bouillon and Marshal de Balagny in the wars of the Ligue. In 1589, this gentleman married Yolaine de Fay d'Athies, a daughter of Charles de Fay d'Athies, one of the Hundred Gentlemen of the King's Household. The grandson of Crespin, Charles de Régnier, also had the title, and seems beside to have been an equerry at the Court. In the eighteenth century, François de Régnier was a Lieutenant-Colonel in the Regiment of Touraine, and Brigadier in the King's army, and a Chevalier of Saint Louis. (*Le Bon Plaisir*, one of Henri de Régnier's novels, which deals with this period, is dedicated to him.) In the eighteenth century also, there is a Gabriel-François de Régnier, who was Brigadier of Light Horse in the King's Guard; and his son, François de Régnier, who was Captain in the Regiment of Royal Dragoons. Both these men were Chevaliers of Saint Louis. When the Revolution came, François de Régnier emigrated and served in the Army of the Princes. His son (the grandfather of the poet) returned to France in 1820, and was made a Chevalier of the Legion of Honour. The poet's father, Henri-Charles de Régnier, held various posts under the government, among others Inspector of Customs at Honfleur, and Receiver at Paris; and (and this is an odd thing) he was the boyhood companion of Gustave Flaubert. On his mother's side, Henri de Régnier's lineage is no less distinguished, his mother being descended from a certain Yves de Bard, who lived in the sixteenth century. The great-grandson of this Yves de Bard married, in 1662, Marie de Saumaise de Chassans, who was the great-grandniece of a celebrated *savant*, Claude de Saumaise, and of Charlotte de Saumaise, who became Comtesse de Brégy, and was lady-in-waiting to Anne of Austria. This lady, although only a many-times-grandaunt of Henri de Régnier, seems to have counted for something in his inheritance, as she wrote "Letters" and "Poems," and was a *précieuse* of distinction. The De Bard family continued, throughout the seventeenth and eighteenth centuries, accruing to themselves lands and surnames, and the great-great-grandfather of the poet, Bénigne du Bard de Chassans, was a Counsellor of the Parliament of Dijon.

I have dwelt so long upon these fatiguing genealogical details, because no one can really understand Henri de Régnier out of his frame — that frame of noble, honourable, virile, cultivated sol-

diers, courtiers, and gentlemen, which surrounds
him on all sides, and which he, himself, seems to be
so atavistically conscious of. One of his novels,
Le Passé Vivant, deals with the strong, almost
terrible, impulsion of the past. And objective as all
Henri de Régnier's work is, I cannot help thinking
that in *Le Passé Vivant* we have an acknowledgment
of a condition of which he is perfectly conscious in
himself, although, of course, in a lesser degree than
he has portrayed it in his characters. But it is not
only in *Le Passé Vivant* that we feel the importunate-
ness of the Past; it vibrates like a muffled organ-
point through all his work.

Yet I must be careful not to give the impression that Régnier is merely the result and echo of
dead generations. So many people are that; and
here, in America, in spite of the generations being
still so few, we see it eating through the present
like a disease. This old French, decadent aristoc-
racy, as we are wont to consider it, seems to main-
tain itself with extraordinary ease and success.
After four hundred years, not of steady rising, but
(much more difficult problem) continued arisen,
this family has produced one of the greatest poets
and novelists which its country has known. Seven
volumes of poetry, fifteen volumes of novels and
stories (and all, mind you, works of the very first
rank), one play, and three volumes of essays, is his
tally up to date. And the man is only fifty-one!

Why ! No stevedore could work so hard ! It is
colossal. And this man is a scion of an old aristocratic family !

Until he was seven years old, Henri de Régnier
lived at Honfleur. In one of his stories, *Le Trèfle
Blanc*, he has given some of his early recollections.
"This time of my life," he says, "has remained
singularly present to my memory, and I feel it still
in a quite particular way. It is as though it were
in suspense within me, and forms an indissoluble
whole." He remembers the minutest details. For
instance, he went with his mother to stay with his
grandfather who was dying. Being left much to
himself, he wandered about and initiated himself
into all the mysteries of the old house. He tells of
"the walls scaling ;" of "the bulging of the canvas
of an old portrait, the cracks in the console, a sliver
of the parquet floor which gave under the foot,
all the imperceptible nothings which I have never
forgotten, all the noises of life and silence to which
I was attentive."

In 1871, Henri-Charles de Régnier, the poet's
father, was appointed Receiver at Paris. And the
family moved there. Three years later, in 1874,
Henri entered the Collège Stanislas, and he seems
to have written his first poem in 1879. Fifteen
years old is not young to attempt writing, and we
may feel at ease in the knowledge that Régnier
was not an infant phenomenon. There is a tale

that one of his professors, catching him writing a poem, at once confiscated it. Schoolmasters would seem to be the same brilliant, sympathetic lot all over the world. But, thank Heaven, our minds do get fed somehow, in spite of the schools. In Régnier's case, there were the *quais*, with their rows of green boxes full of books — delightful, heterogeneous masses of books, classified only by their state of dilapidation. Trees blowing, blue river, spots of bright sunshine, and books! Going to school and coming back, Régnier read them, any of them that happened. There was a reading-room in the rue de Sèvres where he went also, and again read everything: Hugo, Musset, Flaubert, the tragedies of the eighteenth century, and Voltaire's plays. He says now that in those days he liked bad poetry better than good, and perhaps he did. But all nourished him, and helped him over that most dangerous period for a possible writer — his school-days.

He graduated in 1883, and to please his family studied law, and passed an examination for the Diplomatic Service. But that was the end of all thought of, or endeavour about, any career other than letters. During this time he had been writing, and his first verses appeared in a little review, *Lutèce*, under the pen-name of Hugues Vignix, so turning his admiration for Victor Hugo and Alfred de Vigny into a sort of monogram.

Another young man made his literary *début* in *Lutèce* with Henri de Régnier. This was Francis Vielé-Griffin. There was a fencing gallery next door to the office of *Lutèce*, where the young contributors used to disport themselves. An amusing joke of the period had it that they learnt to fight in order to kill their predecessors. For, as we saw in the last essay, these young writers were firmly against the established order, and the established order took it out by not acknowledging their existence.

Régnier, like Samain, had a desire to meet great men, to wear himself smooth by contact with mature minds. Timidly, but firmly, he hazarded a call upon Sully-Prudhomme. He was courteously received, and continued in pleasant relations with the elder poet until Régnier's adherence to *vers libre* separated them.

It was a very quiet, retired life that Régnier led at this time. Reading, studying, learning how. He was thoroughly serious in his work, in his art. He read much Victor Hugo, a master soon to be deserted by his generation. He also read Baudelaire, Vigny, Mallarmé, and the sonnets of José-Maria de Heredia, not yet published, but appearing from time to time in journals and reviews. Another side of his character drew him to memoirs, novels, books which depicted and analyzed life. He has explained himself as he was then, by saying, "I was in some sort double, *Symboliste* and *Réaliste*, loving symbols and anecdotes at the same time, a poem of Mallarmé's or an idea of Chamfort's." De Régnier has remained *Symboliste* and *Réaliste*, neither side of his character has entirely dominated the other, but time has strengthened the realism until it makes a strong and correct base on which the light form of *Symbolisme* can safely stand.

In spite of his realistic leanings, Henri de Régnier was principally *Symboliste* and poet, in these youthful days. If he did not begin writing extraordinarily young, he certainly began publishing in the very green leaf. He left college as we have seen, in 1883, at the age of nineteen, and his first book, *Les Lendemains*, was published in 1885, when he was twenty-one, and in 1886, a second collection of poems, *Apaisement*, came out.

There is nothing very remarkable in these early poems; they show good masters, careful study, and a pleasant imagination. Considering the extreme youth of their author, they gave excellent promise. The theory that a man should serve his apprenticeship in silence, and not give his early work to the public, is a disputable one. The Paris of Régnier's youth was full of young men of remarkable talent; it was full of little reviews publishing the work of these young men. If their circulation was small, at least it was select. It consisted of all the other revolutionary poets, young and old. Printing, publishing, a young man made friends and opened doors. Had Régnier kept his early work shut up between the covers of his portfolio, he might have leapt from his obscurity a few years later armed *cap-à-pie* like Minerva from the head of Jove, but his future would have been harder to make. Coteries would have been formed without him, places he might have had would have been given to others, bands of early friendships would have kept him outside as a late comer. No, we must admit that Régnier did well to publish these two little volumes and the two which succeeded them : *Sites*, in 1887, and *Épisodes*, in 1888. But why his publishers keep them in print is more difficult of comprehension. Yet these poems suggest the Régnier of later years. Take this, for instance :

> J'ai rêvé que ces vers seraient comme des fleurs
> Que fait tourner la main des maîtres ciseleurs
> Autour des vases d'or aux savantes ampleurs.

It was not a bad prophecy. His poems are like the flowers of master carvers. And the words, "gold vases," are almost the keynote of his work. Remy de Gourmont, in the first *Livre des Masques*, mentions his fondness for the words *or* and *mort*. And whether we take *vases d'or* as sound or as sense, it might almost stand as a device in front of any volume of his poems.

The point of view of his group, and his particular

place in it, has been excellently rendered by M. Jean
de Gourmont, one of De Régnier's biographers.
Speaking of the *Symboliste* group, he says, "all the
poets of this group, shut up within their particular
symbols, described . . . the interior of their prison.
M. de Régnier's prison is a palace with onyx columns ;
he walks up and down the length of galleries wain-
scoted with gold. Large windows open upon nature
and life ; he leans out and looks at the spectacle."
That palace with onyx columns we shall see again,
and again, and again. It is one of the truest things
ever said about Henri de Régnier.

At this time, Stéphane Mallarmé was becoming
every moment more certainly the acknowledged
master of these younger writers, soon to be known
as *Symbolistes*. He held a sort of *salon* on Tuesdays,
and received his disciples and admirers. He sat in
a "rocking-chair," under his own portrait by Manet,
and talked. (I believe a rocking-chair to be a purely
American invention, and it must be a matter of
national pride for us to feel that we have not only
given the French poets Poe and Walt Whitman,
whom they understood and admired before we did,
but that we have given one of them at least a
"rocking-chair.") Sitting in comfortable and rhythmic ease — rocking, in fact — and smoking a little,
cheap, red clay pipe, Mallarmé would hold forth ;
and on all the poets who heard him, these Tuesdays
stamped an indelible mark.

The Tuesdays were in full swing when Régnier began to publish in the little reviews. Soon his work attracted the attention of some of the men who frequented them, and soon Régnier, too, was among the constant visitors to the rue de Rome. For many years he went there practically every week. There is a story that one day, full of emotion, he turned to the Master and said, "I am beginning my tenth year." M. Stuart Merrill informs us that at these meetings Régnier acted as a sort of leader of the chorus; that he always occupied the same place, on a sofa at Mallarmé's right, and whenever the great poet's monologue languished a little, he would put in the happy word which started it going again.

There is no doubt that these long conversations count for much in the education of an artist. Perhaps that is one reason t'·· French succeed so marvellously in Art; they talk so well.

In 1887, a new review was started under René Ghil, called *Les Écrits pour l'Art*. Mallarmé and Villiers de l'Isle-Adam were its Great Masters. Beside them, were Émile Verhaeren, Stuart Merrill, Vielé-Griffin, and Henri de Régnier.

It was sometime about 1888, that Régnier made the acquaintance of José-Maria de Heredia, whose receptions at the Bibliothèque de l'Arsenal were crowded with all the literary celebrities of the day. Régnier met Leconte de Lisle there, and Maupassant — a Maupassant already sinking, and a prey to auditory hallucinations.

Heredia had three daughters, all fond of poetry, and perfectly *au courant* with the literary work of the day. His second daughter, Marie, even wrote verses herself, and now as "Gérard d'Houville" is known as a poet of much talent. Henri de Régnier was introduced to Mlle. Marie de Heredia at one of the gatherings at her father's house. Mutual interests naturally brought them together, and in 1896 they were married. I mention this now, because it seems to follow naturally after Régnier's meeting with Heredia, and there is nothing to cause us to remember it at the proper time. Régnier is evidently very reticent about his private life. He has the aristocrat's natural love of privacy. Jean de Gourmont says in his little monograph, "Of M. de Régnier's life I only know some episodes, some facts, which he has discreetly revealed to me." We must not forget that Régnier is still living, and that he is doing so in a country where privacy is both honoured and respected.

A younger brother of the *Mercure de France, Les Entretiens Politiques et Littéraires*, with Vielé-Griffin as editor, was started somewhere about 1890. Régnier became one of its most enthusiastic contributors. Most of the stories, later collected under the title, *La Canne de Jaspe*, appeared in it, and various essays and criticisms which are now to be

M

found in the volume, *Figures et Caractères*. Régnier also contributed to a number of other reviews, among them *La Wallonie*, of which he, Albert Mockel, and Pierre-M. Olin were the editors.

Up to this time, Régnier's life may have been said to be in the experimenting stage. He was laboriously shaping himself into a writer, as it were, working with that indefatigable assiduity which has always characterized him. From 1890, with the publication of *Poèmes Anciens et Romanesques*, his life enters upon another period, the period of constantly increasing accomplishment. In *Poèmes Anciens et Romanesques*, Régnier steps out of the shell of which his four previous volumes were only chippings, and is hatched a full-grown poet. He attempts other metres than the alexandrine, he even essays the uneven *vers libre*, built not upon metre but upon cadence, which is to be his most characteristic form, and in which he surpasses every other French writer. Vielé-Griffin and Stuart Merrill were Americans, Verhaeren was a Belgian, and one of the retorts flung at the *vers libristes* used to be, that the reason they could find this form agreeable was that they were foreigners and therefore had not the peculiar sensitiveness of the native ear. And behold, here was a Frenchman even among Frenchmen, who not only understood and liked it, but wrote it better, more delicately, more audaciously, than any one else. Not even Verhaeren could more variously manipulate it, more certainly guide it.

But it is not in the *Poèmes Anciens et Romanesques* that I first wish my readers to encounter Régnier's *vers libre*. I shall keep that for a later volume, where it is in its magnificent maturity.

Henri de Régnier is "a melancholy and sumptuous poet," as Remy de Gourmont has said. In the first *Livre des Masques* appears the following description: "This man" (Régnier) "lives in an old Italian palace, where emblems and figures are written on the walls. He dreams, passing from room to room; toward evening he descends the marble staircase and wanders about the gardens, which are paved like courts, to dream among the basins and fountains, while the black swans seek their nests, and a peacock, solitary as a king, seems to drink superbly of the dying pride of a golden twilight."

You notice that this is really the palace with the onyx pillars again! It is strange how the same idea seems to occur to every one about Régnier. Perhaps it is because he, himself, has described so many beautiful old houses, so many formal gardens *à la Française*.

Henri de Régnier is the poet of sadness, of gentle melancholy, particularly in his early books. He is also the poet of the nude. He almost attains the chaste and cool treatment of Greek statues. Probably it is this similarity of point of view which makes

him so often choose mythological subjects. But I
am far from suggesting that his attitude is really
Greek, in the historical and pedantic meaning of that
term, but neither is it the sort of Angelica Kauffmann
pastiche of Samain's *Aux Flancs du Vase*. Rather
it is the attitude of certain of our English poets in
treating classical subjects. Beaumont and Fletcher
in "The Faithful Shepherdess," for instance, or
Keats in "Endymion" and "The Grecian Urn."

This little poem will illustrate what I mean:

L'eau des sources où choit, le soir,
La mort unanime des roses
Était heureuse de nous voir
Peigner nos chevelures fauves . . .

Un peu de cette eau nos miroirs!

Les Fontaines étaient sonores
En les bois de Lune et de Nuit;
Cristal où se mire et s'isole
Quelque astre qui du ciel a fui . . .

L'onde est tarie en nos amphores!

Les escaliers courbaient leurs rampes . . .
Oh, les pieds froids sur les pavés! . . .
Les portes et les hautes chambres
Pour le sommeil nu des Psychés . . .

L'huile est figée au fond des lampes!

That is from a poem entitled "The Vigil of the Sands." Here is the first section of another poem called *Le Fol Automne* :

LE FOL AUTOMNE

Le fol automne épuise aux guirlandes ses roses
Pâles comme des lèvres et des sourires ;
Et le mal est d'avoir vécu parmi les roses,
Les masques, les glorioles, les délires !

Les Ægypans rieurs buvaient aux outres neuves
Le vieux vin où survit l'ardeur des Étés ;
Les vignes, égrenant les grappes dans les fleuves,
Gonflaient l'ambre clair de leurs maturités.

Les roses ont fleuri les coupes et les thyrses
Et le pan des robes puériles ; l'âme
Des fontaines pleurait dans l'ombre ; autour des thyrses
Les pampres semblaient un sang de torche en flamme.

L'automne fol s'épuise en suprêmes guirlandes,
Les satyres roux rôdent par les bois,
Et l'on suspend les masques vides par guirlandes
Où le vent rit aux trous des bouches sans voix.

There are many poems in this book which I should like to put in, but there are more important ones waiting in other books. The names of the sections into which the volume is divided will show its trend. Two of them I have already given you. The others are: "Greeting to the Stranger," "Motifs" (this is taken from the *leit-motifs* of Wagner, whose influence was then at its strongest), "Of Legend and Melancholy," "Scenes at Twilight," and "The Dream of the Forest."

In 1892, appeared another volume of poetry, *Tel Qu'en Songe*. The book begins with the following *Exergue*, as a sort of dedication or motto:

EXERGUE

Au carrefour des routes de la forêt, un soir,
Parmi le vent, avec mon ombre, un soir,
Las de la cendre des âtres et des années,
Incertain des heures prédestinées,
Je vins m'asseoir.

Les routes s'en allaient vers les jours
Et j'aurais pu aller avec elles encor,
Et toujours,
Vers des terres, des eaux et des songes, toujours
Jusques au jour
Où, de ses mains magiques et patientes, la Mort
Aurait fermé mes yeux du sceau de sa fleur de paix et d'or.

Route des chênes hauts et de la solitude,
Ta pierre âpre est mauvaise aux lassitudes,
Tes cailloux durs aux pieds lassés,
Et j'y verrais saigner le sang de mon passé,
A chaque pas,
Et tes chênes hautains grondent dans le vent rude
Et je suis las.

Route des bouleaux clairs qui s'effeuillent et tremblent
Pâles comme la honte de tes passants pâles
Qui s'égarent en tes fanges tenaces,
Et vont ensemble,
Et se détournent pour ne pas se voir face à face ;
Route de boue et d'eau qui suinte,
Le vent à tes feuilles chuchote sa plainte,
Les grands marais d'argent, de lunes et de givre
Stagnent au crépuscule au bout de tes chemins
Et l'Ennui à qui veut te suivre
Lui prend la main.

Route des frênes doux et des sables légers
Où le vent efface les pas et veut qu'on oublie
Et qu'on s'en aille ainsi qu'il s'en va d'arbre en arbre,
Tes fleurs de miel ont la couleur de l'or des sables,
Ta courbe est telle qu'on voit à peine où l'on dévie ;
La ville où tu conduis est bonne aux étrangers
Et mes pas seraient doux sur le seuil de ses portes
S'ils n'étaient pas restés le long d'une autre vie
Où mes Espoirs en pleurs veillent des Ombres mortes.

Je n'irai pas vers vos chênes
Ni le long de vos bouleaux et de vos frênes
Et ni vers vos soleils, vos villes et vos eaux,
O routes !
J'entends venir les pas de mon passé qui saigne,
Les pas que j'ai crus morts, hélas ! et qui reviennent,
Et qui semblent me précéder en vos échos,
O routes,

Toi la facile, toi la honteuse, toi la hautaine,
Et j'écoute
Le vent, compagnon de mes courses vaines,
Qui marche et pleure sous les chênes.

O mon âme, le soir est triste sur hier,
O mon âme, le soir est morne sur demain,
O mon âme, le soir est grave sur toi-même!

The last three lines show his point of view at this time. The melancholy is undoubtedly sincere, but it is the melancholy of a very young man, half in love with his own state of mind. But whatever the idea may be, however adolescent the feeling, there is no mistaking the masterly quality of the verse. Here is no immaturity, no hesitating. It is Régnier in the full tide of his perfect *vers libre*. The flow of the poem is exquisite. There is not a single skip-step in the cadence, and never once the dull, pedestrian plodding of a prose line.

The titles of some of the poems are very peculiar. We are in the heyday of *Symbolisme*, remember. And very characteristic are these titles: "Some One Dreams of Dawn and Shadow," "Some One Dreams of Evening and Hope," "Some One Dreams of Hours and Years," "Some One Dreams of Shade and Forgetfulness." Here is the beginning of "Dawn and Shadow:"

QUELQU'UN SONGE D'AUBE ET D'OMBRE

"J'ai cru voir
Ma Tristesse debout sous les saules,
J'ai cru la voir — dit-elle tout bas —
Debout auprès du doux ruisseau de mes pensées
Les mêmes qu'elles tout un soir
Qu'au cours de l'eau passaient surnageantes des roses,
Épaves du bouquet des heures blessées.
Le temps passait avec les eaux passées ;
Elle pensait avec mes pensées
Si longtemps que le bois de bleuâtre fut mauve,
Puis plus sombre et noir."

J'ai cru voir ma Tristesse — dit-il — et je l'ai vue
— Dit-il plus bas —
Elle était nue,
Assise dans la grotte la plus silencieuse
De mes plus intérieures pensées ;
Elle y était le songe morne des eaux glacées,
L'anxiété des stalactites anxieuses ;
Le poids des rocs lourds comme le temps.
La douleur des porphyres rouges comme le sang ;
Elle y était silencieuse,
Assise au fond de mon silence.
Et nue ainsi que s'apparaît ce qui se pense.

Beautiful as this is, it strikes a slightly discordant
note to a modern ear. The desertion of the symbol to plunge into plain allegory is old-fashioned —
was old-fashioned even in the days of the *Symbolistes*,

who attempted a greater subtilty. It is one of De
Régnier's worst faults, and one which, little by
little, he has dropped.

I will quote one more poem from *Tel Qu'en Songe*.
We still have allegory, but more lightly, more indefinitely done. And how cleverly the scene is
sketched in, and all with a sort of pathetic tenderness!
It is one of the divisions of *Quelqu'un Songe d'Heures
et d'Années* :

> Les fruits du passé, mûrs d'ombre et de songe,
> En leur écorce où jutent des coulures d'or,
> Pendent et tombent,
> Un à un et un encor,
> Dans le verger de songe et d'ombre.

> Le crépuscule doux décline et se ravive
> Parfois d'un soleil pâle à travers les arbres,
> Et l'heure arrive
> Où, un à un, arbre par arbre,
> Le vent touche les beaux fruits qui oscillent
> Et heurtent leurs tièdes ors pâles
> Et tremblent encor
> Quand le vent a passé et que l'ombre est tranquille,
> Et tombent, un à un et un encor.

> La Tristesse a mûri ses fruits d'ombre
> Aux doux vergers de notre songe
> Où le passé sommeille, tressaille et se rendort,
> Au bruit de ses fruits mûrs qui tombent,
> A travers l'oubli dans la mort,
> Un à un et un encor.

The first of his prose stories, *Contes à Soi-même*, came out in 1894; and another prose story, *Le Trèfle Noir*, appeared in 1895. The *Contes à Soi-même* are written in a learned and over-stylized prose, very unlike the flowing, rapid manner of his present prose writing. It is evident, indeed we know it from his publications, that at this time Régnier was much more practiced as a poet than as a prose writer. Prose and poetry are different arts, and have to be studied quite separately. Words, ideas, have to be used in almost opposite ways. A man who can succeed in both branches of the difficult art of writing is happy indeed. Few people have done it, and Henri de Régnier is eminent among the few. Both *Contes à Soi-même*, and *Le Trèfle Noir*, with various other poems added to them, were later published under the title, *La Canne de Jaspe*, of which I shall speak when I come to it.

At the moment, poetry still held first place in his interest, and in 1895 also, a new poem, *Aréthuse*, was published, which was included two years later in *Les Jeux Rustiques et Divins*.

Let me deflect a moment to mention the extraordinary charm of Régnier's titles, particularly those of his poetry volumes: "Rustic and Divine Games," "Medals of Clay," "The City of Waters," "The Winged Sandal," "The Mirror of the Hours."

In reading these over in a catalogue, one would know that one had to do with a *Symboliste* poet, and also with a poet of rare grace and elegance. *Les Jeux Rustiques et Divins* is divided into parts, as all Régnier's volumes of poems are. The first part, *Aréthuse*, is subdivided again into three sections; the first and last are called "Flutes of April and September," and the middle part is called "The Man and the Siren." The next large division is "The Reeds of the Flute," followed by "Inscriptions for the Thirteen Gates of the Town," "The Basket of the Hours," and "Divers Poems." I think my contention that Régnier has the gift of titles is fully borne out by these. This, *Le Faune au Miroir*, is one of Régnier's most beautiful pseudo-classical pieces, and written in the alexandrine, which, in spite of its lesser originality, it must be admitted he manages lightly and with ease.

LE FAUNE AU MIROIR

Tristesse, j'ai bâti ta maison, et les arbres
Mélangent leur jaspure aux taches de tes marbres;
Tristesse, j'ai bâti ton palais vert et noir
Où l'if du deuil s'allie aux myrtes de l'espoir;
Tes fenêtres, dans le cristal de leurs carreaux,
Reflètent des jardins de balustres et d'eaux
Où s'encadre le ciel à leur exactitude;
L'écho morne y converse avec la solitude
Qui se cherche elle-même autour de ses cyprès;
Plus loin c'est le silence et toute la forêt,

La vie âpre, le vent qui rôde, l'herbe grasse
Où se marque, selon la stature qui passe,
Un sabot bestial au lieu d'un pied divin ;
Plus loin, c'est le Satyre et plus loin le Sylvain
Et la Nymphe qui, nue, habite les fontaines
Solitaires où près des eaux thessaliennes
Le Centaure en ruant ébrèche les cailloux,
Et puis des sables gris après des sables roux,
Les monstres du Désir, les monstres de la Chair,
Et, plus loin que la grève aride, c'est la Mer.

Tristesse, j'ai bâti ta maison, et les arbres
Ont jaspé le cristal des bassins comme un marbre ;
Le cygne blanc y voit dans l'eau son ombre noire
Comme la pâle Joie au lac de ma mémoire
Voit ses ailes d'argent ternes d'un crépuscule
Où son visage nu qui d'elle se recule
Lui fait signe, à travers l'à jamais, qu'elle est morte ;
Et moi qui suis entré sans refermer la porte
J'ai peur de quelque main dans l'ombre sur la clé ;
Et je marche de chambre en chambre, et j'ai voilé
Mes songes pour ne plus m'y voir ; mais de là-bas
Je sens encor rôder des ombres sur mes pas,
Et le cristal qui tinte et la moire que froisse
Ma main lasse à jamais préviennent mon angoisse,
Car j'entends dans le lustre hypocrite qui dort
Le bruit d'une eau d'argent qui rit dans des fleurs d'or
Et la stillation des antiques fontaines
Où Narcisse buvait les lèvres sur les siennes
Par qui riait la source au buveur anxieux ;
Et je maudis ma bouche, et je maudis mes yeux
D'avoir vu la peau tiède et touché l'onde froide,

Et, quand mes doigts encor froncent l'étoffe roide,
J'entends, de mon passé bavard qui ne se tait,
Les feuilles et le vent de la vieille forêt ;
Et je marche parmi les chambres solitaires
Où quelqu'un parle avec la feinte de se taire,
Car ma vie a des yeux de sœur qui n'est pas morte,
Et j'ai peur, lorsque j'entre, et du seuil de la porte,
De voir, monstre rieur et fantôme venu
De l'ombre, avec l'odeur des bois dans son poil nu,
Quelque Faune qui ait à ses sabots sonores
De la boue et de l'herbe et des feuilles encore,
Et, dans la chambre taciturne, de le voir
Danser sur le parquet et se rire aux miroirs !

L'Homme et la Sirène is an allegory, but written less flatly than many which our poet has perpetrated. And, strangely enough, it is not quite the old story which Régnier has told here. His siren, beautiful, naked, seductive, woos the man, who, dreaming of giving her a soul and making her his true companion, clothes her, covers her with jewels, and awaits the change he expects. It does not come. She, who was nature, simplicity, instinct, he has tricked up into an artificial nothing. He has not understood her, and she cannot reach him. The sea receives her back into its arms, and the man dies, crucified by his own blind prejudice.

Indeed, Henri de Régnier is a thinker as well as a poet. And if his poems are usually merely an expression of a mood, it is because he has other ways of clothing his larger conceptions. He is not tempted to tell stories in verse after the manner of Jammes, and Fort, and other moderns, because he has a prose even more adequate in which to express them. Now we have arrived at what is undoubtedly Régnier's poetic masterpiece: *Le Vase.* It is the first poem in the division *Les Roseaux de la Flûte.* I will not spoil *Le Vase* by describing or analyzing it. Suffice it to say that it is the most perfect presentation of the creative faculty at work that I know of in any literature.

LE VASE

Mon marteau lourd sonnait dans l'air léger
Je voyais la rivière et le verger,
La prairie et jusques au bois
Sous le ciel plus bleu d'heure en heure,
Puis rose et mauve au crépuscule ;
Alors je me levais tout droit
Et m'étirais heureux de la tâche des heures,
Gourd de m'être accroupi de l'aube au crépuscule
Devant le bloc de marbre où je taillais les pans
Du vase fruste encor que mon marteau pesant,
Rythmant le matin clair et la bonne journée,
Heurtait, joyeux d'être sonore en l'air léger !

Le vase naissait dans la pierre façonnée.
Svelte et pur il avait grandi
Informe encor en sa sveltesse,
Et j'attendis,

Les mains oisives et inquiètes,
Pendant des jours, tournant la tête
A gauche, à droite, au moindre bruit,
Sans plus polir la panse ou lever le marteau.
L'eau
Coulait de la fontaine comme haletante.
Dans le silence
J'entendais, un à un, aux arbres du verger,
Les fruits tomber de branche en branche,
Je respirais un parfum messager
De fleurs lointaines sur le vent ;
Souvent,
Je croyais qu'on avait parlé bas,
Et, un jour que je rêvais — ne dormant pas —
J'entendis par delà les prés et la rivière
Chanter des flûtes . . .

Un jour, encor,
Entre les feuilles d'ocre et d'or
Du bois, je vis, avec ses jambes de poil jaune,
Danser un faune ;
Je l'aperçus aussi, une autre fois,
Sortir du bois
Le long de la route et s'asseoir sur une borne
Pour prendre un papillon à l'une de ses cornes.

Une autre fois,
Un centaure passa la rivière à la nage ;
L'eau ruisselait sur sa peau d'homme et son pelage ;
Il s'avança de quelques pas dans les roseaux,
Flaira le vent, hennit, repassa l'eau ;

Le lendemain, j'ai vu l'ongle de ses sabots
Marqué dans l'herbe . . .

Des femmes nues
Passèrent en portant des paniers et des gerbes,
Très loin, tout au bout de la plaine.
Un matin, j'en trouvai trois à la fontaine
Dont l'une me parla. Elle était nue.
Elle me dit : Sculpte la pierre
Selon la forme de mon corps en tes pensées,
Et fais sourire au bloc ma face claire ;
Écoute autour de toi les heures dansées
Par mes sœurs dont la ronde se renoue,
Entrelacée,
Et tourne et chante et se dénoue.

Et je sentis sa bouche tiède sur ma joue.

Alors le verger vaste et le bois et la plaine
Tressaillirent d'un bruit étrange, et la fontaine
Coula plus vive avec un rire dans ses eaux ;
Les trois Nymphes debout auprès des trois roseaux
Se prirent par la main et dansèrent ; du bois
Les faunes roux sortaient par troupes, et des voix
Chantèrent par delà les arbres du verger
Avec des flûtes en éveil dans l'air léger.
La terre retentit du galop des centaures ;
Il en venait du fond de l'horizon sonore,
Et l'on voyait, assis sur la croupe qui rue,
Tenant des thyrses tors et des outres ventrues,
Des satyres boiteux piqués par des abeilles,

N

Et les bouches de crin et les lèvres vermeilles
Se baisaient, et la ronde immense et frénétique,
Sabots lourds, pieds légers, toisons, croupes, tuniques,
Tournait éperdument autour de moi qui, grave,
Au passage, sculptais aux flancs gonflés du vase
Le tourbillonnement des forces de la vie.

Du parfum exhalé de la terre mûrie
Une ivresse montait à travers mes pensées,
Et dans l'odeur des fruits et des grappes pressées,
Dans le choc des sabots et le heurt des talons,
En de fauves odeurs de boucs et d'étalons,
Sous le vent de la ronde et la grêle des rires,
Au marbre je taillais ce que j'entendais bruire ;
Et parmi la chair chaude et les effluves tièdes,
Hennissement du mufle ou murmure des lèvres,
Je sentais sur mes mains, amoureux ou farouches,
Des souffles de naseaux ou des baisers de bouches.

Le crépuscule vint et je tournai la tête.

Mon ivresse était morte avec la tâche faite ;
Et sur son socle enfin, du pied jusques aux anses,
Le grand Vase se dressait nu dans le silence,
Et, sculptée en spirale à son marbre vivant,
La ronde dispersée et dont un faible vent
Apportait dans l'écho la rumeur disparue,
Tournait avec ses boucs, ses dieux, ses femmes nues,
Ses centaures cabrés et ses faunes adroits,
Silencieusement autour de la paroi,
Tandis que, seul, parmi, à jamais, la nuit sombre,
Je maudissais l'aurore et je pleurais vers l'ombre.

Inscriptions pour les Treize Portes de la Ville are always considered among the very finest poems which Régnier has written. They are dedicated to Brunetière, which is a little stroke of malice, for the poems were first printed in the *Revue des Deux Mondes*, of which Brunetière was editor. He accepted them, acknowledged their beauty, but still his conventional soul was severely wounded by certain liberties which their author had permitted himself to take with the classic alexandrine. Finally he consented to print them, with a note appended exonerating the editors from all responsibility in publishing them. Régnier was considerably annoyed by this suggestion at first, but when he was told that this was only the third time that such a thing had been done, and that the other times were, once for Baudelaire, and once for Lamennais, he consented to be labelled with the glorious stigma.

I am going to quote four of these inscriptions; those on the Gates of the Warriors, the Merchants, and the Comedians, and on the "Gate which goes down to the Sea."

POUR LA PORTE DES GUERRIERS

Porte haute! ne crains point l'ombre, laisse ouvert
Ton battant d'airain dur et ton battant de fer.
On a jeté tes clefs au fond de la citerne.
Sois maudite à jamais si la peur te referme ;
Et coupe, comme au fil d'un double couperet,

Le poing de toute main qui te refermerait.
Car, sous ta voûte sombre où résonnaient leurs pas,
Des hommes ont passé qui ne reculent pas,
Et la Victoire prompte et haletante encor
Marchait au milieu d'eux, nue en ses ailes d'or,
Et les guidait du geste calme de son glaive ;
Et son ardent baiser en pourpre sur leur lèvre
Saignait, et les clairons aux roses de leurs bouches
Vibraient, rumeur de cuivre et d'abeilles farouches !
Ivre essaim de la guerre aux ruches des armures,
Allez cueillir la mort sur la fleur des chairs mûres,
Et si vous revenez vers la ville natale
Qu'on suive sur mon seuil au marbre de ses dalles,
Quand ils auront passé, Victoire, sous tes ailes,
La marque d'un sang clair à leurs rouges semelles !

POUR LA PORTE DES MARCHANDS

Sois béni, noir portail, qu'entrant nous saluâmes !
Les coffres durs pesaient à l'échine des ânes ;
Nous apportions, pour les étaler dans les cours,
Ce qu'on taille la nuit, ce qu'on brode le jour,
La pendeloque claire et l'étoffe tissée.
Le plus vieux d'entre nous tenait un caducée ;
C'était le maître exact des trocs et des échanges,
Et la gourde bossue et les perles étranges
Se mêlaient dans nos mains poudreuses, et chacun,
Pourvoyeur de denrée ou marchand de parfum,
Vidait son étalage et gonflait sa sacoche ;
Car tout acheteur cède au geste qui l'accroche
Par un pan de la robe et le bout du manteau . . .

Les plus petits grimpaient sur de grands escabeaux,
Et le plus doucereux comme le plus retors,
Le soir, comptait et recomptait sa pile d'or,
En partant, et chacun, pour qu'à l'ombre des haies
Les détrousseurs d'argent qui guettent les monnaies
Ne nous attendent point sur la route déserte,
O porte ! et pour qu'un dieu fasse nos pas alertes,
Chacun, sans regarder celui qui va le suivre,
Cloue à ton seuil de pierre une pièce de cuivre.

POUR LA PORTE DES COMÉDIENNES

Le chariot s'arrête à l'angle de mon mur.
Le soir est beau, le ciel est bleu, les blés sont mûrs ;
La Nymphe tourne et danse autour de la fontaine ;
Le Faune rit ; l'Été mystérieux ramène
A son heure la troupe errante et le vieux char,
Et celles dont le jeu, par le masque et le fard,
Mime sur le tréteau où pose leur pied nu
La fable populaire ou le mythe ingénu
Et l'histoire divine, humaine et monstrueuse,
Qu'au miroir de la source, au fond des grottes creuses,
Avec leurs bonds, avec leurs cris, avec leurs rires,
La Dryade argentine et le jaune Satyre
Reprennent d'âge en âge à l'ombre des grands bois.
Venez ! l'heure est propice et la foule est sans voix,
Et l'attente sourit déjà dans les yeux clairs
Des enfants et des doux vieillards, et, à travers
Ma porte qui, pour vous, s'ouvrira toute grande,
Hospitalière et gaie et lourde de guirlandes,
Je vous vois qui venez, une rose à la main,

Avec vos manteaux clairs et vos visages peints,
Toutes, et souriant, avant d'entrer, chacune
Met le pied sur la borne et lace son cothurne.

POUR LA PORTE SUR LA MER

Moi, le Barreur de poupe et le Veilleur de proue
Qui connus le soufflet des lames sur ma joue,
Le vent s'échevelant au travers de l'écume,
L'eau claire de l'amphore et la cendre de l'urne,
Et, clarté silencieuse ou flamme vermeille,
La torche qui s'embrase et la lampe qui veille,
Le degré du palais et le seuil du décombre
Et l'accueil aux yeux d'aube et l'exil aux yeux d'ombre
Et l'amour qui sourit et l'amour qui sanglote
Et le manteau sans trous que l'âpre vent fait loque
Et le fruit mûr saignant et la tête coupée
Au geste de la serpe ou au vol de l'épée,
Et, vagabond des vents, des routes et des flots,
De la course marine ou du choc des galops,
Moi qui garde toujours le bruit et la rumeur
De la corne du pâtre et du chant du rameur,
Me voici, revenu des grands pays lointains
De pierre et d'eau, et toujours seul dans mon destin
Et nu, debout encor à l'avant de la proue
Impétueuse qui dans l'écume s'ébroue ;
Et j'entrerai brûlé de soleil et de joie,
Carène qui se cabre et vergue qui s'éploie,
Avec les grands oiseaux d'or pâle et d'argent clair.
J'entrerai par la Porte ouverte sur la Mer !

The poems all purport to be written in the same metre, but notice with what excellent art Régnier varies the movement of each, so that "The Gate of the Warriors" is almost as rhythmic and martial as the steps of the legions passing through it. The *b's* and *d's* in the line: "Ton battant d'airain dur et ton battant de fer," give the heavy tread of the poem at the outset; while with the first line of "The Merchants:" "Soit béni, noir portail, qu'entrant nous saluâmes" something suave, almost cringing, has crept in. The merchants are timid people, or they would not nail a copper coin on the sill of the gate as an offering to the protecting gods that their steps may be rapid and wary, and robbers be eluded. The whole sound of the poem is succulent and sycophantic. Very different again is the light, advancing rhythm of "The Comedians." The two first lines give a feeling of expectation, all the gaiety of an evening of recreation after the day's work:

Le chariot s'arrête à l'angle de mon mur.
Le soir est beau, le ciel est bleu, les blés sont mûrs . . .

The cutting of the last of these two lines into thirds, has given it a skipping, tripping, care-free quality; and the end of the poem, where each comedian, arrayed and made up for the play, puts her foot up on the pedestal of the gate to be certain that her sandal-lace is adjusted and will not trip her, is most simple and charming. There is a certain fresh, swirling, blowing movement about "The Gate of the Sea," hard to define, but very evident, nevertheless. We feel the proud, almost haughty lifting and falling of the figurehead :

Avec les grands oiseaux d'or pâle et d'argent clair.
J'entrerai par la Porte ouverte sur la Mer !

Now we come to a form which Régnier invented for himself, and called *Odelette* — Little Ode. It is often spoken of as being his greatest contribution to poetry ; which is nonsense. His greatest contribution is his *vers libre* as a whole, and these *Odelettes* are merely short, evanescent poems in *vers libre*, and should hardly be dignified by being called a form. But they are as satisfying as they are slight, and have a piercingly sweet little melody that I can remember nowhere else. The first one is perhaps the most successful of all he has done.

ODELETTE I

Un petit roseau m'a suffi
Pour faire frémir l'herbe haute
Et tout le pré
Et les doux saules
Et le ruisseau qui chante aussi ;
Un petit roseau m'a suffi
A faire chanter la forêt.

Ceux qui passent l'ont entendu
Au fond du soir, en leurs pensées,

Dans le silence et dans le vent,
Clair ou perdu,
Proche ou lointain . . .
Ceux qui passent en leurs pensées
En écoutant, au fond d'eux-mêmes,
L'entendront encore et l'entendent
Toujours qui chante.

Il m'a suffi
De ce petit roseau cueilli
A la fontaine où vint l'Amour
Mirer, un jour,
Sa face grave
Et qui pleurait,
Pour faire pleurer ceux qui passent
Et trembler l'herbe et frémir l'eau ;
Et j'ai, du souffle d'un roseau,
Fait chanter toute la forêt.

This is what he calls an ode. The difference in
weight and rhythm is very marked.

ODE III

Je t'ai connue,
Chère Ombre nue,
Avec tes cheveux lourds de soleil et d'or pâle,
Avec ta bouche de sourire et de chair douce.
Du plus loin de mes jours, là-bas, tu es venue
Au bout des vieux chemins de blés et de mousses,
Le long des prés, au bord du bois,
Alors que je suivais la sente et le ruisseau,

Joyeux du ruisseau clair et de la sente fraîche,
Et qu'à mes mains,
Entre mes doigts,
La fleur cueillie à l'herbe épaisse
Était toute moite de rosée
Et tremblante de l'or d'une abeille posée,
Au temps d'avril où les roseaux
Chantaient d'eux-mêmes,
Auprès des eaux et des fontaines,
Au moindre vent,
Je t'ai connue, assise au porche sur le seuil
De la Vie et du Songe et de l'An,
Jadis, toi qui, du seuil,
Regardais venir l'aube et tressais des couronnes.

Je t'ai revue,
Chère Ombre nue,
Avec tes cheveux rouillés d'or roux,
Graves de tout le poids de leur automne ;
Le vieux vent d'Est pleure dans les haies,
Lourd d'avoir rôdé, l'aile basse ;
Le pampre se desserre au tronc qu'il désenlace
Et la terre s'éboule au talus qui l'étaie ;
La joie est brève et l'heure passe,
Et chacun marche vers un autre qui recule,
Et la fleur de l'aurore est fruit au crépuscule
Et le fruit d'or du soir est cendre dans la nuit.

Je t'ai revue,
Tu étais nue,

Comme à l'aube où je vins par la route des blés,
Moi qui reviens vers toi par le chemin des chaumes
Avec le soir qui tremble et le pas de l'automne
Aux échos de ma vie où riait le printemps ;
Que vas-tu mettre aux mains que le retour te tend ?
Car j'ai perdu l'obole et la bague et la clé
Et la couronne en fleurs d'espoir d'où j'ai senti,
Feuille à feuille, tomber la rose et le laurier ;
L'opale s'est rompue à l'anneau desserti
Et ma voix de nouveau hésite à te prier,
Car, debout à jamais et le doigt sur la bouche,
Comme pour écouter l'écho du temps qui fuit,
Ton silence obstiné, patient et farouche
Regarde venir l'ombre et pleure vers la nuit.

La Canne de Jaspe, which I mentioned a few moments ago, came out the same year as *Les Jeux Rustiques et Divins*, in 1897. It is not my intention to go into Henri de Régnier's prose books with any minuteness. Here, we are dealing with him as a poet, and in that capacity alone he has given us quite enough to do. But there is a little prose poem in the Preface to *La Canne de Jaspe* which I can by no means let pass. Speaking of the contents of his book, he says : "There are swords, mirrors, jewels, dresses, crystal goblets and lamps, with, sometimes, outside, the murmur of the sea and the breeze of forests. Listen also to the singing of the fountains. They are intermittent and unceasing ; the gardens which they enliven are symmetrical. The statue there is either of marble or of bronze; the yew is trimmed. The bitter smell of box perfumes the silence; the rose blossoms next to the cypress. Love and Death kiss each other on the mouth. The water reflects the foliage. Make the round of the basins. Go through the labyrinth; wander about the grove; and read my book, page by page, as though, with the end of your tall jasper cane, Solitary Stroller, you turned over on the dry gravel of the walk a beetle, a pebble, or some dead leaves." What is this but the palace with the onyx pillars once more! It seems as though it were such an exact simile, that even Régnier himself could not escape it.

The strange haunting by the past is also here, in the preface and in the book. Régnier's novels are divided into two kinds. Those which picture the past, and those where the scenes are laid in the present. There is one novel which, like the Colossus of Rhodes, spans the division, and has a foot in either territory. That is *Le Passé Vivant*, which I mentioned at the beginning of this essay.

The first of Régnier's long novels belongs to the group of the past. It is *La Double Maîtresse*, and was published in 1900. This book has been much admired, much abused, and widely read. My copy is nine years old, and dates therefore only from the sixth year of its publication, yet the title page says "seventh edition." It is perhaps the one of Régnier's novels in which the Rabelaisian humour I have spoken of is most apparent. But there is a great deal else in it. Among other things, a tragedy, none the less terrible because it borders on the ludicrous; and an excellent and penetrating psychology. Even in its coarseness there is something broad and sane — very different from the perverted innuendoes and everlasting under-suggestions of so much of Remy de Gourmont's work. How it is possible for a man of Régnier's delicacy to be so coarse, is a problem for the psychologist. But it is undoubtedly true that this fastidious gentleman enjoys a very loud laugh at times. *La Double Maîtresse* is certainly a masterpiece. Many critics call it his finest novel. It is hard to say "finest" where all are so fine. I content myself with saying "one of them."

But Régnier was not done with poetry, nor has he ever done with it. That is the most astonishing thing about him. It is not as though the poet in him had preceded the novelist merely. On the contrary, they both run along cheerfully and rapidly side by side. The same year that saw the publication of *La Double Maîtresse*, saw also a new volume of Régnier's poems, *Les Médailles d'Argile*.

Yes, *Le Vase*, which I quoted a little while ago, is Régnier's best poem. And yet — and yet — there is nothing finer than the Introduction to this new book, or some of the sonnets to Versailles in *La Cité des Eaux*.

In *Les Médailles d'Argile*, the poet speaks of his poems under the metaphor of clay medals, upon which he models his gods. His gods, which he says are the visible essences of the Thing which underlies everything in Heaven or Earth. Pantheism, I suppose some people would call it. Perhaps — does it matter? It is all his philosophy in a nutshell, and in this Henri de Régnier seems to be less a Frenchman than a citizen of the world. At least, there is no trace of the superstition which I mentioned in the last chapter. This is the Introduction:

J'ai feint que des Dieux m'aient parlé;
Celui-là ruisselant d'algues et d'eau,
Cet autre lourd de grappes et de blé,
Cet autre ailé,
Farouche et beau
En sa stature de chair nue,
Et celui-ci toujours voilé,
Cet autre encor
Qui cueille, en chantant, la ciguë
Et la pensée
Et qui noue à son thyrse d'or
Les deux serpents en caducée,
D'autres encor . . .

Alors j'ai dit: Voici des flûtes et des corbeilles,
Mordez aux fruits;
Écoutez chanter les abeilles
Et l'humble bruit
De l'osier vert qu'on tresse et des roseaux qu'on coupe.

J'ai dit encor : Écoute,
Écoute,
Il y a quelqu'un derrière l'écho,
Debout parmi la vie universelle,
Et qui porte l'arc double et le double flambeau,
Et qui est nous
Divinement . . .

Face invisible ! je t'ai gravée en médailles
D'argent doux comme l'aube pâle,
D'or ardent comme le soleil,
D'airain sombre comme la nuit ;
Il y en a de tout métal,
Qui tintent clair comme la joie,
Qui sonnent lourd comme la gloire,
Comme l'amour, comme la mort ;
Et j'ai fait les plus belles de belle argile
Sèche et fragile.

Une à une, vous les comptiez en souriant,
Et vous disiez : Il est habile ;
Et vous passiez en souriant.

Aucun de vous n'a donc vu
Que mes mains tremblaient de tendresse,
Que tout le grand songe terrestre
Vivait en moi pour vivre en eux
Que je gravais aux métaux pieux,
Mes Dieux,
Et qu'ils étaient le visage vivant
De ce que nous avons senti des roses,

De l'eau, du vent,
De la forêt et de la mer,
De toutes choses
En notre chair,
Et qu'ils sont nous divinement.

Is anything in any language more lovely than that? If so, I do not know it.

True to his *flair* for divisions and titles, Régnier has divided this book into "Votive Medals," "Love Medals," "Heroic Medals," and "Marine Medals." Then, deserting his metaphor, we have several other sections of which only the last, "The Passers-by of the Past," invites mention. In almost every poem of the medal section, Régnier has kept to the idea of the modeller. It is nearly always brought in, as though he enjoyed the difficulty of writing poems of many kinds and writing them by this central symbol, and yet treating each one differently, and avoiding any suggestion of monotony. When I say that there are sixty-seven poems in the medal section, it will be seen what a task this was. This is one of the "Votive Medals:"

LA FILEUSE

Fileuse! L'ombre est tiède et bleuâtre. Une abeille
Bourdonne sourdement dans le jour qui s'endort,
Et ton rouet se mêle à cette rumeur d'or
Ailé qui peu à peu s'engourdit et sommeille.

Il est tard. C'est le soir. Le raisin à la treille
Pend et sa grappe est mûre à l'essaim qui la mord,
Mais, pour la vendanger demain, il faut encor,
Avant que vienne l'aube et que le coq s'éveille,

Que j'aie en cette argile obéissante et douce
Arrondi de la paume et façonné du pouce
Cette amphore qui s'enfle entre mes mains obscures,

Tandis que mon labeur écoute autour de lui
Ton rouet imiter de son rauque murmure
Quelque guêpe invisible éparse dans la nuit.

This is a " Marine Medal : "

ODE MARINE

J'entends la mer
Murmurer au loin quand le vent
Entre les pins, souvent,
Porte son bruit rauque et amer
Qui s'assourdit, roucoule ou siffle, à travers,
Les pins rouges sur le ciel clair . . .

Parfois
Sa sinueuse, sa souple voix
Semble ramper à l'oreille, puis recule
Plus basse au fond du crépuscule
Et puis se tait pendant des jours
Comme endormie
Avec le vent
Et je l'oublie . . .

Mais un matin elle reprend
Avec la houle et la marée,
Plus haute, plus désespérée,
Et je l'entends.

C'est un bruit d'eau qui souffre et gronde et se lamente
Derrière les arbres sans qu'on la voie,
Calmée ou écumante
Selon que le couchant saigne ou rougeoie,
Se meurt ardent ou s'éteint tiède . . .

Sans ce grand murmure qui croît ou cesse
Et roule ou berce
Mes heures, chacune, et mes pensées,
Sans lui, cette terre crue
Et crevassée
Que çà et là renfle et bossue
Un tertre jaune où poussent roses
De rares fleurs chétives qui penchent,
Sans lui, ce lieu âpre et morose
D'où je ne vois qu'un horizon pauvre
De solitude et de silence
Serait trop triste à ma pensée

Car je suis seul, vois-tu. Toute la Vie
M'appelle à son passé encor qui rit et crie
Par mille bouches éloquentes
Derrière moi, là-bas, les mains tendues,
Debout et nue ;
Et moi, couché
Sur la terre durcie à mes ongles en sang,
Je n'ai pour y sculpter mon rêve frémissant

Et le rendre éternel en sa forme fragile
Qu'un peu d'argile,
Rien d'autre
Pour façonner mes médailles mélodieuses
Où je sais dans la glaise ocreuse
Faire, visage d'ombre ou profil de clarté,
Sourire la Douleur et pleurer la Beauté . . .

Mais dans mon âme au loin l'amour gronde ou roucoule
Comme la mer, là-bas, derrière les pins rouges.

Now I am going to skip over to "Passers-by of the Past." These are wonderful little vignettes of eighteenth century characters. Did writing *La Double Maîtresse* put them into his head? Or are they merely another sign of that urging of the past upon him which we come across so often?

The first picture is a battle scene, or rather a portrait with a battle scene for background :

TABLEAU DE BATAILLE

Il est botté de cuir et cuirassé d'airain,
Debout dans la fumée où flotte sur sa hanche
Le nœud où pend l'épée à son écharpe blanche ;
Son gantelet se crispe au geste de sa main.

Son pied s'appuie au tertre où, dans le noir terrain,
La grenade enflammée ouvre sa rouge tranche,
Et l'éclair du canon empourpre, rude et franche,
Sa face bourguignonne à perruque de crin.

Autour de lui, partout, confus et minuscule,
Le combat s'enchevêtre, hésite, fuit, s'accule,
Escarmouche, mêlée et tuerie et haut fait;

Et le peintre naïf qui lui grandit la taille
Sans doute fut loué jadis pour avoir fait
Le héros à lui seul plus grand que la bataille.

This next one is of a pet monkey:

LE SINGE

Avec son perroquet, sa chienne et sa négresse
Qui lui tend le peignoir et sèche l'eau du bain
A son corps qui, plus blanc sous cette noire main,
Cambre son torse souple où sa gorge se dresse,

Elle a fait peindre aussi, pour marquer sa tendresse,
Par humeur libertine ou caprice badin,
Le portrait naturel de son singe africain
Qui croque une muscade et se gratte la fesse.

Très grave, presque un homme et singe en tapinois,
Velu, glabre, attentif, il épluche sa noix
Et regarde alentour, assis sur son séant;

Et sa face pelée et camuse où l'œil bouge
Ricane, se contracte et fronce en grimaçant
Son turban vert et jaune où tremble un plumet rouge.

Here is the most charming one of all:

L'AMATEUR

En son calme manoir entre la Tille et l'Ouche,
Au pays de Bourgogne où la vigne fleurit,
Tranquille, il a vécu comme un raisin mûrit.
Le vin coula pour lui du goulot qu'on débouche.

Ami de la nature et friand de sa bouche,
Il courtisa la Muse et laissa, par écrit,
Poèmes, madrigaux, épîtres, pot-pourri,
Et parchemins poudreux où s'attestait sa souche.

En perruque de crin, par la rue, à Dijon,
S'il marchait, appuyé sur sa canne de jonc,
Les Élus de la Ville et les Parlementaires

Saluaient de fort loin Monsieur le Chevalier,
Moins pour son nom, ses champs, sa vigne et son hallier
Que pour avoir reçu trois lettres de Voltaire.

The three letters of Voltaire have a nice irony about them.

I am going to give myself the pleasure of printing just one more of this group. It is not a portrait, it is a thing. One of those bright, Dresden china clocks, all painted porcelain flowers and twining bronze branches. Henri de Régnier has a profound affection for what Voltaire calls, "ce superflu si nécessaire."

LA PENDULE DE PORCELAINE

Le jardin rit au fleuve et le fleuve soupire
Du regret éternel de sa rive qu'il fuit,
La glycine retombe et se penche vers lui,
Le lilas s'y reflète et le jasmin s'y mire.

Le liseron s'élance et le lierre s'étire ;
Un bouton qui germait est corolle aujourd'hui ;
L'héliotrope embaume l'ombre et chaque nuit
Entr'ouvre un lys de plus pour l'aube qui l'admire ;

Et dans la maison claire en ses tapisseries,
Une pendule de porcelaine fleurie
Contourne sa rocaille où l'Amour s'enguirlande,

Et tout le frais bouquet dont le jardin s'honore
Survit dans le vieux Saxe où le Temps pour offrande
Greffe la fleur d'argent de son timbre sonore.

Gathering up his scattered essays contributed to various reviews and particularly *Les Écrits pour L'Art*, Régnier brought them out in 1901, in a volume. With this book we have nothing to do. The same year produced *Les Amants Singuliers*, a harking back to the style of tales with which he began ; and the next year, a long novel, *Le Bon Plaisir*, with the seventeenth century for scenery, and dedicated to his many-times-removed grandfather, as I said before. Again, in the same year, came another volume of poems, *La Cité des Eaux*.

The title of this book is taken from Michelet's line : "Versailles, Cité des Eaux." Henri de Régnier is in love with Versailles. Here, as nowhere else, can he solace his taste for old French garden architecture, for stately buildings, and for the melancholy of vanished generations. With that feeling for style which he has to so unusual a degree, with unerring taste, he has chosen the formal sonnet, the classic French alexandrine sonnet (a far inferior brand to the Italian sonnet, be it said), for his tribute to Versailles. Versailles, model of formality and stately etiquette!

The dedication, *Salut à Versailles*, is too long to print in its entirety. I will quote the first part (of course it is in several parts), and let me hastily add that it is not a sonnet.

SALUT A VERSAILLES

Celui dont l'âme est triste et qui porte à l'automne
Son cœur brûlant encor des cendres de l'été,
Est le Prince sans sceptre et le Roi sans couronne
De votre solitude et de votre beauté.

Car ce qu'il cherche en vous, ô jardins de silence,
Sous votre ombrage grave où le bruit de ses pas
Poursuit en vain l'écho qui toujours le devance,
Ce qu'il cherche en votre ombre, ô jardins, ce n'est pas

Le murmure secret de la rumeur illustre,
Dont le siècle a rempli vos bosquets toujours beaux,

Ni quelque vaine gloire accoudée au balustre,
Ni quelque jeune grâce au bord des fraîches eaux ;

Il ne demande pas qu'y passe ou qu'y revienne
Le héros immortel ou le vivant fameux
Dont la vie orgueilleuse, éclatante et hautaine
Fut l'astre et le soleil de ces augustes lieux.

Ce qu'il veut, c'est le calme et c'est la solitude,
La perspective avec l'allée et l'escalier,
Et le rond-point, et le parterre, et l'attitude
De l'if pyramidal auprès du buis taillé ;

La grandeur taciturne et la paix monotone
De ce mélancolique et suprême séjour,
Et ce parfum de soir et cette odeur d'automne
Qui s'exhalent de l'ombre avec la fin du jour.

I should like to quote all these sonnets, one after the other — and only in this way can you get the whole effect — but as I cannot do that, I have picked out a few here and there. The first is *La Façade*.

LA FAÇADE

Glorieuse, monumentale et monotone,
La façade de pierre effrite au vent qui passe
Son chapiteau friable et sa guirlande lasse
En face du parc jaune où s'accoude l'Automne.

Au médaillon de marbre où Pallas la couronne,
La double lettre encor se croise et s'entrelace ;
A porter le balcon l'Hercule se harasse ;
La fleur de lys s'effeuille au temps qui la moissonne.

Le vieux Palais, miré dans ses bassins déserts,
Regarde s'accroupir en bronze noir et vert
La Solitude nue et le Passé dormant ;

Mais le soleil aux vitres d'or qu'il incendie
Y semble rallumer intérieurement
Le sursaut, chaque soir, de la Gloire engourdie.

Already the note is struck : mournful, echoing.
We are watching the dissolution of something beautiful, fragile, but doomed. And yet, how lovely it
is in its decay, how much more sympathetic than
strident vigour ! Listen to this of *Le Bassin Vert* :

LE BASSIN VERT

Son bronze qui fut chair l'érige en l'eau verdie,
Déesse d'autrefois triste d'être statue ;
La mousse peu à peu couvre l'épaule nue,
Et l'urne qui se tait pèse à la main roidie ;

L'onde qui s'engourdit mire avec perfidie
L'ombre que toute chose en elle est devenue,
Et son miroir fluide où s'allonge une nue
Imite inversement un ciel qu'il parodie.

Le gazon toujours vert ressemble au bassin glauque.
C'est le même carré de verdure équivoque
Dont le marbre ou le buis encadrent l'herbe ou l'eau.

Et dans l'eau smaragdine et l'herbe d'émeraude,
Regarde, tour à tour, errer en ors rivaux
La jaune feuille morte et le cyprin qui rôde.

How the creeping of the moss up the shoulder of
the statue gives, in one line, the sense of decay!
Here is another called *La Nymphe.* Notice how
slightly and yet certainly it is done. With how
little he gives the colours and reflections in the water.

LA NYMPHE

L'eau calme qui s'endort, déborde et se repose
Au bassin de porphyre et dans la vasque en pleurs
En son trouble sommeil et ses glauques pâleurs
Reflète le cyprès et reflète la rose.

Le Dieu à la Déesse en souriant s'oppose ;
L'un tient le sceptre et l'arc, l'autre l'urne et les fleurs,
Et, dans l'allée entre eux, mêlant son ombre aux leurs,
L'Amour debout et nu se dresse et s'interpose,

Les talus du gazon bordent le canal clair ;
L'if y mire son bloc, le houx son cône vert,
Et l'obélisque alterne avec la pyramide ;

Un Dragon qui fait face à son Hydre ennemie,
Tous deux du trou visqueux de leurs bouches humides
Crachent un jet d'argent sur la Nymphe endormie.

Oh, they are beautiful, these poems! I know nothing more perfect in any language.
Now let us take an interior. He is no less happy there, as you will see. And when it comes to the smell of the box through the window, we must admit that words can do no more.

LE PAVILLON

La corbeille, la pannetière et le ruban
Nouant la double flûte à la houlette droite,
Le médaillon ovale où la moulure étroite
Encadre un profil gris dans le panneau plus blanc ;

La pendule hâtive et l'horloge au pas lent
Où l'heure, tour à tour, se contrarie et boite ;
Le miroir las qui semble une eau luisante et moite,
La porte entrebâillée et le rideau tremblant ;

Quelqu'un qui est parti, quelqu'un qui va venir,
La Mémoire endormie avec le Souvenir,
Une approche qui tarde et date d'une absence,

Une fenêtre, sur l'odeur du buis amer,
Ouverte, et sur des roses d'où le vent balance
Le lustre de cristal au parquet de bois clair.

La Cité des Eaux has other divisions. And they are interesting, if you have the fortitude to begin the volume in the middle. But if you start with *Versailles*, I predict that you will always remain there.

La Cité des Eaux was followed, in 1903, by his first modern novel, *Le Mariage de Minuit*, and again in the same year by another, *Les Vacances d'un Jeune Homme Sage*. This last is a delightful story of a boy in his late school-days, and is done with complete sympathy and seriousness. No vestige of a sneer ever mars it. The author never patronizes his creation, young boy though he is. By the people who find *La Double Maîtresse* a little too extreme, *Les Vacances d'un Jeune Homme Sage* is usually considered Régnier's best novel.

Les Rencontres de M. de Bréot, published in 1904, was a return to the seventeenth century, but in rather a different manner. *M. de Bréot* is a series of scenes rather than a novel, and it is a very strange mixture of realism and fantasticality. The two sides of Régnier have each had a hand for a while, and the result is a book which utterly defies classification. But when, in 1905, *Le Passé Vivant* appeared, Régnier had flung a bridge over the chasm in himself, and produced a book which rested upon both of his personalities.

Le Passé Vivant is too big a book, a book with too many overtones, to be discussed in a paragraph.

Perhaps the poetical side of Régnier comes out more strongly in it than in most of his novels, though they are all impregnated with poetry. It is a tragic story of a young man who is so obsessed by the past that he feels called upon to reproduce in his own person, as much as possible, the ancestor whose name he bears. The result is a series of circumstances which make life so hideous that the duplicate ends by the young man killing himself on the spot where his ancestor had died of a wound received in battle.

It is easy to sneer at this book as a fairy story, or a ghost story of an unusual kind. It is neither of these things, but a profound study of a fact, which, in a lesser, saner degree, I feel sure Henri de Régnier knows from personal experience to be true.

La Sandale Ailée, a return to poetry again, appeared in 1906. The quality of Régnier's verse has not exactly deteriorated, and yet there is nothing in this volume to equal *Le Vase*, the introduction in *Les Médailles d'Argile*, or the sonnets to Versailles. Yet there is one poem which is among the poet's finest work. It is a new note of vigour, almost a joy of living. The particular kind of *Symbolisme* of his early books is fading out of these last volumes. There is a greater robustness, a dashing quality. But here let me print "September:"

SEPTEMBRE

Avant que l'âpre vent exile les oiseaux,
Disperse la feuillée et sèche les roseaux
Où j'ai coupé jadis mes flèches et mes flûtes,
Je veux, assis au seuil qu'encadre la lambrusque,
Revoir, avec mes yeux déjà demi fermés
Sur ces jours, un à un, que nous avons aimés,
La face que l'Année, en fuyant, mois à mois,
Détourne, en souriant, de l'ombre qui fut moi.

Septembre, Septembre,
Cueilleur de fruits, teilleur de chanvre,
Aux clairs matins, aux soirs de sang,
Tu m'apparais,
Debout et beau,
Sur l'or des feuilles de la forêt,
Au bord de l'eau,
En ta robe de brume et de soie,
Avec ta chevelure qui rougeoie
D'or, de cuivre, de sang et d'ambre,
Septembre,
Avec l'outre de peau obèse
Qui charge ton épaule et pèse
Et suinte à ses coutures vermeilles
Où viennent bourdonner les dernières abeilles !

Septembre !
Le vin nouveau fermente et mousse de la tonne
Aux cruches ;
La cave embaume, le grenier ploie ;

La gerbe de l'Été cède au cep de l'Automne ;
La meule luit des olives qu'elle broie.

Toi, Seigneur des pressoirs, des meules et des ruches,
O Septembre, chanté de toutes les fontaines,
Écoute la voix du poème !
Le soir est froid ;
L'ombre s'allonge de la forêt,
Et le soleil descend derrière les grands chênes.

Oh, how good that *vers libre* is, and how unerring
Régnier's judgment to know when it is indispen-
sable ! Could that movement of speed and delight
have been got in the alexandrine, do you think?
No — "other times, other manners ;" new metres
suit new minds.

Another volume of essays in 1906, a series of
Venetian sketches, also in 1906. A modern novel,
and a singularly successful one, in 1907. A play,
which it must be admitted amounts to very little,
in 1908. Another modern novel, *L'Amphisbène,* in
ᵀ912, and the year before, 1911, the last collection
of poems that he has published so far, *Le Miroir des
Heures.*

Again, the poems retain their extraordinary technique, but to any one who knows his earlier books,
Le Miroir des Heures offers nothing either exception-
ally good like *Septembre,* in *La Sandale Ailée,* or
particularly new. For the first time, some of the
Rabelaisian quality of certain scenes in certain of
his novels has crept into his poems, in the section :

Sept Estampes Amoureuses. Many of the poems are records of travel in Turkey and Italy. They are pleasant, adequate — but unarresting. I do not think it necessary to quote anything from *Le Miroir des Heures.* I prefer to leave *Septembre* as the last quotation.

Another novel, *Romaine Mirmault,* came out in the Summer of 1914, and still another, which had been running in a review, was to have been published soon after. I suppose the war has delayed it.

The wonder in reading Henri de Régnier's life is how on earth he has been able to accomplish all he has. His novels show him to be a man of the world, observant, experienced, but the labour of producing twenty-six books in exactly twenty-nine years is enormous. And the genius (when practically all the books are masterpieces) is incalculable. Never once in the fatigue of this constant production has Régnier lowered his artistic standards. He has told us how he writes his novels, re-writing them entirely three or four times before they are ready for publication.

In 1911, Henri de Régnier was elected to the French Academy, succeeding Melchior de Vogue.

Symbolisme is over. The younger men are more preoccupied with life, they need new tools to express new thoughts. In the next essay we begin with the Moderns. Henri de Régnier himself has said, "We dreamed; they want to live and to say they have lived, directly, simply, intimately, lyric lly. They do not want to express man in his syr ols, they want to express him in his thoughts, i is sensations, in his sentiments."

Whether this great genius who is H de Régnier will ever renew himself in his poetry he has in his prose, remains for time to show. is the fashion at the moment to consider him only as a novelist, and to disparage his poetry in the light of his prose. But even taking that into consideration, and admitting him to be, in poetry, the voice of a vanishing quarter of a century, he is still the greatest French poet alive to-day, and one of the greatest poets that France has ever had.

P

FRANCIS JAMMES

FRANCIS JAMMES

I SAID in the last chapter that, in this, we should begin to study the Moderns. Perhaps it would be well, at the outset, to inquire a little what is modern. What is this modern spirit which distinguishes Francis Jammes and Paul Fort from the men of the *Symboliste* group? If I were obliged to define it in a word, I should say that it was "exteriority" versus "interiority."

Since the days of Musset, a long line of poets had been weeping their miseries in beautiful verse. Baudelaire, Verlaine, Samain, Régnier, all of them, had found life disillusion (or said they had), and none of them hesitated to complain through the length of charming volume after charming volume. Romantics, Realists, *Naturalistes*, *Symbolistes*, were all united by one common bond, they were convinced that a man who did not find the world dust and ashes was a philistine. They could be happy for a few brief moments in some *brasserie*, provided they were rather noisy and vulgar about it, but it was quite understood between them and an indul-

gent world that they were only spending a few moments in cheating the misery which was devouring them, that the next morning they would be as
unhappy as ever.   And the *brasserie* saw to it that
they were.

It was the convention that a poet loved rather
decrepit and faded things (how often we find the
word *fané* in their poems).   *Volupté* is another word
they loved, and here we have the companion picture
to the *brasserie*.   They were a pack of individualists,
egoists, living in a city, and inoculating one another
with the microbe of discontent.

I am far from saying that they were not great
poets — the foregoing chapters will have shown you
how much I admire their work — but these men
were born with a great talent.   They would have
been poets no matter where they lived or what they
thought, for one feels with them that it is their
poetry which counts and not their ideas.   (Of course,
I except Verhaeren from this statement.   As I said
in the first essay, Verhaeren flew over the interven-
ing period, during those years of illness in London,
and emerged a fully developed modern, some years
ahead of anybody else.)

Neither do I wish to convey the idea that none
of this long line of poets was a cynic by nature.
Musset, Baudelaire, and Verlaine had every reason
to be unhappy, both because of their temperaments,
and because of the events their temperaments led

them into. But what was undoubtedly true of a few men, was equally undoubtedly a convention with the majority. "Interiority" was the fashion; a poet examined his mental processes under a microscope until he was like the gentleman in the story who had everything but "housemaid's knee."

Such a state of things was really utterly insupportable. Musset drank himself to death; Verlaine and Huysmans fell exhausted into the arms of the Church; Rimbaud took refuge in the Orient, married a native wife, and wrote no more poems; and the greater number undoubtedly learned to enjoy their little pleasures and comforts with agreeable calm, although they continued to write as though suicide were just round the corner.

Somehow, that fashion worked itself out, and "exteriority," as I have called the characteristic modern touch, came in. By this extremely awkward word, "exteriority," I mean an interest in the world apart from oneself, a contemplation of nature unencumbered by the "pathetic fallacy." It is the reason of the picture-making of the modern poet. Picture-making these other men gave us, but the Modern gives us picture-making without comment. A somewhat old-fashioned editor once said to me that poetry was losing its nobility, its power of inspiration, because the young poets were only concerned with making pictures. I longed to ask him whether he would find a portrait by Van

Dyck or Romney more appealing, if there were a little cloud issuing from the mouth of the sitter upon which, somewhere in an upper corner, his or her sentiments might be read, after the manner of our comic papers.

Well, whether editors like it or not, this making of pictures is one side of the modern manner. Another is a certain zest in seeing things and recording them. (*Chansons pour me Consoler d'Être Heureux* is the title of one of Fort's books.) The "modern" poet dares to be happy and say so. Still another side of "modernity" is the feeling of unity. *Unanisme*, they call it in France. The knowledge that the world is all interrelated, that each part of it is dependent upon every other. That the butcher, the baker, and the candlestick-maker are performing important functions, of which he, the poet, is merely performing another; and that love is hardly more necessary in making the world go round than a host of other little shoves given by trade, and science, and art, collectively.

Again let me ward off misunderstanding by remarking that I do not wish to imply that "Moderns" never write about themselves, nor that the elder poets never wrote purely descriptive poems. It is general temper which makes a type, not sporadic departures from it. Any poet may feel sad and write sad verses, it is only when he writes no others that we are justified in calling it a *mode*.

Francis Jammes is the poet of contentment, of observation, of simplicity. He is the poet of hills, and fields, and barns, not of libraries and alcoves. His poetry blows across the scented verses of the '90's like the wind from one of the snow-capped peaks of his native Pyrenees.

In 1893, there drifted to Paris a little volume of poems called simply *Vers*. It was privately issued, and bore the name of a provincial printer : J. Goude-Dumesnil, Orthez. The author's name was quite unknown to the *literati* of Paris. Orthez was a little town in the Basses-Pyrénées ; that seemed the only tangible thing about the book. ᛫ But the poems were worthy of notice for their candour and simplicity, and they piqued curiosity by what seemed to the critics their anonymity. The *Mercure de France* for December, 1893, contained a notice which said : "This slim volume presents itself in a mysterious and very particular manner. The name of the author is unknown. Is it a pseudonym ? And it seems as though the spelling were not very careful : James would be more exact. The book is dedicated to Hubert Crackanthorpe and Charles Lacoste. M. Hubert Crackanthorpe exists. He is a young English writer who has published a volume of stories, which are, it appears, very remarkable, somewhat in the manner of Maupassant, and entitled 'Wreckage.' The second name is unknown to me."

So the author must be an Englishman named

"James," or an English boy, for farther on this astute commentator says, "The few words, written by hand on the copy I have before my eyes, are in the writing of an awkward little schoolboy." In his dedication, Jammes had written, "My style stammers, but I have told my truth." Of course he stammered, because he was English and so writing in a foreign tongue. The Pyrenees is one of the favourite haunts of the English; it was settled: the author was English, and his name was James.

But Jammes was not English; he was the descendant of an old Pyrenean *bourgeois* family. His great-grandfather was a notary in the town of Albi, and the family were of enough consequence to have a neighbouring village named after them. The sons of this gentleman left home to seek their fortunes, and the grandfather of the poet, Jean-Baptiste Jammes, became a doctor at Guadeloupe. At first he prospered, and souvenirs of the interesting and exotic life he lived in the West Indies seem to have left an indelible impression upon the mind of his grandson. But he was ruined by an earthquake, and died without returning to France.

Jean-Baptiste had married a Creole, and a little son was born at Pointe-à-Pitre, before the earthquake. This boy was sent back to France when he was seven years old, to be brought up by some aunts who lived at Orthez. Jammes has written with feeling of the old dining-room, and the corner of it where his father sat, a little waif, seven years old, just arrived from Guadeloupe.

M. Jammes, the father, grew up and married — whom, I have been unable to find out — and settled in the town of Tournay in the Hautes-Pyrénées, where his son, Francis Jammes, was born on the second of December, 1868.

Never was any one more rooted to a countryside than Jammes to the Midi. "My bed," he writes, "is set down between that grain of sand : the Pyrenees, and that drop of water : the Atlantic Ocean. I live in Orthez. My name is inscribed at the *mairie*, and I am called Francis Jammes." But I anticipate ; Orthez came later. His early childhood was passed at Tournay. He has given some of his early recollections in a series of poems called *Souvenirs d'Enfance* :

> J'allai chez Monsieur Lay l'instituteur.
> Mon alphabet était comme des fleurs.
> Je me souviens du poële et de la bûche
> que chaque enfant du village apportait
> lorsque le Ciel est une blanche ruche
> et qu'on réveil on dit : "Il a neigé !"

> Je me souviens aussi de la gaîté
> de mon tablier, aux jours mûrs d'Été
> quand je quittais l'école un peu plus tôt.
> Petit petit j'avais encore les Cieux
> dedans les yeux comme une goutte d'eau
> à travers quoi l'on peut voir le Bon Dieu.

Already, suggested though not stated, is that blue of the sky which Jammes always seems to be in love with. All his books are cool and white like snow, and threaded with the blue of skies, of snow-shadows, of running water.

In these reminiscences, he tells us how he "suffered because the nightingale preferred the green rose-bush to my heart," as he expresses it. He tells of being taken, one Sunday, to lunch with the notary, and being told off to play with the notary's niece; of how they wandered in the orchard and "the birds upon the branches were confiding." We see the old apothecary, with his red wig and his hat "*à la Murger*," coming to take care of him when he is ill. He goes fishing and catches a white fish. He is taken to Pau and sees some performing monkeys, and stands up on his chair with excitement. One of the monkeys is supposed to be a soldier who has tried to desert and is shot, and the little boy is terribly affected, he says:

> . . . la vision du Singe qu'on fusille
> tu le sais bien, elle est toujours en moi.

His love for animals is very beautiful, his books are full of dogs, cats, donkeys; of hares, and wood-cock, and quail, and butterflies, and dragonflies. His love of nature began at Tournay:

> Eau, feuillage, air, sable, racines, fleurs,
> sauterelles, lombrics, martin-pêcheurs,

brume tombant sur quelque champ de raves,
vrilles de vigne au toit du tisserand :
ô doux génies qui m'avez fait esclave !
Vous m'amusiez, moi petit, vous si grands !

When Jammes was five years old, his father was
made Receiver of Records at Bordeaux, and the
family went there to live. For a brief time during
the moving, Jammes was sent to school in Pau. It
was a "dame-school," directed by two ladies.
Jammes was a petulant little boy, and probably the
restraint of a city was irksome to him ; apparently
the only thing which he remembers with pleasure
about this period, is chasing butterflies on his way
home from school. But Bordeaux was another
story. It was full of endless interests for a growing
boy — the quays, with their big ships perpetually
loading and unloading, and that spicy smell which
haunts vessels trading with the Indies or the Orient ;
the ship-chandlers' shops, with their suggestion of
deep waters ; and the innumerable bird-sellers' shops,
full of parrots and other gay-plumaged, tropical
birds, fit to rouse the imagination of the stolidest
youngster that ever was born. And Jammes was
anything but a stolid youngster. He was avid of
impressions, and untiring in the intelligence he
brought to bear upon them.

The big ships forever sailing away, and returning
laden with strange fruits and tropical merchandise,
filled the boy with a sort of nostalgia for those

distant, sun-basking ports. His grandfather had
lived in one of them, and his mind wrapped itself in
a delicious dreaming about those luxuriant islands
of which he had heard so much. He fell to imagin-
ing his grandfather in his big planter's hat and light
blue coat, wandering round among bamboos and
cocoa-trees :

> O Père de mon Père, tu étais là, devant
> mon âme qui n'était pas née et sous le vent
> les avisos glissaient dans la nuit coloniale.

or sleeping :

> . . . au pied de la goyave bleue, parmi
> les cris de l'Océan et les oiseaux des grèves.

All the mementoes of this West Indian life he
cherished like sacred things : his grandfather's
letters ; his grandmother's shawl, embroidered with
flowers and birds ; a trunk of camphor-wood, full
of the murmuring of seas and forests.

In one of his poems he speaks of the old letters :

TU ÉCRIVAIS . . .

> Tu écrivais que tu chassais des ramiers
> dans les bois de la Goyave,
> et le médecin qui te soignait écrivait,
> peu avant ta mort, sur ta vie grave.

Il vit, disait-il, en Caraïbe, dans ses bois.
Tu es le père de mon père.
Ta vieille correspondance est dans mon tiroir
et ta vie est amère.

Tu partis d'Orthez comme docteur-médecin,
pour faire fortune là-bas.
On recevait de tes lettres par un marin,
par le capitaine Folat.

Tu fus ruiné par les tremblements de terre
dans ce pays où l'on buvait
l'eau de pluie des cuves, lourde, malsaine, amère . . .
Et tout cela, tu l'écrivais.

Et tu avais acheté une pharmacie.
Tu écrivais : "La Métropole
n'en a pas de pareille." Et tu disais : "Ma vie
m'a rendu comme un vrai créole."

Tu es enterré, là-bas, je crois, à la Goyave.
Et moi j'écris où tu es né :
ta vieille correspondance est très triste et grave.
Elle est dans ma commode, à clef.

Perhaps something of this exotic life had really crept into his blood. He is said to look like a Creole, with "a great black beard, eyes nearly as green as the sea, and a sharp voice." His early books are full of this preoccupation with the tropical islands of the West Indies.

Side by side with this dreaming, another interest was growing upon Jammes, he was becoming interested in flowers. Bordeaux has an excellent botanical garden. One afternoon, when the poet was fourteen years old, he went into this garden for the first time. It made such an impression upon him that he even remembers that it was a Thursday, a hot Thursday afternoon in Summer. He says that there was " a white sun, with thick blue shadows," and that " the perfumes were so heavy they were almost sticky."

From that moment, Jammes' love for old maps, old marine charts, the lovely French names of the New World — *La Floride, La Louisiane, La Caroline, La Martinique* — and all they evoked, had a rival in his love for flowers. He became an *habitué* of the Botanical Gardens, and might be found there, defying the heat, with his handkerchief tucked into his collar to keep off the sun, studying the classification of plants. At that time, an old botanist, Armand Clavaud, frequented the Gardens, and taught botany to occasional pupils. Jammes became one of these, and not only learnt that "seul le papillon-aurore à l'aube du Printemps visite la cardamine," but found a friend who listened while he read the poems he was beginning to write.

Jammes does not seem to have carried on his botany with a very scientific finality. Rather, he seems to have dabbled in it, with the heart of a poet and the mind of a delighted amateur. Jean-Jacques

Rousseau began to rival the figure of his grand-father in his dreams and affections. His favourite book became the *Confessions*, which he called "son livre ami." He never lost this interest in Rousseau; one of his best prose pieces is *Sur Jean-Jacques Rousseau et Madame de Warens aux Charmettes et à Chambéry*, and one of his best poems is to *Madame de Warens*. He constantly refers to Rousseau, "triste botaniste" as he calls him, and his love of peri-winkles. It is interesting to note that the little blue periwinkle is almost the same colour as the blues of the sky and water, which I have said so pervade the work of Jammes.

His father dying in Bordeaux, Francis Jammes and his mother returned to Orthez, and the young man went into the office of a notary in that town. It is needless to say that nothing could have been more at variance with his tastes. The dusty proximity of deeds and registers was obnoxious to him, and it is rather amusing to notice that their dull and un-romantic present entirely obscured their past, which may very well have been as full of suggestion as the maps and charts he loved.

But Nature was too much for Jammes, and Nature is very importunate in the South of France. He wanted to strap his little flower-box on his back and be off "botanizing" in the fields; he wanted to race along the banks of the Gave with his dogs; he wanted to do anything except attend to business.

Q

To pass his days in the close atmosphere and powdery sunshine of a lawyer's office was horrible. But his observant eye was everywhere. Of the common, sordid, dull people he met while he was with the notary he has made his novel in verse, *Existences*. If the picture is a true one, we can hardly blame him for chafing to get away.

Meanwhile, three little volumes had slipped into being, all privately printed, of which the one I mentioned at the beginning of this essay was the last. The *Mercure de France* does not mention works that are entirely insignificant; Jammes was justified in determining to follow the business of literature. So the office was abandoned, and Jammes was free to pursue the career of poet.

Francis Jammes and his mother settled down in the old house so full of memories. The old house of the great-aunts, whither his father had been sent from Guadeloupe. Charles Guérin has written of this house :

> O Jammes, ta maison ressemble à ton visage.
> Une barbe de lierre y grimpe, un pin l'ombrage
> Éternellement jeune et dru comme ton cœur.

and Edmond Pilon, Jammes' friend and biographer, describes it also : "This cottage of Jammes', all twittering with birds, humming with bees, and surrounded with roses, in a garden which is loud with beehives, and shaded by a pine tree, stands on the slopes of Orthez. The countryside extends all about it, divided by the Gave, and watered by torrents. Here are villages, and over there are farms; the flocks climb the flanks of the mountains; two-wheeled carriages bring the peasants to market; a cart makes a rut in the plain; the sun has warmed the grains in the earth; the rain follows; the plums in the orchard are blue; a girl dressed in foulard sings in the lane, and the churlish beggar has gone down the road."

But I think, after all, that Jammes can describe it best himself:

LA MAISON SERAIT PLEINE DE ROSES . . .

La maison serait pleine de roses et de guêpes.
On y entendrait, l'après-midi, sonner les vêpres;
et les raisins couleur de pierre transparente
sembleraient dormir au soleil sous l'ombre lente.
Comme je t'y aimerais. Je te donne tout mon cœur
qui a vingt-quatre ans, et mon esprit moqueur,
mon orgueil et ma poésie de roses blanches;
et pourtant je ne te connais pas, tu n'existes pas.
Je sais seulement que, si tu étais vivante,
et si tu étais comme moi au fond de la prairie,
nous nous baiserions en riant sous les abeilles blondes,
près du ruisseau frais, sous les feuilles profondes.
On n'entendrait que la chaleur du soleil.
Tu aurais l'ombre des noisetiers sur ton oreille,
puis nous mêlerions nos bouches, cessant de rire,

pour dire notre amour que l'on ne peut pas dire;
et je trouverais, sur le rouge de tes lèvres,
le goût des raisins blonds, des roses rouges et des guêpes.

So much for the outside of the house. And this is
the inside:

LA SALLE A MANGER

Il y a une armoire à peine luisante
qui a entendu les voix de mes grand'tantes,
qui a entendu la voix de mon grand-père,
qui a entendu la voix de mon père.
A ces souvenirs l'armoire est fidèle.
On a tort de croire qu'elle ne sait que se taire,
car je cause avec elle.

Il y a aussi un coucou en bois.
Je ne sais pourquoi il n'a plus de voix.
Je ne veux pas le lui demander.
Peut-être bien qu'elle est cassée,
la voix qui était dans son ressort,
tout bonnement comme celle des morts.

Il y a aussi un vieux buffet
qui sent la cire, la confiture,
la viande, le pain et les poires mûres.
C'est un serviteur fidèle qui sait
qu'il ne doit rien nous voler.

Il est venu chez moi bien des hommes et des femmes
qui n'ont pas cru à ces petites âmes.
Et je souris que l'on me pense seul vivant

quand un visiteur me dit en entrant :
— comment allez-vous, monsieur Jammes ?

With ink and paper and his beloved pipe, which he
adores and apostrophizes in prose and verse, for
inside ; and the blue sky, and the flowering fields
and shady trees, with the Gave "blue like air,"
church bells ringing in the evening, and the quiet
moon over the magnolia trees, what more could
any poet desire for the outside ? But there was
more — there were old iron gates of great parks
leading up to some half-deserted château ; there
were legends, and the houses which contained them.
These things hitched themselves on to his old dreams
of Guadeloupe and Martinique, and gave the poet
a whole new gamut of imaginary possibilities.

The natural preoccupation of a young man peopled
his châteaux with girls. Not the girls of to-day,
but the frail, graceful girls of fifty years ago. How
well Jammes evokes them when he says, "Leurs
grands chapeaux de paille ont de longs rubans."
And the names he gives them ! Clara d'Ellébeuse,
who lived "au fond du vieux jardin plein de tulipes ;"
Almaïde d'Etremont ; Pomme d'Anis, whose real
name is Laure. These three are all in prose stories,
which resemble no other prose stories in the world,
and should really be called poems. They are full
of the details which show "de quelles vieilles fleurs
son âme est composée." There is L'Oncle Tom in
Pomme d'Anis, whose joy is in his greenhouse, and

whose greatest desire is to make a heliotrope seed, found in the tomb of an ancient Egyptian lady, blossom. There is M. d'Astin in *Clara d'Ellébeuse*, who lives all alone in an old house ; on one of his walls hangs "a marine chart browned like an old shell. Underneath it one reads 'Indian Ocean.'" It is he who gave to his friends, the D'Ellébeuses, "two pretty engravings, one representing 'a Mongolian woman in her dress of ceremony : summer ;' the other, 'the eldest daughter of the Emperor.'" Slight touches, but so deftly done as to evoke the whole room, with the furniture of the time.

But, as I have said, these are prose stories. Let me show you somewhat the same thing in a poem :

J'ÉCRIS DANS UN VIEUX KIOSQUE . . .

> J'écris dans un vieux kiosque si touffu
> qu'il en est humide et, comme un Chinois,
> j'écoute l'eau du bassin et la voix
> d'un oiseau — là, près de la chute (chutt ! !)

> d'eau. Je vais allumer ma pipe.
> Ça y est. J'en égalise la cendre.
> Puis le souvenir doucement descend
> en inspiration poétique.

> "*Je suis venu trop tard dans un monde
> trop vieux*" et je m'embête, je m'embête
> de ne pas assister à une ronde
> de petites filles aux grands chapeaux étalés.

— Cora ! tu va salir le bas de ton
pantalon, en touchant à ce vilain chien.
Voilà ce qu'eussent dit, dans un soir ancien,
les petites filles au bon ton.

Elles m'auraient regardé, en souriant,
fumer ma pipe tout doucement,
et ma petite nièce eût dit gravement :
Il rentre faire des vers maintenant.

Et ses petites compagnes, sans comprendre,
auraient arrêté une seconde
le charmantage de leur ronde,
croyant que les vers allaient *se voir* -   eut-être.

— Il a été à Touggourt, ma chère,
eût dit le cercle des écolières
plus âgées. Et Nancy eût déclaré :
il y a des sauvages et des dromadaires.

Puis, j'aurais vu déboucher sur la route
le caracolement des ânes
de plusieurs messieurs et de plusieurs dames
revenant, le soir, d'une cavalcade.

Mon cœur, mon cœur, ne retrouveras-tu
que dans la mort cet immense amour
pour ceux que tu n'as pas connus
en ces tendres et défunts jours ?

Jammes' life at this time was made up of dreams and reality, but few poets have understood so well as he how to combine the two. How to make his very accurate observation give an air of perfect naturalness to his most fantastic tales. But all the time that he was evoking a beautiful, delicate past in his imagination, he was really living in the little rose-covered house, smoking his pipe in the old tapestry room, or tramping the fields and woods, and breathing the bright, sparkling air which was blown from the snow-capped Pyrenees.

The place got into his blood. He loved it. "Here is a bucolic poet," exclaims Remy de Gourmont in the *IIme Livre des Masques*, "no kind of poet is more unusual." Yes, Jammes is a bucolic poet, such a poet as France has never seen before. England has had bucolic poets in no mean number, but the habit for centuries in France of all men of parts running to the capital as early in their lives as possible, has left no one behind to sing the labours of the fields.

By what happy chance Fate has permitted a poet of the first rank to remain in the country, we do not know. But he is in the country, and a country so far away as to make an annual journey to Paris all he cares to undertake.

Let me quote part of a poem called *Le Calendrier Utile*, which, for accuracy, might be taken from some Farmer's Almanac :

LE CALENDRIER UTILE

Au mois de Mars (le Bélier ♈) on sème
le trèfle, les carottes, les choux et la luzerne.
On cesse de herser, et l'on met de l'engrais
au pied des arbres et l'on prépare les carrés.
On finit de tailler la vigne où l'on met en place,
après l'avoir aérée, les échalas.

Pour les bestiaux les rations d'hiver finissent.
On ne mène plus, dans les prairies, les génisses
qui ont de beaux yeux et que leurs mères lèchent,
mais on leur donnera des nourritures fraîches.
Les jours croissent d'une heure cinquante minutes.
Les Soirées sont douces et, au crépuscule,
les chevriers traînards gonflent leurs joues aux flûtes.
Les chèvres passent devant le bon chien
qui agite la queue et qui est leur gardien.

So much for the description of March labours.
Now read this of Palm Sunday :

Ensuite vient le beau dimanche des RAMEAUX.
Quand j'étais enfant, on m'y attachait des gâteaux,
et j'allais à vêpres, docile et triste.
Ma mère disait : dans mon pays il y avait des olives . . .
Jésus pleurait dans le jardin des oliviers . . .
On était allé, en grande pompe, le chercher . . .
A Jérusalem, les gens pleuraient en criant son nom . . .
Il était doux comme le ciel, et son petit ânon
trottinait joyeusement sur les palmes jetées.
Des mendiants amers sanglotaient de joie,

en le suivant, parce qu'ils avaient la foi . . .
De mauvaises femmes devenaient bonnes
en le voyant passer avec son auréole
si belle qu'on croyait que c'était le soleil.
Il avait un sourire et des cheveux en miel.
Il a ressuscité des morts . . . Ils l'ont crucifié . . .
Je me souviens de cette enfance et des vêpres,
et je pleure, le gosier serré, de ne plus être
ce tout petit garçon de ces vieux mois de Mars,
de n'être plus dans l'église du village
où je tenais l'encens à la procession
et où j'écoutais le curé dire la PASSION.

No one is so tender and charming in Bible stories
as Jammes.　Here is a catalogue of March flowers,
beginning (and one cannot help smiling) with "peri-
winkles of milk-blue, loved by Jean-Jacques : "

Il te sera agréable, au mois de Mars,
d'aller avec ton amie sur les violettes noires.
A l'ombre, vous trouverez les pervenches bleu de lait
qu'aimait Jean-Jacques, le triste passionné.
Dans les bois, vous trouverez la pulmonaire
dont la fleur est violette et vin, la feuille vert-
de-gris, tachée de blanc, poilue et très rugueuse.
Il y a sur elle une légende pieuse ;
la cardamine où va le papillon-aurore,
l'isopyre légère et le noir hellébore,
la jacinthe qu'on écrase facilement
et qui a, écrasée, de gluants brillements ;

la jonquille puánte, l'anémone et le narcisse
qui fait penser aux neiges des berges de la Suisse ;
puis le lierre-terrestre bon aux asthmatiques.

Jammes does not like small townspeople. That
is if his novel, *Existences*, gives his real point of view.
But his whole soul is in sympathy with the shepherds,
the village people, the workers in the fields. "These
are the works of man," he says, "which are great."

CE SONT LES TRAVAUX . . .

Ce sont les travaux de l'homme qui sont grands :
celui qui met le lait dans les vases de bois,
celui qui cueille les épis de blé piquants et droits,
celui qui garde les vaches près des aulnes frais,
celui qui fait saigner les bouleaux des forêts,
celui qui tord, près des ruisseaux vifs, les osiers,
celui qui raccommode les vieux souliers
près d'un foyer obscur, d'un vieux chat galeux,
d'un merle qui dort et des enfants heureux ;
celui qui tisse et fait un bruit retombant,
lorsqu'à minuit les grillons chantent aigrement ;
celui qui fait le pain, celui qui fait le vin,
celui qui sème l'ail et les choux au jardin,
celui qui recueille les œufs tièdes.

That the poet knew practically nothing about any
other life except his own, and superficial glimpses
while in the lawyer's office, did not in the least
trouble him. Jammes has never been moved by

reason. His is an emotional nature, entirely swayed by his sentiments. Any judgment given by the intellect alone would undoubtedly seem to him cold and repellent. Francis Jammes is a charming child on one side, and a most lovable genius on the other. But a man of mature and balanced intellect he certainly is not. He loves with all his heart, and that is a most unusual and very refreshing thing. How he loves this little village and all its familiar sights and sounds!

LE VILLAGE A MIDI . . .

Le village à midi. La mouche d'or bourdonne
    entre les cornes des bœufs.
    Nous irons, si tu le veux,
si tu le veux, dans la campagne monotone.

Entends le coq . . . Entends la cloche . . . Entends le paon . . .
    Entends là-bas, là-bas, l'âne . . .
    L'hirondelle noire plane.
Les peupliers au loin s'en vont comme un ruban.

Le puits rongé de mousse! Écoute sa poulie
    qui grince, qui grince encor,
    car la fille aux cheveux d'or
tient le vieux seau tout noir d'où l'argent tombe en pluie.

La fillette s'en va d'un pas qui fait pencher
    sur sa tête d'or la cruche,

sa tête comme une ruche,
qui se mêle au soleil sous les fleurs du pêcher.

Et dans le bourg voici que les toits noircis lancent
au ciel bleu des flocons bleus ;
et les arbres paresseux
à l'horizon qui vibre à peine se balancent.

And so I have given much of Jammes' first real
book before we have got to it. Never mind, chronologically we are the more accurate, for it was undoubtedly written before it was printed. *De l'Angélus de l'Aube à l'Angélus du Soir* was published
by the *Société du Mercure de France*, in 1898. Two
little books had preceded it. *Un Jour*, also published by the *Mercure de France*, in 1896, and *La
Naissance du Poète*, printed in Brussels, in 1897.
But, as both these poems are now included in the
Angélus volume, I prefer to speak of them as a part
of it. (Another volume called *Vers* was printed by
Ollendorf, Paris, in 1894. But, although I am not
absolutely sure, I imagine it to have been just a
reprint of the book which first attracted the *Mercure's* attention.)

La Naissance du Poète and *Un Jour* are now followed by a companion piece, *La Mort du Poète*.
These are a series of three stories, vague and un-
solved allegories, which Jammes pleased himself by
writing. Doubtless they were done to soothe his
own feelings, for his biographers hint at "intimate

sorrows" lived down. Jammes, like so many young Frenchmen, had ceased to be a practising Roman Catholic. But, with his childlike, unreasoning, and clinging mind, no other solution of life was really possible to him, and it can have been no surprise to his friends when he became a professing Roman Catholic again. But we are anticipating by some seven years. At the time of *Un Jour* and *La Naissance du Poète*, Jammes was not an active member of the Church, but that his hereditary religion was neither distasteful nor indifferent to him, is shown by the fact that *Un Jour* ends by the Poet and his *fiancée* kneeling, one on either side of the wall partition which divides their bedrooms, and praying.

I wonder whether the dedication in my volume of *De l'Angélus* is contemporary or subsequent. Mine is the sixth edition, issued in 1911, and from the tone of this dedication I believe it to have been tacked on later. If it is not so characteristic of the Jammes of 1898, it is very characteristic of the later Jammes: "My God, you have called me among men. Here I am. I suffer and I love. I have spoken with the voice which you have given me. I have written with the words that you taught my father and mother and which they have transmitted to me. I pass upon the road like a laden ass at whom the children laugh and who lowers his head. I will go where you will, when you will.

The Angelus rings."

As we shall see later, Francis Jammes approaches his religion with the beautiful simplicity of Saint Francis of Assisi. Just now, we must concern ourselves with another trait in Jammes' character. His humour. Few Frenchmen have his delightful, innocent, happy sense of humour. We shall see it cropping out again and again, as we go through his books. Let me give you a specimen of it from this first volume :

ÉCOUTE, DANS LE JARDIN . . .

Écoute, dans le jardin qui sent le cerfeuil,
chanter, sur le pêcher, le bouvreuil.

Son chant est comme de l'eau claire
où se baigne, en tremblant, l'air.

Mon cœur est triste jusqu'à la mort,
bien que de lui plusieurs aient été, et une soit — folles.

La première est morte. La seconde est morte ;
— et je ne sais pas où est une autre.

Il y en a cependant encore une
qui est douce comme la lune . . .

Je m'en vais la voir cet après-midi.
Nous nous promènerons dans une ville . . .

Ce sera-t-il dans les clairs quartiers
de villas riches, de jardins singuliers ?

Roses et lauriers, grilles, portes closes
ont l'air de savoir quelque chose.

Ah! si j'étais riche, c'est là
que je vivrais avec Amaryllia.

Je l'appelle Amaryllia.   Est-ce bête!
Non, ce n'est pas bête.   Je suis poète.

Est-ce que tu te figures que c'est amusant
d'être poète à vingt-huit ans?

Dans mon porte-monnaie, j'ai dix francs
et deux sous pour ma poudre.   C'est embêtant.

Je conclus de là qu'Amaryllia
m'aime, et ne m'aime que pour moi.

Ni le *Mercure* ni *l'Ermitage*
ne me donnent de gages.

Elle est vraiment très bien Amaryllia,
et aussi intelligente que moi.

Il manque cinquante francs à notre bonheur.
On ne peut pas avoir tout, et le cœur.

Peut-être que si Rothschild lui disait:
Viens-t'en . . . Elle lui répondrait:

non, vous n'aurez pas ma petite robe,
parce que j'en aime un autre . . .

Et que si Rothschild lui disait : quel est
le nom de ce . . . de ce . . . de ce . . . poète?

Elle lui dirait : c'est Francis Jammes.
Mais ce qu'il y aurait de triste en tout cela :

c'est que je pense que Rothschild ne saurait pas
qui est ce poète-là.

To be published by the *Mercure* was a great honour
for a young poet (who was not so very young any
more, being thirty), but no regular publishing house
could print fast enough to satisfy him. In 1898
also, he printed at Orthez, *Quatorze Prières*. Nothing more beautiful, more touching, than these
prayers, can be conceived. In them he shows the
"simpleness" (I choose the word advisedly) of his
soul. A few of the titles of these poems will serve
to show Jammes' sweet, gentle nature : *Prière pour
que les Autres Aient le Bonheur, Prière pour Avoir
une Étoile, Prière pour Être Simple, Prière pour que
le Jour de ma Mort Soit Beau et Pur, Prière pour
Offrir à Dieu de Simples Paroles.* I will print one :

R

PRIÈRE POUR ALLER AU PARADIS AVEC LES ANES

Lorsqu'il faudra aller vers vous, ô mon Dieu, faites
que ce soit par un jour où la campagne en fête
poudroiera. Je désire, ainsi que je fis ici-bas,
choisir un chemin pour aller, comme il me plaira,
au Paradis, où sont en plein jour les étoiles.
Je prendrai mon bâton et sur la grande route
j'irai, et je dirai aux ânes, mes amis :
Je suis Francis Jammes et je vais au Paradis,
car il n'y a pas d'enfer au pays du Bon-Dieu.
Je leur dirai : Venez, doux amis du ciel bleu,
pauvres bêtes chéries qui, d'un brusque mouvement d'oreille,
chassez les mouches plates, les coups et les abeilles . . .

Que je vous apparaisse au milieu de ces bêtes
que j'aime tant parce qu'elles baissent la tête
doucement, et s'arrêtent en joignant leurs petits pieds
d'une façon bien douce et qui vous fait pitié.
J'arriverai suivi de leurs milliers d'oreilles,
suivi de ceux qui portèrent au flanc des corbeilles,
de ceux traînant des voitures de saltimbanques
ou des voitures de plumeaux et de fer-blanc,
de ceux qui ont au dos des bidons bossués,
des ânesses pleines comme des outres, aux pas cassés,
de ceux à qui l'on met de petits pantalons
à cause des plaies bleues et suintantes que font
les mouches entêtées qui s'y groupent en ronds.
Mon Dieu, faites qu'avec ces ânes je vous vienne.
Faites que dans la paix, des anges nous conduisent
vers des ruisseaux touffus où tremblent des cerises

lisses comme la chair qui rit des jeunes filles,
et faites que, penché dans ce séjour des âmes,
sur vos divines eaux, je sois pareil aux ânes
qui mireront leur humble et douce pauvreté
à la limpidité de l'amour éternel.

Jammes loves all animals, but apparently dogs and donkeys best. In another book, we shall find a whole series of poems to the latter. In 1899, *La Petite Collection de l'Ermitage*, Paris, brought out *La Jeune Fille Nue*. It is another of Jammes' allegories, — the poet seeking solace from his dissatisfaction — and full of the woods and moonlight. It is punctuated with beautiful things like this :

... C'est un chien vielleur qui aboie
au clair de lune dont l'ombre bouge sur les roses,

or this :

Nous l'attendions à l'heure rouge où les Midis
balancent aux clochers paysans leur ailes bleues.

In 1899, the first of Jammes' prose tales was published by the *Mercure de France* : *Clara d'Ellébeuse, ou l'Histoire d'une Ancienne Jeune Fille*. I mentioned this book in another connection a little while ago, and I am not going into it any farther now. It is all aroma, all evanescent, fleeting sensation. To rehearse the story heavy-footedly would be like dissecting a butterfly to prove how pretty it was. In it, Jammes has twined a three-stranded cord of his greatest delights. One strand is his love of the past; one, his love of the West Indies; and one, his deep-rooted affection for the high, blue sky, the quick, blue streams, and the long, white roads of the Basses-Pyrénées.

During these years, Jammes had travelled. Not much, it must be admitted. He dreamed of travelling, revelled in the idea of it, sitting at home in his armchair; one of his pipes was "round and black like the breast of a little negress," he tells us, and presto — he was off to his beloved Islands in the Southern Sea, growing sugar cane and bartering spices as his grandfather had done. "For years," he says, "I lived there, where my grandfather and my great-uncle went, in the flowering Antilles."

But his grandfather's were not the only travels he mused about. We have seen in *Clara d'Ellébeuse* that China attracted him. Adventure in far countries he found irresistible; by preference the countries should be tropical, or at least richly caparisoned. From a child he had loved Sinbad and Robinson Crusoe, we find both these gentlemen in his poems. So he smoked and dreamed, and — managed to get as far as Amsterdam on the North, and Algiers on the South.

One of his most charming poems in *Le Deuil des Primevères*, published by the *Mercure* in 1901, is on Amsterdam.

AMSTERDAM

Les maisons pointues ont l'air de pencher. On dirait
qu'elles tombent. Les mâts des vaisseaux qui s'embrouillent
dans le ciel sont penchés comme des branches sèches
au milieu de verdure, de rouge, de rouille,
de harengs saurs, de peaux de moutons et de houille.

Robinson Crusoë passa par Amsterdam,
(je crois, du moins, qu'il y passa), en revenant
de l'île ombreuse et verte aux noix de coco fraîches.
Quelle émotion il dut avoir quand il vit luire
les portes énormes, aux lourds marteaux, de cette ville ! . . .

Regardait-il curieusement les entresols
où les commis écrivent des livres de comptes ?
Eut-il envie de pleurer en resongeant
à son cher perroquet, à son lourd parasol
qui l'abritait dans l'île attristée et clémente ?

"O Éternel ! soyez béni," s'écriait-il
devant les coffres peinturlurés de tulipes.
Mais son cœur attristé par la joie du retour
regrettait son chevreau qui, aux vignes de l'île,
était resté tout seul et, peut-être, était mort.

Et j'ai pensé à ça devant les gros commerces
où l'on songe à des Juifs qui touchent des balances,
avec des doigts osseux noués de bagues vertes.
Vois ! Amsterdam s'endort sous les cils de la neige
dans un parfum de brume et de charbon amer.

Hier soir les globes blancs des bouges allumés,
d'où l'on entend l'appel sifflé des femmes lourdes,
pendaient comme des fruits ressemblant à des gourdes.
Bleues, rouges, vertes, les affiches y luisaient.
L'amer picotement de la bière sucrée
m'y a râpé la langue et démangé au nez.

Et, dans les quartiers juifs où sont les détritus,
on sentait l'odeur crue et froide du poisson.
Sur les pavés gluants étaient des peaux d'orange.
Une tête bouffie ouvrait des yeux tout larges,
un bras qui discutait agitait des oignons.

Rebecca, vous vendiez à de petites tables
quelques bonbons suants arrangés pauvrement . . .

On eût dit que le ciel, ainsi qu'une mer sale,
versât dans les canaux des nuages de vagues.
Fumée qu'on ne voit pas, le calme commercial
montait des toits cossus en nappes imposantes,
et l'on respirait l'Inde au confort des maisons.

Ah ! j'aurais voulu être un grand négociant,
de ceux qui autrefois s'en allaient d'Amsterdam
vers la Chine, confiant l'administration
de leur maison à de fidèles mandataires.
Ainsi que Robinson j'aurais devant notaire
signé pompeusement ma procuration.

Alors, ma probité aurait fait ma fortune.
Mon négoce eût fleuri comme un rayon de lune

sur l'imposante proue de mon vaisseau bombé.
J'aurais reçu chez moi les seigneurs de Bombay
qu'eût tentés mon épouse à la belle santé.

Un nègre aux anneaux d'or fût venu du Mogol
trafiquer, souriant, sous son grand parasol !
Il aurait enchanté de ses récits sauvages
ma mince fille aînée, à qui il eût offert
une robe en rubis filé par des esclaves.

J'aurais fait faire les portraits de ma famille
par quelque habile peintre au sort infortuné :
ma femme belle et lourde, aux blondes joues rosées,
mes fils, dont la beauté aurait charmé la ville,
et la grâce diverse et pure de mes filles.

C'est ainsi qu'aujourd'hui, au lieu d'être moi-même,
j'aurais été un autre et j'aurais visité
l'imposante maison de ces siècles passés,
et que, rêveur, j'eusse laissé flotter mon âme
devant ces simples mots : là vécut Francis Jammes.

I hope you observed Robinson Crusoe.
The *Primevères* begins with seventeen *Élégies*.
The first one, to Albert Samain, I quoted in the
second essay. These are followed by a reprint of
La Jeune Fille Nue, and *Le Poète et l'Oiseau* (which
had been published two years before by *L'Ermitage*),
a half-a-dozen new poems, and the fourteen poems
printed at Orthez.

Some time ago, I mentioned a poem on Madame
de Warens, as being one of Jammes' best and most
famous poems. This is it:

MADAME DE WARENS

Madame de Warens, vous regardiez l'orage
plisser les arbres obscurs des tristes *Charmettes*,
ou bien vous jouiez aigrement de l'épinette,
ô femme de raison que sermonnait Jean-Jacques!

C'était un soir pareil, peut-être, à celui-ci . . .
Par le tonnerre noir le ciel était flétri . . .
Une odeur de rameaux coupés avant la pluie
s'élevait tristement des bordures de buis . . .

Et je revois, boudeur, dans son petit habit,
à vos genoux, l'enfant poète et philosophe . . .
Mais qu'avait-il? . . . Pourquoi pleurant aux couchants roses
regardait-il se balancer les nids de pies?

Oh! qu'il vous supplia, souvent, du fond de l'âme,
de mettre un frein aux dépenses exagérées
que vous faisiez avec cette légèreté
qui est, hélas, le fait de la plupart des femmes . . .

Mais vous, spirituelle, autant que douce et tendre,
vous lui disiez: Voyez! le petit philosophe! . . .
Ou bien le poursuiviez de quelque drogue rose
dont vous lui poudriez la perruque en riant.

Doux asiles ! Douces années ! Douces retraites !
Les sifflets d'aulne frais criaient parmi les hêtres . . .
Le chèvrefeuille jaune encadrait la fenêtre . . .
On recevait parfois la visite d'un prêtre . . .

Madame de Warens, vous aviez du goût
pour cet enfant à la figure un peu espiègle,
manquant de repartie, mais peu sot, et surtout
habile à copier la musique selon les règles.

Ah ! que vous eussiez dû pleurer, femme inconstante,
lorsque, le délaissant, il dut s'en retourner,
seul, là-bas, avec son pauvre petit paquet
sur l'épaule, à travers les sapins des torrents . . .

*Almaïde d'Etremont ou l'Histoire d'une Jeune Fille
Passionée* appeared in 1901. The same remarks
which apply to *Clara d'Ellébeuse* apply to this story.
It is too lovely to be garbled. I leave it to those
who are sufficiently interested to read it.

Jammes' next volume of poems was published in
1902, and marks the end of an epoch, as far as his
poetry is concerned. His next book of poems was
written after his conversion, and the change is very
noticeable.

Le Triomphe de la Vie contains only two poems :
Jean de Noarrieu, and the long novel in verse,
Existences. Jean de Noarrieu is a rich farmer, in
love with his own waiting-maid, who, in turn, loves

one of his shepherds. The old triangle! Yes, of course, but Jammes is not engaged with literature, but with life as he sees it in the little villages of the Pyrenees. Whatever conventional morality is preached there, it seems certain that such villages share the common lot of rural communities and do not live it. At any rate, Lucie, the servant, permits her master to make love to her, and writes affectionate letters to the shepherd then on the mountain with his flocks, at the same time. The conventional novelist or poet would have worked up to a fine tragedy. Jammes is too truthful to do any such thing. Jean is careless, but not bad ; Lucie is unreliable, but not vicious. Autumn comes, and the shepherd returns from the mountain. Jean sees, from the way in which he and Lucie greet each other, that they are in love ; he has a momentary pang, but in the end does the sensible thing — hands the girl over to her lover. The unromantic end gives a hint that Jean may console himself elsewhere.

Not much of a story, except for its unusual finish. But what is really interesting in the poem is the long succession of pictures of landscapes, and places, and labours. The book smells of hay, and freshly dug earth, and the sweet breath of cows.

The poem begins with this passionate cry of delight at the passing seasons :

> Je ne veux pas d'autre joie, quand l'été
> reviendra, que celle de l'an passé.

Sous les muscats dormants, je m'assoirai.
Au fond des bois qui chantent de l'eau fraîche,
j'écouterai, je sentirai, verrai
tout ce qu'entend, sent et voit la forêt.

Je ne veux pas d'autre joie, quand l'automne
reviendra, que celle des feuilles jaunes
qui racleront les coteaux où il tonne,
que le bruit sourd du vin neuf dans les tonnes,
que les ciels lourds, que les vaches qui sonnent,
que les mendiants qui demandent l'aumône.

Je ne veux pas d'autre joie, quand l'hiver
reviendra, que celle des cieux de fer,
que la fumée des grues grinçant en l'air,
que les tisons chantant comme la mer,
et que la lampe au fond des carreaux verts
de la boutique où le pain est amer.

Je ne veux pas, quand revient le printemps,
d'autre joie que celle de l'aigre vent,
que les pêchers sans feuilles fleurissant,
que les sentiers boueux et verdissants,
que la violette et que l'oiseau chantant
comme un ruisseau d'orage se gorgeant.

That is a sort of invocation. The opening of the story follows, with a vivid picture of Jean de Noarrieu, his kitchen, and the flitting shadow of the little servant, Lucie:

Comme un troupeau en fumée et laineux,
le ciel marchait sous le vent pluvieux.
La pluie luisait sur les ardoises bleues.
Près du portail cria un char à bœufs.
Un coq piqua un coq. Et, sur le vieux
banc de noyer, bâilla Jean de Noarrieu.

On entendit remuer la servante.
La cheminée, obscure et rougeoyante,
flamba plus fort sous le chaudron luisant.
Près du bahut noir, graissé par le temps,
elle éclaira la gourde au lisse ventre,
et le labrit s'étira en bâillant.

Midi sonna. Le lard dans le poêlon
grésilla. Et, contre le landier long,
Lucie brisa avec précaution
deux œufs de poule à coque rousse. Et l'on
vit se gonfler à côté du lard blond
les œufs qui criaient en faisant des bonds.

Here is a little vignette of plates which gives the brightness of the kitchen, in a nutshell :

Sur le dressoir sont les belles assiettes
où sont peints des oiseaux ornés d'aigrettes,
de jaunes fruits et des fleurs violettes.
Lucie remue, dans le panier d'osier,
l'argenterie qui sonne toute claire,
change l'assiette et sourit à son maître.

Easter comes, and the poet seems to shout and snap
his fingers for sheer happiness :

> Et Pâques fleuries vint. Alléluia !
> Oh ! Douce fête ! L'harmonium gronda
> au ventre des églises. Alléluia !
> Le vert des prairies luisantes se dora.
> Les grillons crièrent. Alléluia !
> Dans la nuit bleue luirent les lilas.
>
> Un soir béni et doux, Alléluia,
> on entendit tout à coup ces lilas
> interpeller lentement les étoiles.
> C'était, c'était, c'était, Alléluia,
> le rossignol, la lune ruissela,
> le rossignol en fleurs. Alléluia !
>
> Renais, nature ! Oh ! Dans le jardin, vois
> le merisier tout blanc. Alléluia !
> Le cœur éclate . . .

Lucie and Jean go to drive, and cross a river by a
little bridge :

> Ils passent le pont léger du torrent
> d'un vieux petit moulin tourbillonnant
> tout fait de mousse et de rire d'argent,
> d'un torrent joli comme en un roman,
> plein de cresson et de soleil tremblant
> et de cailloux sur des cailloux roulant.

Il rebondit.   Ils voient et ils entendent
le frisson clair dont tremble l'eau courante.
La roue, chargée de mousse transparente,
ruisselle et brille, comme brille au printemps,
quelque vallée d'émeraude et d'argent
dans l'azur creux de Bigorres riantes.

Here is a hot day in July.   They are cutting the corn :

Ce fut la canicule de Juillet :
les stigmates des maïs s'argentèrent,
et leurs étamines se desséchèrent.
Le geste rond dont on étend le blé
avec la faux au rateau attachée
sonna dans le tremblement du soleil.

La faux qui pousse un clair gémissement
rasa le blé et les liserons blancs,
la salicaire et le chardon volant.
La chaleur fit crépiter dans les champs
la paille creuse, aiguë, ronde et brisante.
Et éclata la cigale grinçante.

Son cri prit feu, soudain, comme la poudre,
se continuant d'arbre en arbre, et toute
la plaine bleue courbée sur le blé roux,
à l'heure de la sieste où rien ne bouge,
fit ce sifflement qu'entre ses dents pousse
un enfant qui excite un chien sur la route.

Tout, hors ce cri déchirant, fit silence.

I have no words to describe the effect those three stanzas have on me. They carry me back to terribly hot days of my childhood, when the locusts scraped and sang so loud they seemed to make it hotter. Notice the wonderful accuracy and beauty of saying that the grasshopper's cry "took fire like powder and ran from tree to tree." Listen to this description of a quiet, moonlit, Summer night:

Dehors, la nuit coupe la lune claire.
Les arbres sont de l'ombre plus épaisse,
une ombre si épaisse qu'on dirait
qu'ils ont en eux l'ombre de la journée,
et que cette ombre en eux s'est retirée
pour y dormir jusqu'à la matinée.

Quel silence d'amour que n'interrompt
que le grésillement du crapaud qu'on
entend sous quelque pierre du perron . . .
La lune, à travers le catalpa, monte.
On distingue ses continents que ronge
une lumière où s'endorment des songes . . .

Le jardin prie. On sent battre le cœur
des pêches dans le silence de Dieu.
Elles sont duvetées comme la lueur
des joues éclatantes de ces danseuses
qui, à Laruns, pareilles à des fleurs,
se déploient en lentes rondes paresseuses.

Les fruits pèsent davantage la nuit.
La nuit semble s'appuyer sur les fruits.

Ils s'inclinent comme Jean et Lucie.
On aime en tremblant. Les baisers finissent
plus lentement, comme ces rondes rides
que sur l'eau font naître et mourir les brises.

Et les étoiles se lèvent une à une.
Et Jean, au milieu des vitres obscures,
les voit briller, blanches, jaunes et pures.
Au sud, lentement, se traînent des nues
gonflées d'orage qui, parfois, sur la lune,
passent un instant puis la laissent nue.

What a genius the man is!

Existences is a sordid enough tale, relieved by the poet who is the chief character in it. It is wonderfully clever. Far and away the best thing I know for the realistic treatment of a story in verse. And it is really realistic too, for that there is beauty in the world is admitted by the author and mentioned by the poet. Most "realistic" novels stoutly deny it, I believe. Again in *Existences*, we have the sharply etched pictures, and they are all I am going to give of this long poem of one hundred and seventy-two pages. Those who can bear the somewhat broad stating of malodorous facts will find the novel most interesting, other people should not attempt to read it. It is certainly very remarkable, but I do not say that it is pleasant.

Here is a description of the utter boredom and monotony of a little town:

Comme toutes ces boutiques sont parallèles !
Toutes les petites villes sont pareilles.
A droite : Épicerie. A gauche : Teinturerie.
A droite : Gendarmerie. A gauche : Pharmacie.
A droite : Auberge. A gauche : Mégisserie.
A droite : Avoué. A gauche : Médecin.
Puis dix ou douze maisons bourgeoises, avec jardins
pleins de feuillages bleus et de roses trémières
et la chaleur luisante et rose de lumière.
Là-bas ? C'est la mairie et son paratonnerre,
et la place carrée, d'ormeaux, avec des chaînes . . .

Zola and Jammes are the only men who have known enough about life to mingle poetry with their "realism." Witness this :

Qu'elle est belle la nuit sur la petite ville !
Onze heures bleues ! Le tulipier de ce jardin
sur l'ombre de la lune est plus doux que n'est douce
la ligne des coteaux d'argent bleu dans le loin.
Lune claire ! On ne sait, tant il fait beau et clair,
pourquoi l'on ne vit pas, la nuit, comme les lièvres.
Personne dans la rue. Un grillon crie. Un chat
tousse, il a sans doute une angine.
Je voudrais ne pas me coucher dans mon lit, m'étendre
dans un champ, et nager dans cette lueur bleue.

Le Roman du Lièvre came out in 1903. The two earlier stories were included in it, and the notes of Jammes' journey to Algiers, and his pilgrimage to *Les Charmettes*. M. Henri Bordeaux encountered

s

him there, and has written how they both searched vainly for the forgotten grave of Madame de Warens in the little cemetery of Saint-Pierre-de-Lémenc. There are many other things in *Le Roman du Lièvre*; among them, the history of the poor little hare himself, chased by dogs, and killed with a gun.

Jammes loves animals, as I said before. Since the days when the shooting of the monkey set him trembling, he has suffered with them, and for them. His dog figures often in his poems. There are many creatures in his books: cats, kingfishers, larks, butterflies. He has sung of wasps, their humming, their flight, when they seem like golden balls. La Fontaine's rabbit, the beasts which followed Saint Francis of Assisi, and those with whom Robinson Crusoe consoled himself on his Island, Jammes has loved them and written about them all.

As a child, his sensibility was extreme. A natural kindness of heart caused him to dower even minerals and vegetables with a nervous system like his own, and in consequence he suffered profoundly whenever he thought they must be suffering. "A piece of furniture riddled with worms," he says, "a gun with a broken spring; a swollen drawer, or the soul of a violin suddenly drawn false, such are the sorrows which agitate me."

Jammes' is a heart full of compassion. For every being, for every thing. Little by little, his pity, his compassion, his love for the simple, beautiful side of the Church brought him back to it. The conversion was finished by a friend of his (Claudel, I think), lately returned from the Far East, who worked over him and persuaded him. From this moment, there is a change in Jammes' work. Certain of his most pronounced characteristics disappear. Has it changed for the better or for the worse? I thought for the worse until his last book, *Feuilles dans le Vent*, came out. When its contents were written I do not know, but they are no whit inferior to any of the best things he has done. It must be admitted that Jammes' Catholicism is a very sweet and lovable thing. He is certainly cousin-german to Saint Francis in his whole manner of thinking.

Pensée des Jardins was published in 1906, preceded by *Pomme d'Anis ou l'Histoire d'une Jeune Fille Infirme*, another of Jammes' graceful, fanciful stories of fifty years ago. Perhaps this is the loveliest of all his tales, and again I must not spoil it by touching it ill-advisedly.

Pensée des Jardins is an adorable little book in both poetry and prose, full of animals and flowers. The prose part consists of notes, apparently just jotted down for safe keeping. One, entitled *Sur le Chat*, says: "Le Chat, ce chien des pauvres . . ." and that is the whole of it. In another, called *Premières Journées de Printemps*, is this enchanting line: "J'aime ce qui est nacré, ce qui est phosphorescent comme un jardin d'Avril." Here is another nice thing: "C'est la fragilité des hautes branches qui protège la fragilité des nids." *Pensée des Jardins* ends with seven poems called "Some Donkeys." Christ's donkey is here, and Sancho Panza's, and Beatrice's; there is a learned donkey, and a donkey who has been beaten; finally, there is the gardener's donkey, so packed with vegetables that he looks like an ambulatory garden.

The first one of Jammes' purely poetic books to be published after his conversion was *L'Église Habillée de Feuilles*, 1906. The church which he here describes is the little chapel of Noarrieu, whose spire dominates three valleys. Jammes has said that "prayer is the sister of the birds." Here, in this little church hidden in the leaves, we can well understand that Jammes found the sympathy of surrounding that he desired. M. Touny Lérys, a friend of his, wrote in an article published in *L'Année Poétique*: "I remember one evening going to church with Francis Jammes, and seeing him pray. He troubled me profoundly, as much by the *abandon* of his body as by the expression of his face, and I felt that he was not really there any more, but away, very far away . . . with God." One poem from *L'Église Habillée de Feuilles* will show what he has lost, what he has gained, what he has kept. Perhaps there is rather less high spirits, and more tenderness:

La paix des champs s'étend autour de la chapelle.
Et, au carrefour poudreux, parmi les avoines,
les menthes, les chicorées et les aigremoines,
se dresse un grand Christ de bois creux où les abeilles
ont fait leur nid. Et on peut voir, dans le soleil,
aller, venir, ces affairées pleines de miel
comme des lettres noires écrites dans le ciel.

De quoi nourrir son Dieu si ce n'est pas de miel?
Parfois le cantonnier qui casse des cailloux
lève la tête et voit le Christ, le seul ami
qu'il ait sur cette route où palpite Midi.
Pour casser les cailloux l'ouvrier est à genoux
dans l'ombre de ce Christ dont le flanc est vermeil.
Et tout le miel alors chante dans le soleil.

Le poète contemple et médite. Il se dit,
devant le lent frisson des champs, que chaque épi
est du peuple de Dieu la sage colonie
dont chaque grain attend, pour être vivifié,
que des grottes du Ciel l'eau se soit élancée.
Il se dit que ce grain désormais va pousser
dans l'azur précieux que tout approfondit
et, qu'image du Fils de Dieu, né lui aussi
dans une grotte, il nourrira ceux qui ont faim.
Et l'épi qui naîtra à son tour de ce grain
aura la forme d'un clocher dans une aurore.

Another book of poems, *Clairières dans le Ciel*,
came out in 1906. One is glad to find in it, along
with the new tenderness, all the old, merry, wise
humour. For instance:

L'ENFANT LIT L'ALMANACH . . .

L'enfant lit l'almanach près de son panier d'œufs.
Et, en dehors des Saints et du temps qu'il fera,
elle peut contempler les beaux signes des cieux :
Chèvre, Taureau, Bélier, Poissons, et cætera.

Ainsi peut-elle croire, petite paysanne,
qu'au-dessus d'elle, dans les constellations,
il y a des marchés pareils avec des ânes,
des taureaux, des béliers, des chèvres, des poissons.

C'est le marché du Ciel sans doute qu'elle lit.
Et, quand la page tourne au signe des *Balances*,
elle se dit qu'au Ciel comme à l'épicerie
on pèse le café, le sel et les consciences.

Sometime about this period, the poet married. But
whom, we, the public, are not told in any of the
books about Jammes. But one day the little church
in its leaves

> . . . allègrement sonnait
> Car la fille d'un métayer se mariait.

From this time, Jammes' work takes on a greater
peace and contentment. In a poem, *Le Poète et sa
Femme*, we have the companion picture to *Un Jour*,
*La Naissance du Poète, La Mort du Poète, La Jeune
Fille Nue*, and *Le Poète et l'Oiseau*. But how very
different the picture is ! In this poem, in spite of
its sad ending, there is a sense of happiness and

satisfaction pervading the whole. The poet speaks
to his wife and she replies :

DENIS

Que le vent est léger ! Il soulève la treille . . .
Reste ainsi, mon amie, dans cette molle veille . . .
Tantôt je regardais tes bras quand tu fanais . . .
Ils savent purement vers ton cœur se courber.
Quelle est l'émotion, quand je touche tes yeux,
qui fait que je ne pense à rien d'autre qu'à eux ?
Quel est le sentiment, si je t'entends chanter,
qui fait que c'est ma voix qui me semble empruntée ?
Qu'est-ce qui fait que quand tu poses sur mon cœur
ton cœur, je nous confonds dans la même douceur ?

LUCIE

Que tu sais me parler avec des mots jolis !
Moi qui ne sais, hélas ! répondre en poésie,
je t'aime cependant. Si je ne sais te rendre
l'amour en vers charmants, crois bien que je sais prendre
toute l'émotion que tu veux me donner,
et que je suis à toi avec simplicité.
Béni soit le travail s'il inflige à mes bras
la courbe que tu veux et qui t'enlacera . . .
C'est que la poésie est l'âme de la vie.
C'est moi qui la cultive et toi qui la fleuris.
Denis, je ne suis rien que la pauvre servante
qui écoute avec foi la parole savante.

The sequel to *Le Poète et sa Femme* is a little prose
book, *Ma Fille Bernadette*, 1910, which records the

birth and early babyhood of Jammes' little daughter. The dedication to *Marie de Nazareth, Mère de Dieu* is really a miracle of prose beauty :

A MARIE DE NAZARETH, MÈRE DE DIEU

En Vous dédiant cette œuvre, je Vous dédie aussi ma fille Bernadette dont la patronne, dans mon pays natal qui est la Bigorre montagneuse, Vous a vue.

Les vieux botanistes Vous dédiaient aussi leurs flores et on Vous peignait à la première page, debout, Votre fils dans les bras, tout entourée de lilas, de radiées bleues, de roses, de gloxinias, de weigélias, de pivoines, de boules-de-neiges, de lis, de ces mille fleurs qui ne reviendront plus parce qu'elles ne sont plus cueillies pour Vous par les robustes rêveuses qui se levaient au matin des myosotis et s'endormaient au couchant des capucines.

Vous êtes la mère de tous les hommes et de Dieu. Vous êtes née à Nazareth aussi simplement que ma Bernadette à Orthez. On a dit la vérité. On n'a pas inventé pour Vous une origine extraordinaire. Je Vous tiens dans mon cœur comme une certitude. Je suis inintelligent, c'est possible, mais l'encens de toutes les fleurs créées s'élève pour Vous de la terre et Vous le changez en amour comme ce rosier grimpant qui s'élance à la cime des cèdres.

Vous voyez que je ne sais plus bien ce que j'écris, mais ma pensée s'attache à Vous ainsi que cette liane fleurie et je Vous dédie cette pauvre œuvre comme une servante son pot de résédas, et il tremble dans mes mains élevées.

Little Bernadette is followed in her uprising and downsitting. She cuts her first tooth, sees her first snow storm, is vaccinated, has croup, is taught to say her prayers. And all with an ineffable sweetness, delicacy, and charm. The father loves his little daughter so much that the pages of the book seem warm, like the palm of a hand.

It is amusing to see, however, that this new life which has entered his, only makes the poet hark back, by a natural process, to those which have preceded them both. The last part of the volume is given over to Bernadette's ancestors, and here we encounter once more that grandfather who played so large a part in the poet's youthful imagination, and have again those souvenirs of Guadeloupe which hang like a faint perfume over the poet's personality.

Jammes' last book of poems is *Les Géorgiques Chrétiennes*, 1912. How much of a Catholic he has become, may be best understood by quoting in full a note at the beginning of the book. "On the threshold of this book I confirm that I am a Roman Catholic, submitting very humbly to all the decisions of my Pope, His Holiness Pius X, who speaks in the name of the True God, and that I do not adhere either closely or at a distance to any schism, and that my faith does not permit any sophism, neither the modernist sophism, nor other sophisms; under no pretence will I separate myself from the most uncompromising and most loved of dogmas: the Roman Catholic dogma which is the truth come from the mouth of our Lord Jesus Christ by his

Church. I reprove in advance all forestalling which the ideologues, the philosophers, and the reformers would wish to do with this poem." *Les Géorgiques Chrétiennes* is a whole book dealing with the agricultural labours of a year. It must be admitted that it is a little tedious. The following stanzas are interesting as showing his method, not merely in this poem, but in many:

C'est ainsi que le vers dont j'use est bien classique,
Dégagé simplement par la seule logique.

Après un grand combat où j'avais pris parti
Je regarde et comprends qu'on s'est peu départi.

Devenu trop sonore et trop facile et lâche
Le pur alexandrin, si beau jadis, râbache.

Le vers libre ne nous fit pas très bien sentir
Où la strophe s'en vient commencer et finir.

Mais quelques libertés, quand il les voulait toutes,
Ce dernier les conquit. Elles ouvrent la route.

Si rares qu'elles soient, elles sont bien assez.
Les vers seront égaux et pas assonancés

Comme l'oiseau répond à son tour à l'oiselle
La rime mâle suit une rime femelle.

Quoique les vers entre eux ainsi soient reliés
J'accepte qu'un pluriel rime à un singulier,

Encor tel que l'oiseau, qui du ciel prend mesure,
Le rythme ici et là hésite à la césure.

L'hiatus quelquefois vient à point rappeler
Celui qui est poète au plus simple parler.

Alors que l'*e* muet s'échappe du langage
Je ne veux pas qu'il marque en mon vers davantage.

Les syllabes comptées sont celles seulement
Que le lecteur prononce habituellement.

Ayant fixé ce bref mais sûr art poétique,
Mon inspiration me rouvre son portique.

Jammes' last book is called *Feuilles dans le Vent*, and was published in 1913. It contains some reprints, among others *Pomme d'Anis*, and some of the *Notes* from *Pensée des Jardins*. But the interesting things in it are two stories, *L'Auberge des Douleurs* and *L'Auberge sur la Route*. This is from the latter tale, and it is in prose, but I submit that it is nevertheless very beautiful poetry :

Le vent courait sur la soie bleue des blés et la ridait, et la crécelle des cri-cris tremblait comme un timbre de petite gare. La ligne de l'horizon dormait, étendue au-dessus des épis, et les feuilles des chaumes se soulevaient et retombaient telles que des oriflammes de mâts pour sauterelles. Parfois, on apercevait dans le ciel un nuage comme un bosquet d'ombres qui se serait enlevé de la colline, et, cependant qu'il glissait, elle s'illuminait, s'obscurcissait, s'illuminait à nouveau.

L'Auberge des Douleurs is even more delightful, but I will not spoil any of it by breaking a little piece off.

Francis Jammes is still living at Orthez. He is still in the prime of life: forty-seven. It is impossible to suppose that he will not go on producing for some time to come. He has already had a great effect upon the younger generation, and if there do not seem to be any poets who can be exactly called his disciples, it is partly because he has never sought disciples, and partly because the best part of him cannot be copied.

Paul Fort.

PAUL FORT

PAUL FORT

IN preparing this chapter, I learnt a strange thing. I had half suspected it before, but now I know it beyond peradventure of a doubt — the world, which is always affected by exteriors, carries that principle even to typography.

It so happened that I was unable to get a biography of Paul Fort, which I needed, from abroad. Hoping they might have it, I tried the Public Library. I was not surprised that that particular volume was not forthcoming, but I was surprised when the library proved to contain not one single volume of Paul Fort.

The reason that this is so strange is that Paul Fort is the one poet writing in French, who (as soon as he becomes known) is certain to share with Verhaeren the unqualified admiration of English-speaking people. Both in matter and manner, we cannot fail to understand him. His admiration for the English poets is unbounded, and he tells us that he has modelled himself upon them.

Are his books hard to get, are they few and far between? — you will ask. Not at all. In the past nine years, he has published sixteen volumes of verse. They are the ordinary paper-covered volumes of modern French commerce, lemon-hued and inviting, selling at the usual price of three francs, fifty centimes, and they are for sale at every book-shop in Paris.

Then what is the matter? — you will ask again. The matter (idiotic though it may sound) is a question of typography. Paul Fort prints his poems as prose. That is the obscuring veil which keeps him from being known. You print words in a line — long lines, short lines, uneven lines (thank Heaven! you are permitted so much liberty) — and they are instantly recognized as poetry. You print the same lines in a block, like prose, and you are undone. If some unwary reader, sitting down to a good bit of prose, should happen to read it aloud, behold, it is poetry! The reader is confused, then angry. Things are not what they seemed, not, in fact, what they purported to be. To find one's self inveigled into reading poetry when one thought it was prose, when by every typographical sign it should have been prose, 'tis a charlatan's trick, rank dishonesty! Or, if not quite that, at any rate it makes one feel very uncomfortable.

Paul Fort says that he has sacrificed his popularity to his theory. And at first that was no doubt true. But he has won the game at last, in his own country. He has been elected by popular suffrage

"Prince des Poètes," a fact which I shall come back
to later. Only, the excellent gentlemen who buy the
French books for the public libraries are a bit behind the times, and a prose which jumps at one in
unexpected rhymes is a fearsome thing in a foreign
language. It is probably the same all over England
and America, and so this most universal genius of
all living Frenchmen remains very little known out
of France. The "Nineteenth Century" for December, 1914, contained a sympathetic article by a
young English poet of much promise, James Elroy
Flecker, on Fort, recommending him to his coun-
trymen. A pathetic interest attaches to this article,
in that its author was already dying when it appeared, and his subsequent death makes it the last
word he felt it important to say, the last effort
worth making.

Paul Fort classes himself as a *Symboliste*; why, it
is a little hard to say, except that he regards *Symbolisme* as another term for liberty. And Fort is
fairly intoxicated with the idea of liberty. But he
employs his liberty for quite other purposes than
those of the real *Symbolistes*. Paul Fort is the
modern man. Exteriorizing, full of vitality and
vigour, and "la joie de vivre." I know no one except
Sam Weller who seems to me so bubblingly alive.
He positively bounces with delight through poem
after poem. He is intensely interested in everything, and a good motto for his sixteen volumes

T

would be Stevenson's

> The world is so full of a number of things,
> I am sure we should all be as happy as kings.

Nature, people, books, all fill him with enthusiastic interest, and to all he gives an equal share of himself, having the power to devote himself entirely to whichever one he is occupied with for the moment.

More than that, he is so genuinely sympathetic, that, almost unconsciously it would seem, his style changes with his subject. He is master of what Matthew Arnold would have called "the grand style," but he is also past-master of a hail-fellow-well-met diction to sing the preoccupations of the Breton sailors. Not even Byron has so fine an irony as he; and Henri de Régnier in *Les Vacances d'un Jeune Homme Sage* has not caught the naïve simplicity of adolescence any better, any more delicately, than he has done in *Paris Sentimental*.

Let me illustrate. Here are two poems which have for subject nothing at all but the extreme happiness of being alive. The "great intoxication," as it is to him.

LA GRANDE IVRESSE

Par les nuits d'été bleues où chantent les cigales, Dieu verse sur la France une coupe d'étoiles. Le vent porte à ma lèvre un goût du ciel d'été! Je veux boire à l'espace fraîchement argenté.

L'air du soir est pour moi le bord de la coupe froide où, les yeux mi-fermés et la bouche goulue, je bois, comme le jus pressé d'une grenade, la fraîcheur étoilée qui se répand des nues.

Couché sur un gazon dont l'herbe est encor chaude de s'être prélassée sous l'haleine du jour, oh! que je viderais, ce soir, avec amour, la coupe immense et bleue où le firmament rôde!

Suis-je Bacchus ou Pan? je m'enivre d'espace, et j'apaise ma fièvre à la fraîcheur des nuits. La bouche ouverte au ciel où grelottent les astres, que le ciel coule en moi! que je me fonde en lui!

Enivrés par l'espace et les cieux étoilés, Byron et Lamartine, Hugo, Shelley sont morts. L'espace est toujours là; il coule illimité; à peine ivre il m'emporte, et j'avais soif encore!

The second is one of those *Chansons* for which Fort is so famous.

LE CIEL EST GAI, C'EST JOLI MAI

La mer brille au-dessus de la haie, la mer brille comme une coquille. On a envie de la pêcher. Le ciel est gai, c'est joli Mai.

C'est doux la mer au-dessus de la haie, c'est doux comme une main d'enfant. On a envie de la caresser. Le ciel est gai, c'est joli Mai.

Et c'est aux mains vives de la brise que vivent et brillent des aiguilles qui cousent la mer avec la haie. Le ciel est gai, c'est joli Mai.

La mer présente sur la haie ses frivoles papillonnées.   Petits
navires vont naviguer.   Le ciel est gai, c'est joli Mai.

La haie, c'est les profondeurs, avec des scarabées en or.   Les
haleines sont plus vilaines.   Le ciel est gai, c'est joli Mai.

Si doux que larme sur la joue, la mer est larme sur la haie qui
doucement descend au port.   Mais on n'a guère envie de pleurer.

— "Un gars est tombé dans le port!" — "Mort dans la
mer, c'est jolie mort."   Mais on n'a guère envie de pleurer.   Le
ciel est gai, c'est joli Mai!

I am at a loss to know what to do among these
sixteen volumes.   I do not know where to begin.
To note them chronologically is of no value, for Paul
Fort is not one of the poets who grows old.   He re-
news himself perpetually, but the renewal is only
to greater vigour, farther delight.   And this is perhaps natural, for in spite of the immense amount of
work he has done, Fort is still a young man.   Yet
that does not always follow.   Usually, a man would
seem to have only a certain amount in him.   Sometimes he matures slowly and begins to produce late.
I have heard it said that Shakespeare was thirty
before he began to write, and we know that the
painter Gauguin was forty before he touched a
brush.   Daniel Webster, too, was some thirty odd
before he made his first remarkable speech.

The contrary is often true: a man whose creative power exhausts itself in early youth. Are we so sure that Keats was unlucky to die young? The dismal and academic "Hyperion," so praised by the conventional critic, makes us pause and consider the question. In our own time, William Butler Yeats is a case in point. His excellent and brilliant work was all done in his twenties. Since then he has been like a haunted man, pursued by the ghost of his own poetry.

It is characteristic of Paul Fort, characteristic of the robustness of his nature, physical and mental alike, that, beginning young, he should still be writing with unimpaired vigour.

Paul Fort was born in Rheims on the first of February, 1872. In a pathetic letter, written recently, he tells that he was born right opposite the Cathedral — "la Cathédrale assassinée," as he calls it. What the destruction of the Cathedral must have meant to him, we can faintly understand, loving it, as we must, only as a beautiful, strange thing. In a poem written since the burning of Rheims, he tells as much as he can of its place in his childhood. He tells of his father crying out at the first sign of real notice in his baby eyes, "Il voit! il voit! il voit!" and turning him toward "l'église sublime;" how, as he grew

... elle naquit pour moi, réelle, grande, immense et rêvée à la fois.

Elle naquit pour moi, devinée par mes yeux, un matin de printemps au cri des hirondelles. Mes menottes ont cru la prendre au bleu cieux! Renassant chaque aurore elle m'était fidèle, tout habitée de saints, de rois et de héros, et d'anges à mi-vol, comme un arbre d'oiseaux.

Grand jouet de mon âme, O française forêt de pierres, et vos tours, mes immense hochets, vous êtes demeurés le seul Jeu de mon âme, avec les trois hauts porches, en triangle de flamme, et dessus eux la Rose ou l'on voit voltigée des pigeons becquetant les reflets passagers.

Puis quand je suis enfin venu, ma Cathédrale, mêler un cerf-volant aux ailes de tes anges, que j'ai de tous mes cris fait sonner ton parvis et, les cheveux au vent et poursuivant mes cris, entouré tes vieux murs des cent jeux de l'enfance . . .

The poem is too long to quote entire, but is it surprising that it has this stanza, constantly repeated as a refrain?

Monstrueux général baron von Plattenberg, si je vous dois ce chant d'amour à mon église, je vous donne en retour, bien qu'immortalisent, le soufflet de poètes et l'échafaud du Verbe, — mais je tiens magazin de haine consacrée à tous les Allemands que j'ai pu rencontrer.

Who were Fort's parents, and how, and why, he went to Paris, the lack of the volume I have mentioned makes it impossible for me to say. But to

Paris he went, and there, at the incredibly early age of eighteen, he founded a little theatre, the *Théâtre d'Art*.

It was a protest against the naturalistic generation who held sway over the *Théâtre Libre*, and, oddly enough, this audacious undertaking had a certain success. What are we to make of a youth of eighteen who, alone, almost without resources, conceives such an idea, and carries it through? Fort's actors were engaged to receive no wages; his scenes were painted for him, presumably by enthusiastic and unpaid friends, among them being Gauguin and Maurice Denis; and plays were submitted, plays in manuscript and quite unactable, which were acted nevertheless. For Fort stuck at nothing in pursuit of his theory; what he wished to do should be done, and thanks to his energy and brains, was done.

Fort was possessed of the idea that the old and excellent, even if forgotten, should be mixed with the new. Everything which was intrinsically worthy of dramatic representation should have its turn. On they went — pell-mell. An assortment of a kind to make the ordinary and experienced theatrical manager faint dead away.

The *Théâtre d'Art* mounted Shelley's "Cenci," of all extraordinary ventures; and, perhaps not quite so queer, but still sufficiently unusual, the "Dr. Faustus" of Christopher Marlowe. In both these pieces, Fort took a part himself. It seems as though at this time he expected to become an actor.

For modern plays, the *Théâtre d'Art* gave *Les Uns et Les Autres*, by Verlaine; *L'Intruse* and *Les Aveugles*, by Maeterlinck; *La Voix du Sang* and *Madame La Mort*, by Rachilde; *Théodat*, by Remy de Gourmont; *Les Flaireurs*, by Van Lerberghe; it even gave *Le Concile Féerique*, by Signoret; and *Le Corbeau*, by Mallarmé. How it gave the latter, unless it was merely read, possibly in costume, I fail to understand, as *Le Corbeau* is simply a translation of Poe's "Raven." But nothing seems to have been unattemptable to Fort, who went so far as to dare to produce an adaptation of the first book of the "Iliad."

Gourmont says in his *Promenades Littéraires*, that Sarcey enjoyed these performances so much that he never missed one, and that he wrote happily in an article on the subject: "These studio-farces took until two o'clock in the morning to finish." From this remark it is quite obvious that Fort's public was, composed of young and enthusiastic students of the arts like himself. But he certainly had a public; and when the *Théâtre d'Art* moved from the Marais to Montparnasse, and from Montparnasse to Montmartre, the public went with it.

The *Théâtre d'Art* broke up in 1893. Why, I do not know, possibly from lack of funds, that most important factor in all theatrical enterprises, even when the actors work for nothing and the performances last until two o'clock in the morning. Or possibly Fort had discovered that acting was not his vocation.

In 1890, the year he started his theatre, Fort had published a little play of inconsiderable importance, *La Petite Bête*. This, you see, was just in the heyday of his preoccupation with the theatre. But three years as an actor and manager taught him that the theatre offered no scope to his particular talents. Description, in which he excels, has no place in theatrical writing. Fort definitely abandoned it for the free medium of verse, pure and simple.

There is no doubt, however, that the years in the theatre were of the utmost value to Fort as a poet. A keen dramatic instinct he must always have had, but the practical training of this instinct gave him an extraordinary mastery over the difficult art of dramatic verse. Dramatic verse in contradistinction to drama. One of the reasons for the dullness of most narrative poems is that their authors do not understand the manipulation of the dramatic. Dullness is the one unpardonable sin in all the arts, but in the theatre it is suicidal. A play must "get over," or it is damned. Now this quality of "getting over" Fort has to an eminent degree. Let me illustrate by two selections from *Le Roman de Louis XI*. The first one is where the king, having heard of the death of his natural son, goes incognito and by night to find out if the rumour is true:

JOACHIM

La nuit glisse épaisse et froide dans Paris. Deux ombres dans l'ombre, deux petites ombres maigres s'agitent frileusement, puis glissent dans la nuit.

— Doux sire, j'ai juré. Cette nuit, nous partons.
— C'est bien, suis-moi, suis-moi.

De petites ruelles en petites ruelles, deux petites ombres maigres s'agitent dans le froid, — puis s'arrêtent.

Là, devant une masure à demi enterrée, une voix, une petite voix aigre-douce, aigrelette, une petite voix que mouillent des sanglots :

— Je ne suis lion, ni loup, ni renard, je suis un homme, Croy. Frappe à cette porte, Croy ! Ici, bien. Appelle : Dame Simonne des Chaînes !

— Dame Simonne des Chaînes !

— Bien. Écoute, écoute ! . . . Demande s'il n'est pas mort, hier, quelqu'un chez elle.

— Dame Simonne ! Est-il mort, hier, quelqu'un ici ?

— Hélas, doux seigneur ! vous le savez donc, vous ? Mon fils Joachim, mon fils, la nuit dernière.

— Je ne suis lion, ni loup, ni renard, je suis un homme. Croy, reviens, soutiens-moi ! Joachim ! . . . Croy ! je ne suis lion, ni loup, ni renard, je suis tous trois. Croy, je suis un homme. Adieu, ô petit être ! . . . Joachim ! Joachim ! Allons, bien ! partons. Dame Simonne me fut . . . Dame Simonne m'était . . . Je suis un homme, Croy, je pleure un petit être . . . Joachim ! Hélas ! . . . mon petit enfant . . .

La nuit glisse épaisse et froide dans Paris, deux petites ombres maigres butent, glissent, s'agitent. Oh ! quelle petite voix aigrelette, aigrelette . . . Oh ! ses petits cris déchirés.

The second is a gay account of Louis, with his gentlemen and their attendant mistresses, fishing in the Seine :

LA PÊCHE MIRACULEUSE

La nouvelle était si charmante, — un oncle mort si à propos ! — mon doux petit Louis XI voulut bien la fêter, mais intimement, en gentille société.

Maître Tristan, tout imagination, conseilla une partie dans l'herbe, et, comme il clignait de ses yeux roux malins : — "Compris, dit le roi, tu n'es qu'un vaurien."

Le lendemain matin, sous le paradis bleu, gais et contents, mon doux petit Louis XI, Tristan l'Ermite et leurs folles amantes, Simonne des Chaînes et Perrette du Trésor, s'en vinrent taquiner le goujon de Seine, aux pieds en roseaux de la Tour de Nesle.

Maître Olivier, puceau, faisait le guet sur la berge, à longues enjambées froissant l'herbe. Il bayait aux corneilles avec mélancolie : la chute de Buridan occupait son esprit.

Simonne des Chaînes, âme et cœur liés au cœur et à l'âme de son roi bien-aimé, comme un lys d'eau penchant sur un vieux nénuphar, penchait, sur l'épaule râpée de son amant, son cou de neige, son front de lait, son petit nez de velours blanc ;

et, de temps en temps, le gracieux roi Louis de France lui demandait un asticot. Alors, c'était avec un si grand charme qu'elle en puisait un, dans une petite boîte verte, c'était avec un charme si troublant qu'elle le présentait au roi, tout frétillant, que Louis ne se tenait plus de lui baiser l'oreille (non point à l'asticot, mais à Simonne des Chaînes), voire de lui chuchoter amoureusement ces mots: "M'amie, vous assisterez aux États Généraux."

*   *   *   *   *   *   *

Maître Olivier, puceau, faisait le guet sur la berge, à longues enjambées froissant l'herbe. Il bayait aux corneilles avec mélancolie : la chute de Buridan occupait son esprit.

Il regardait, d'un œil inattentif, certain maître Villon, fleur de berge s'il en fût, courant dans les roseaux après les libellules et qui, parfois, tournait des yeux pleins d'anarchie vers ces bourgeois pêchant là-bas, et leurs amies. Maître Olivier, puceau, avait l'esprit ailleurs . . . A peine vit-il, dans les roseaux, maître Villon se dévêtir. A peine murmura-t-il, comme on murmure en rêve: "Sans doute, ce monsieur nu ne m'est pas inconnu."

Et Tristan n'attrapait rien. Et le roi n'attrapait rien. Les asticots filaient, filaient . . . Et François Villon, prenant une pleine eau, soufflait aux poissons, tout en faisant la planche: "Vive la liberté! ne vous laissez pas prendre."

*   *   *   *   *   *   *

— "Paix! cria le roi, ou je manque ce turbot!"

— "Un turbot, seigneur, est un poisson de mer . . . risqua timidement la tendre Simonne. J'en ai vendu, avec ma mère,

au grand marché Saint-Honoré, du temps de ma virginité." —
"Un poisson de mer?... Hé, c'est bien pour cela que je l'ai
manqué!" répondit le roi sans se déconcerter.

— "Le temps passé ne revient pas," fredonnait Perrette en
ajustant ses bas. — "Oui! la jeunesse n'a qu'un temps," en-
tonna Tristan, avec conviction. Alors, la timide, la tendre
Simonne roucoula sur un air encore peu connu : "Voici vingt
ans que j'ai perdu ma mère . . ." Il n'en fallait pas plus,
Tristan fondit en larmes, — tandis que le roi, tout en pêchant
du vent, chantait à tue-tête : "Non! mes amis, non, je ne veux
rien être! . . ."

Et Tristan n'attrapait rien. Et le roi n'attrapait rien. Les
asticots filaient, filaient . . . Et les goujons spirituels, battant
des ouïes, applaudissaient. — ("Applaudissaient," sans doute,
n'est qu'une image. Mais sait-on bien ce qui se passe dans
l'eau?)

Aux pieds en roseaux de la Tour de Nesle, les deux com-
mères, le roi et le bourreau chantaient, en chœur, comme des
oiseaux. Et les goujons, autour des bouchons, valsaient, valsaient agréablement.

Maître Olivier, puceau, faisait le guet sur la berge . . .

Soudain, Perrette pouffa de rire dans sa jupe! Mon doux
petit Louis XI, levant sa ligne avec ardeur, venait d'accrocher
un martin-pêcheur. — Tristan dit : "Un gage!" Simonne :
Poisson vole! et maître Olivier s'arrêta, tout net, sur une en-
jambée.

— "Par m'âme! je me serai trompé, se dit François Villon
nageant entre deux eaux. Au lieu d'un goujon pêcher un oiseau
. . . Ce bourgeois n'est pas dépourvu de lyrisme!"

Et les goujons, autour des bouchons, valsaient, valsaient
agréablement.

The theatre definitely abandoned, Fort turned to
literature, and published a number of little books of
verse, got up something like chap-books, very slim,
and very unpretentious. The first one, *Plusieurs
Choses*, appeared in 1894, followed the same year by
two others, *Premières Lueurs sur la Colline* and
Monnaie de Fer. The next year came others, *Presque les Doigts aux Clés* and *Il y a là des Cris*. But
it was not until 1896, that he started what may be
considered as his life work in the publication, by the
indefatigable *Mercure de France*, of the first volume
of his *Ballades Françaises.* It contained all the
poems already published, with new ones added, and
was a large book of three hundred and fifty pages.
Those three hundred and fifty pages tell the story
of Fort's life, his enormous fecundity, his over-
fecundity, I fear it must be admitted. Fort is like
some kinds of fishes, who spawn an incredible number of eggs, of which some, at least, are bound to
survive. And in Fort's case, it is astonishing how
many are perfect, and fashioned to resist all the

accidents of time. Particularly is this true in these early volumes.

All Fort's succeeding volumes have been *Ballades Françaises*. No matter how various the subjects, he has given them all the same generic title. And it is an excellent title, and hitches them all together into the soul of France better than anything else could do. For this most English of French poets is at the same time the very embodiment of France. One of his critics (and to my mind at once the most sprightly and the most illuminating of the lot, and their names have been legion) says : "Paul Fort is a mask, and I know well what is underneath : it is the familiar demon of the soil of France. . . . Intrepid innovator and firm partisan of freedom, Paul Fort is nevertheless the most traditional of our poets. The demon of French soil, I have just said, lives in him. Disdainful of expected rhythms and domesticated sentiments, he has taken poetry again at its beginning, from the moment when it spouts out of the earth, when it is still hot and moving, full of dissolved salts and living germs. He has listened to the instinctive songs in which the soul of the race shivers ; which are born, so to speak, of themselves, each like the others, clumsy and sincere, with indistinct onomatopœias, with cadences balanced like peasant rounds danced in sabots, with rough and new words, impregnated by the fat earth. It is there, the raw, inexhaustible treasure, which germinates through the length of the centuries in epics and odes, in epigrams, in romances, in legends, in tales full of *bonhomie* and in fables full of roguishness. Thérould comes, and of this lyrism the *Chanson de Roland* is made; Rabelais comes, and of this spirit *Pantagruel* is composed. One can understand everything, say everything, sing or chatter in every fashion, when one is in France."

Singing and chattering in every fashion — that is a paraphrase of Paul Fort. His *Choix de Ballades Françaises*, a modest little tome of five hundred and sixty-nine pages into which he has condensed his sixteen ample volumes, is divided under headings. These headings, invented by himself, will give a more comprehensive idea of the many kinds of his work than any arbitrary list which I could make would do. They are: *Hymnes*; *Chansons*; *Lieds*; *Élégies*; *Poèmes Antiques*; *Poèmes Marins*; *Odes et Odelettes*; *Romans*; *Petites Épopées*; *Fantaisies à la Gauloise*; *Complaintes et Dits*; *Madrigaux et Romances*; *Épigrammes à Moi-même*.

Now, I think it is time to speak of Fort's versification. That new and original versification which has caused so much commotion among the critics. That strange and baffling style to which Fort says he has sacrificed his books.

It is very hard for an English reader not to smile at the earnestness and great length with which all Fort's commentators deal with the subject. We must constantly remind ourselves that French is an artificially-made language, and is hedged about with any number of set rules. In France, there is a right and a wrong in pronunciation, there is a correct construction of sentences, and, above all, there is an exact system of versification. We, in the English-speaking countries, are constantly bemoaning the fact of the absence of standards, and the consequent decay of the language. A decay, let it be whispered, which has been loudly wailed over ever since the days of Chaucer. Whether we lose most or gain most by our freedom to talk and write as we please will probably always be a disputed question. Each system has its advantages. In France, everybody can write at least correctly, everybody who makes a pretence of being educated, that is. In England, and even more in America, the language is open to the enrichment of interpolated words and forms. (The picturesque and vitalizing influence of American slang has hardly yet been noticed by students; some day we shall have monographs upon the subject.) The corresponding disadvantages of each system are, that although in England and America there is a flexible, strong, and excessively rich language to make use of, only a handful of writers have sufficient taste and training to manipulate it and bring out its possibilities. English is not really inferior to French at any point except in its paucity of rhymes, and

U

occasionally in its lack of shaded meanings. But, as a rule, the skill of English (and here I would include American) writers is behind that of the French. On the other hand, the very clarity and precision of the French tongue makes it difficult for it to change with sufficient speed. Life, in France, is ahead of its official language. Hence the poet who attempts any innovation, no matter how obvious the advantage of the change may be, has to fight a long series of battles before he is admitted to have proved his point.

The *vers libristes* had hardly been accorded permission to exist, in the minds of the crowd, before Paul Fort appeared with a still greater innovation. Briefly it was this : — He alternated prose and verse at will, going from one to the other without any transition, sometimes changing from one to another in the same stanza. To make this possible, he printed his poems as prose, and the change into rhyme only became evident when the poem was read ; with the greater number of readers, undoubtedly, this change was never noticed until the poem was read out loud. He never attempted to write *vers libre*, nor is he to be classed among the *vers libristes*. His verse is almost always the alexandrine, pure and simple ; sometimes, however, his lines are of eight syllables or of ten. In very few cases has he departed from either strict prose or strict verse. Only, he says that he follows the colloquial pronunciation of the *Ile de France*, which means really Paris. In other words, he practically suppresses the mute *e*, after the fashion of conversation, instead of counting it in the traditional manner of French verse (and often pronouncing it too, sometimes drawing it out in the disagreeable mannerism of the *Comédie Française*). The only thing which I can compare this to in English, is the very bad and foolish tradition of singing English, in which "wind" is pronounced "winde," and "pretty" — "pritty," and the consonants, for some unknown reason, are blurred so that nothing is sharp. Even this is not quite the same thing, as the English singing habit has nothing to recommend it, whereas the French poetic tradition is at least based upon a bygone pronunciation.

What seriously troubles Fort's critics is that he does not always suppress the mute *e*. In a case where one cannot safely count out twelve feet, and be sure, by that, whether the *e* is to be suppressed or not, such uncertainty is very confusing. Again, to the English sense, this does not seem to matter. M. Louis Mandin, in his *Étude sur les "Ballades Françaises,"* points out that "if our traditional prosody is based upon the rigid fixity of the number of syllables, other idioms leave to many of their vocables the faculty of contracting or distending themselves according to the movement of the rhythm." And he cites as examples, our word "wandering," which may be either two or three syllables to suit the metre; or again, "Heaven," which may be either one or two.

Fort's mute *e's* are to be counted or not according to the flow of the verse when pronounced in the usual Parisian fashion. The only sensible way to read Fort's poems is to read them ahead as they are written. So done, they will at once fall into their natural rhythm, be it prose, be it verse. Fort has such an excellent sense of rhythm, of cadence, that you may safely trust him to bring out what he wishes in his poems; only read him as he is written, he will do the rest. Here is a very little poem. It is one of the most beautiful that Fort has done, and one of the best known; it is also one of the very few that are written in lines. It is, as you see, in regular alexandrines:

LA FILLE MORTE DANS SES AMOURS

Cette fille, elle est morte, est morte dans ses amours.

Ils l'ont portée en terre, en terre au point du jour.

Ils l'ont couchée toute seule, toute seule en ses atours.

Ils l'ont couchée toute seule, toute seule en son cercueil.

Ils sont rev'nus gaîment, gaîment avec le jour.

.Ils ont chanté gaîment, gaîment : "Chacun son tour.

"Cette fille, elle est morte, est morte dans ses amours."

Ils sont allés aux champs, aux champs comme tous les
jours . . .

Here is a stanza from another poem, *Richard
Cœur de Lion*, which is quite uneven, the lines being
ten, eleven, or twelve feet long. (Perhaps I should
repeat here, what I think I mentioned in the first
essay, that French being an unaccented language,
they have not our variety of feet, all of which are
based upon accent. In French prosody, a foot is a
syllable, so that the alexandrine, which is a line of
twelve feet, is simply a line containing twelve
syllables.)
This is the uneven stanza :

Non, me faut aimer, me faut traîner ma peine, pleurer contre
la pierre ici, que voici, où j'inscrivis son nom entre un hélian-
thème, et cet œillet couleur de cœur. — Suis transi ! — Je vais
herborisant au clair de la lune, cherchant sous la mousse l'herbe
qui rajeunit.

For one who is not a Frenchman and therefore in
love with the alexandrine, I think this last quotation far more interesting than regular verse. The
unexpected popping up of the rhymes is pungent
and delightful, and the assonances give a very rich

effect and are most satisfying. One cannot help
wishing that Fort had gone farther into this irregular
verse, but he has stuck very faithfully to his original
plan, given in the preface to *Le Roman de Louis XI* :
"I have sought a style which could pass, at the will
of the emotion, from prose to verse and from verse
to prose, rhythmic prose furnishing the transition.
The verse follows the natural elisions of the language.
It is presented as prose, all difficulty of elision dis-
appearing in this form . . . Prose, rhythmic prose,
and verse, are only a single instrument, graduated."
Paul Fort is not seeking a new verse form, and when
he stumbles upon the possibility of one, as in the
quotation I have just read, he passes it by as a mere
accident of no importance. What he is seeking is
to connect prose and verse more closely than they
have ever been connected before, and that he has
succeeded in doing in an extraordinarily satisfactory
manner.

But here I am, fallen into the usual pit which
betrays all Fort's commentators. I am devoting
far too much space to the metrical side of his work.
Let me scramble out as best I can by the aid of this
admirable quotation from M. Octave Béliard, the
critic whom I cited above. "When one of the genii
of free space," he says, "trembling and intoxicated
with life, falls into the midst of our humanity, he
begins by giving himself air, somersaulting over
barriers, upsetting categories, throwing our poor

symmetrical ideas arranged like ninepins, one on top of the other. He puts life where there was immobility and silence. We, careful busybodies, had pasted tags everywhere: This is a theatre and this is a novel. . . . This is verse. . . . This is prose. . . . Paul Fort unfastens the labels, plays unplayable plays at his theatre, rhymes novels, puts prose into verse and verse into prose, vibrates to every wind, chatters like a brook, makes poetry of everything, and amuses himself like a god. . . . And suddenly all these volatile, wandering syllables unite themselves into the regular verses of an epic, as if, recreation time finished, the hour of hymn and prayer had rung."

The first volume of *Ballades Françaises* contained a little of everything. It was divided into six books as follows: Book I: The Sea. The Bells. The Fields. The Hamlet. Book II: The Seasons. Night. A Book of Love. The Fields. The Road to Atre. The Storm. Book III: Orpheus Charming the Animals. Endymion. Indian Bacchus, etc. Louis XI, Curious Man. Heavy Blows of the Door Knocker. The Birth of Coxcomb. Book IV: Madmen and Clowns. Death and Satan. Peasants and Knights. Nobles and Kings. Book V: First Steps. There are Cries There. Book VI: The Young Ladies of my Dreams. The Friend without Sin.

It seems as if in this first book, Fort had set out to cover everything in the universe. Let us begin with one of the simplest songs in the volume:

LA RONDE

Si toutes les filles du monde voulaient s'donner la main, tout
autour de la mer elles pourraient faire une ronde.

Si tous les gars du monde voulaient bien êtr' marins, ils
f'raient avec leurs barques un joli pont sur l'onde.

Alors on pourrait faire une ronde autour du monde, si tous les
gens du monde voulaient s'donner la main.

Here is another, describing a peasant wedding,
with the refrain of the traditional *Chanson Populaire*:

LA NOCE

Ah! que de joie, la flûte et la musette troublent nos cœurs
de leurs accords charmants, voici venir les gars et les fillettes, et
tous les vieux au son des instruments.

Gai, gai, marions-nous, les rubans et les cornettes, gai, gai,
marions-nous, et ce joli couple, itou!

Que de plaisir quand dans l'église en fête, cloche et clochettes
les appellent tertous, — trois cents clochettes pour les yeux de
la belle, un gros bourdon pour le cœur de l'époux.

Gai, gai, marions-nous, les rubans et les cornettes, gai, gai,
marions-nous, et ce joli couple, itou!

La cloche enfin tient nos langues muettes. Ah! que de
peine quand ce n'est plus pour nous . . . Pleurez, les vieux, sur
vos livres de messe. Qui sait? bientôt la cloche sera pour vous?

Gai, gai, marions-nous, les rubans et les cornettes, gai, gai,
marions-nous, et ce joli couple, itou!

Enfin c'est tout, et la cloche est muette. Allons danser au
bonheur des époux. Vive le gars et la fille et la fête! Ah! que
de joie quand ce n'est pas pour nous.

Gai, gai, marions-nous, les rubans et les cornettes, gai, gai,
marions-nous, et ce joli couple, itou!

Que de plaisir, la flûte et la musette vont rajeunir les vieux
pour un moment. Voici danser les gars et les fillettes. Ah!
que de joie au son des instruments!

It is amusing to note that this is one of the *Ballades
des Cloches.*

Robert de Souza in his *Poésie Populaire* says:
"Rondes et pastourelles, aubades, romances et guil-
lonées, berceuses et brunettes, ballades narratives,
complaintes d'amour, chansons de fêtes et de métiers,
qwerziou et soniou bretons, lieds ou saltarelles, il
semble qu'aucun des modes lyriques populaires ne
soit absent du livre de M. Fort." And he quotes
this Breton song with its fantastic refrain:

ET YOU YOU YOU

Et you, you, you, c'est le pêcheur qui meurt, et you, you, yu, et toute la mer dessus.

Et you, you, you, c'est la bergère qui pleure, et you, you, ya, c'est l'amour qui s'en va.

Et you, you, you, c'est-y la mer qui bêle, et you, you, yon, ou c'est-y les moutons?

Et you, you, you, les plaisirs sont au ciel, et you, you, you, les nuages par-dessous.

But Paul Fort has other peasant songs. Songs with overtones of sadness :

LA VIE

Au premier son des cloches : "C'est Jésus dans sa crèche . . ."

Les cloches ont redoublé : "O gué, mon fiancé!"

Et puis c'est tout de suite la cloche des trépassés.

Songs tinged with a gay irony :

LES BALEINES

Du temps qu'on allait encore aux baleines, si loin qu'ça fai-sait, mat'lot, pleurer nos belles, y avait sur chaque route un

Jésus en croix, y avait des marquis couverts de dentelles, y avait la Sainte-Vierge et y avait le Roi !

Du temps qu'on allait encore aux baleines, si loin qu'ça faisait, mat'lot, pleurer nos belles, y avait des marins qui avaient la foi, et des grands seigneurs qui crachaient sur elle, y avait la Sainte-Vierge et y avait le Roi !

Eh bien, à présent, tout le monde est content, c'est pas pour dire, mat'lot, mais on est content ! . . . y a plus d' grands seigneurs ni d'Jésus qui tiennent, y a la république et y a l'président, et y a plus d'baleines !

All the poems which I have quoted, with the exception of *Les Baleines* and *La Vie*, are from this first volume, and Fort has never done anything better in this line. I cannot leave it without quoting one more, from the section " Madmen and Clowns." It is irony, pure and simple, keen and flickering like a sword-blade :

LES DEUX CLOWNS

— Synthétic Clown-Clown, hip, hip, tournez !

— Six pirouettes bleu blanc blanc bleu, voilà le Ciel ! six pirouettes bleu vert vert bleu, voilà la Mer ! six pirouettes vert jaune jaune vert, c'est le Désert ! six pirouettes or jaune jaune or, c'est le Soleil !

— Bravo, bravo, un p'tit bravo, messieurs. Analytic Clown-

Clown, à vous, tournez!

Soit. Messieurs, décomposons, suivez-moi bien : Violet,
deux pirouettes, Indigo, trois pirouettes, Bleu, cinq pirouettes,
Vert, deux pirouettes, Jaune, trois pirouettes, Orangé, cinq
pirouettes, Rouge, dix pirouettes. Total : trente pirouettes.
Attention, Messieurs! guignez l'arc de Noé . . . Deux trois
cinq, deux trois cinq dix, rrrrrrran!

— Cessez, Analytic, cessez, assez! Il va se rompre . . .
Dieu! . . . Ah!

Synthétic se tord, puis dans la sciure du cirque inscrit d'un
doigt profond cette sombre épitaphe :

Ci-Git
ANALYTIC
ce clown qu'on disait sage
— très fol
et mort de rage
de n'avoir pu tourner dans un orage.

The next volume of *Ballades Françaises* was called
Montagne, Forêt, Plaine, Mer, and was published in
1898. Fort has as great a love for scenery as
Francis Jammes, again and again he delights himself with describing it. Only, unlike Jammes, he
loves to paint towns as well as countrysides. He
notices all the changes of light and shadow, all the
effects of trees, and houses, and steeples, and always

with that intoxication of delight. Nature strikes him and sets him singing. "Tout mon corps," he cries, "est poreux au vent frais du printemps. Partout je m'infinise et partout suis content." Spring fills him with an almost uproarious happiness: "Rendez-vous des muguets! rendez-vous des coucous! et de toutes les fleurs dont les prairies abondent, au son de la trompette à Phébus. Rendez-vous d'abeilles et d'oiseaux! Un empire se fonde."
Here is the little town of Senlis in the morning mist:

SENLIS MATINALE

Je sors. La ville a-t-elle disparu ce matin? Où s'est-elle envolée? Par quel vent, dans quelle île? Je la retrouve, mais n'ose plus étendre les mains. Senlis est vaporeuse comme une mousseline.

Moi, déchirer Senlis? prenons garde. Où est-elle? Toits et murs sont un transparent réseau de brume. Notre-Dame livre à l'air sa gorge de dentelle, son cou si fin, son sein léger couleur de lune

où bat l'heure irréelle, que seuls comptent les anges, tant l'écho s'en étouffe dans l'oreiller du ciel fait des plumes doucement étendues de leurs ailes, où Dieu repose un front qui vers Senlis se penche.

This is a curious *paysage*, considered in the light of recent events; it appeared in 1909, in his tenth volume:

HORIZONS

Du côté de Paris, mais vers Nemours la blanche, un bouvreuil ce matin a chanté dans les branches.

Du côté d'Orléans, vers Nemours envolée, au cœur du jour l'alouette a chanté sur les blés.

Du côté de la Flandre, au crépuscule d'or, loin de Nemours la pie a caché son trésor.

Le soir, criant vers l'est, l'Allemagne et la Russie, la troupe des corbeaux quitta ce pays-ci.

Mais dans mon beau jardin par Nemours abrité, toute la nuit d'étoiles, Philomène a chanté!

The third volume of the *Ballades, Le Roman de Louis XI*, came out also in 1898. On the fly-leaf, Fort has put: "I have wanted to write a book of 'good humour.' I call it 'The Novel of Louis XI,' which means that I do not pretend to the exactitude of a severe historian."

What can one say of such a book as *Louis XI*? It is one of Fort's most original and amusing works. The picture of the King, with his hat bordered by medals and images, occupied with his prayers, and suddenly stooping to pick a chestnut or two out of the fire, is inimitable. We see him dictating to his barber "certaines petites lois." We see him fishing, as in the passage I quoted a little while ago. We see him riding "along the white road whistling with larks, by the side of the thorn hedges covered with linen hung out to dry." We see him sleeping peacefully on his horse, "entends-tu le coucou, malurette? — Non, je dors." We see him at the siege of Beauvais. And truly this same siege of Beauvais is one of the most astounding things in all literature. This account of the things the besieged threw down upon the besiegers, and the noise they made in falling, out-Marinettis Marinetti on his own ground :

Et lorsqu'avec ses gens il grimpait à l'échelle, que leur jetait-on, dites-moi? — des poulets? non pas, — des radis? du beurre? vous êtes dans l'erreur, — des agneaux? des bœufs? plus souvent! — des fraises à la crème? des melons? des salsifis? fi! vous vous moquez! — On leur jetait du plomb fondu dans les prunelles; sur le nez, sous le nez, des torches enflammées (comme roses écloses, bonnes à humer); et par tout le corps un joyeux pêle-mêle de meubles, de pavés, d'ardoises, de boulets, de crachats, d'os rongés, d'ordures variées, de petits clous, de grands clous, d'enclumes, de marteaux, de casseroles, de piots, de papinettes en fer, d'assiettes, de fourchettes, de poêles, de cuillers, d'encre, de graisse et d'huile bouillantes, que sais-je? de tombeaux, de margelles, de cloisons, de gouttières, de toits, de clochers, de cloches, de clochettes qui tintinnabulaient gracieusement sur les têtes.

Que leur jetait-on encore pour ne point mentir?

Ah! Maints objets moult contondants, tranchants, affûtés,

affilés, en boule, en douille, grenus, cornus, en scie, en soc, de terre, de tôle, de pierre de taille, de fer, d'acier, arqués, hérissés, tordus, confus, tout mal fichus, moussus, rouillés, éraillés, en lanières, en coin, en creux, en crible, en croix, en cric, en croc, sonnants, crissants, sifflants et ronflants, faisant humph, ouf, louf, pouf, bring, sring, tringle, balaam, bottom, betting, batar, arara, raraboum, bul, bul, breloc, relic, relaps, mil, bomb, marl, broug, batacl, mirobol, pic, poc, quett, strict, pac, diex, mec, pett, sec, sic, soïf, flic, faïm, bric, broc, brrrrrr . . ., qui enfonçaient les crânes, élargissaient les nez, tricotaient les oreilles, écarquillaient les bouches, faisaient voler les dents, les doigts, les coudes, les bras, les mentons, les pommettes, mariaient les yeux, en dédaignaient l'omelette, désossaient les épaules, abrutissaient le thorax, décourageaient les cœurs, mettaient l'intrus au ventre, scrutaient une fesse puis l'autre, en tiraient faux boyaux, de cuisses cuissettes, de rotules billes et développaient les pieds ou coupaient l'homme en cinq, six, sept, voire.

Oui-da, encore, que leur jetait-on?

Des cadavres, des injures, des merdailles et des flèches?

Bien mieux! (frissonnez avec moi) — des maisons. Et peu s'en fallut que, par-dessus la ville, on ne leur jetât la ville entière!

Here I must skip over four volumes and quote what I believe to be Fort's masterpiece. It is in the same *genre* as *Louis XI*, but where one is diffused throughout a long novel, the other is condensed into eight pages. Eight pages in which is contained the whole Middle Ages. I give the poem entire.

HENRI III

I

Les rideaux des croisées sont clos. Les meubles dorment. Parfois le lit royal pousse un long gémissement. C'est le bois qui se plaint, c'est l'âme du vieux chêne. Écoutez. . . . Aussi bien, cela gémit à peine. Écoutez. L'âtre obscur se ranime et frissonne. Trois petites flammes bleues dansent sur le foyer, jetant de grands adieux aux murs fleurdelisés.

Plus rien. L'obscurité chasse les quatre murs.

Aussitôt, un éclat du foyer les ramène. Le lit tout grelottant pousse une plainte humaine ; et Philippe de Valois se détache d'un mur. Vite il ouvre un bahut, s'y plonge et le referme.

Louis XI précautionneux se glisse en chattemite ; sur son chaperon noir tourne une souris blanche ; et voici, l'écusson de Bretagne à la manche, se dévorant des yeux, Louis XII et Charles VIII. Ils ouvrent le bahut, s'y plongent et le referment.

Le gamin François II dans l'âtre va vomir. Le lit, soulevant ses draps, semble un fantôme en peine. Que les règnes sont courts dans la chambre des rois ! Avez-vous vu bâiller le grand coffre de bois ?

Plus rien. L'obscurité chasse les quatre murs.

Aussitôt, un éclat du foyer les ramène, et devant Henri II boite François Ier. Ils songent, le front bas, à Diane de Poitiers, puis s'abîment ensemble et ferment le couvercle.

x

C'est Charles V qui le relève de son sceptre, et le Roi-Sage
est rouge d'un reflet de bûcher. Il saute. Est-ce que la pourpre
empêche de sauter? Il roule dans sa pourpre et jette le bâton. La main de justice vole de serrure en serrure (cric! crac!)
tournant les clefs.

Car voici Jean le Bon.

Voûté, couvert de chaînes mélodieuses et tristes, il a mau-
vais sourire et les yeux bleus du Christ. Le dément Charles
VI le flagelle en cadence, du morion aux pattes, avec des lys de
France, et Charles VII, l'ivrogne, ramassant les pétales, baisse la
trogne. Mais il titube. Il a trop bu. Trois chutes sépulcrales
font sonner le bahut.

Les rois valois sont en rumeur. Le lit tressaille. Les onze
rois valois en appellent un autre. Là, et dans les miroirs, voyez,
le coffre bâille. La Mort s'exerce-t-elle à des métamorphoses?
A chaque bâillement des cornes de Satyres soulèvent le couvercle
et vite se retirent.

Puis grand silence. . . .

Enfin, sortant de la pénombre, un blanc visage monte comme
la lune monte. Et le lit voit passer Charles IX aux yeux noirs.
Houp! le bahut l'aspire et tout s'évanouit. Une souris grignote
au fond de l'infini.

II

Les rideaux des croisées sont clos. Les meubles dorment. Parfois le lit royal pousse un long gémissement. C'est le bois qui se plaint, c'est l'âme du vieux chêne ou, peut-être, aux flambeaux, verrait-on là un homme? . . . Et tenez! l'âtre obscur se ranime et frissonne; trois petites flammes bleues allongent leurs reflets qui fauchent la moisson des murs fleurdelisés. Le plafond s'en éclaire et paraît s'exhausser; le lit, resté dans l'ombre, s'abîmer sous son dôme.

La chambre où tout vacille est en proie aux fantômes.

Une lueur dernière frappe sur le bahut la ronde qui s'échappe de son gouffre entr'ouvert.

Une lueur vivante frappe aux flancs du bahut la ronde qui tournoie sur son bois en rumeur.

Le reflet des miroirs isole et fait saillir la ronde aux bonds lascifs de douze grands Satyres, entourant de leurs membres un bouc épouvanté, — tandis qu'en ces miroirs, trente fois répété, un Hercule de bronze fait tournoyer sa masse.

Il a du Béarnais le sourire en grimace. Lui vraiment! Tout craché!

L'ombre est chaude. Un cri couve. . . .

En silence, au galop, poussé par la tempête silencieuse des Temps et des Temps et des Temps, en silence, au galop de son cheval de fer, Charlemagne traverse la salle d'un coup bref.

Henri de Guise le suit sur son haut cheval noir, mais ayant fait fausse route se perd dans un miroir. Et puis voici Catherine, sa grande et belle figure — horrible à voir!

C'est alors qu'Henri tire, de sa stupeur, un cri comme il en vient la nuit du fond des plaines, ce cri des solitudes qui s'enfle et passe et traîne, décourageant la vie au cœur du voyageur; et c'est l'instant où, pris dans l'étoffe agitée, le fer d'une hallebarde soulève à la croisée que l'occident allume, un rideau qui s'allège.

Au dehors le jour tombe, rose, avec de la neige.

III

Le roi, vêtu de noir, a sauté hors du lit et va dans les miroirs interroger sa face, recule à sa pâleur, et tout tremblant se coiffe. Alors, son chapeau noir isole sa pâleur. "Viendras-tu réveiller un sang stupéfié (dit-il), ô toi, liqueur! . . ." A ses pieds la coupe tombe. Ouvrant doucement la porte, il écoute l'antichambre, tout allumée d'épées et pleine de cliquetis.

Les gants. La canne d'ébène. Et le voilà parti.

"Le roi, Messieurs. Le roi!" — Une hallebarde sonne. Voix, chuchotis, bruits de chaises. La lueur crépusculaire souligne en pétillant les solives dorées. L'antichambre est confuse, pleine d'ombres vassales, penchées vers un couloir où s'avance un point blanc.

Là-bas, le lit royal est blotti sous son dôme, tout au bout d'un couloir où s'avance un point blanc.

"Le roi!" — Deuxième écho. — Une hallebarde sonne.

Quelle blancheur ovale, à hauteur de visage, remue deux perles longues comme la lune en pleurerait? Visage et perles longues, Henri III apparaît. Et les ombres vassales, toutes les ombres se courbent.

Un vol de feuilles mortes est-il ici tombé? . . .

— "Toi qui risques un œil, regarde : le crépuscule souligne-t-il encore les solives dorées?

— Oui, mais le roi?

— Le roi, mon fils? . . . Il est passé.

— Quélus, mon bon ami, cela tient du prodige.

— Maugiron, Saint-Mégrin, écoutez la merveille : ce soir l'Ombre du roi dans le palais voltige, masquée de clair de lune et deux larmes aux oreilles.

— Va-t-elle retrouver Catherine en ses nuages? Elle monte l'escalier.

— C'est au second étage!"

Une hallebarde sonne. Voix, chuchotis, bruits de chaises. Au dehors le jour tombe, rose, avec de la neige.

IV

Cependant que le roi court dans l'escalier vide, Chicot survient berçant sa lanterne allumée : on entoure le Fou qui ricane et s'esquive, et reparaît, haussant et berçant sa lanterne, ainsi qu'un encensoir, au bas de l'escalier.

"Continuez, Messieurs, je cherche un roi," dit-il.

L'antichambre est obscure avec de grands coins pâles, où déjà les flambeaux s'allument sous des mains. L'un d'eux jette une flamme de neige et de carmin. Vite les mains s'écartent. — On voit toute la salle. — Légères, au bout des bras les épées s'incendient et, se liant par deux, peuplent l'air d'étincelles: quelques lames fredonnent, d'autres sont en cliquetis, et des ombres de torses font bouger les murailles, et les pieds des Mignons frou-froutent sur les dalles.

— "Chicot, s'écrie Quélus, l'Ombre du roi voltige. Que fais-tu là, Chicot? Veux-tu bien voltiger? Armé de ta chandelle, tu la verras monter.

— Mais non, je vois descendre.

— Qui donc?

— Henri de Guise.

— Diable! il est en Espagne . . . (A vous, Monsieur, touché!)

— Pardon, mon cher seigneur, il descend l'escalier.

— Chicot, prends garde à toi! . . . C'est parbleu vrai, Messieurs. *Je l'ai vu.*"

Les épées retombent sur les dalles.

Cependant que le roi court dans l'escalier vide, seul, jusque chez sa mère Catherine en ses nuées, et ne sent pas glisser la cuirasse limpide de monseigneur de Guise qui se range au palier. Le duc est bien en chair pourtant. Son cœur bat fort. Mais

non pas jusqu'à faire tinter le froid métal que monseigneur
dérobe, du chapeau, en saluant.

Tout au bas l'escalier flamboie. Le duc descend. Il descend marche à marche comme un discret fantôme. On se
presse, on le voit. Le duc revient d'Espagne comme un discret fantôme — et même il en revient par la chambre à coucher
de la reine !

— "Incroyable," dit Maugiron.
— "Ce Guise est fort," dit Saint-Mégrin.
— "Place à monseigneur-duc !"

La cuirasse limpide entraîne les épées. Tout s'écoule.
Tout s'éteint.

V

Henri III, cependant, mi-couché sur la rampe, du haut de
l'escalier a tout vu cette fois. Il tire de son cou un sanglot de
colombe, puis se relève.

Un mur s'entr'ouvre pour le roi.

VI

Ici, rien qu'une lampe éclairant une main.

Tout, sinon cette lampe et sauf le parchemin, où cette main
potelée, vieillotte, amidonnée, guide la plume d'oie ou cherche
l'encrier, ici tout est dans l'ombre. La main, par aventure,

disparaissant un peu, laisse de l'écriture. Alors, voici ce que la flamme pourrait lire, qui sur les caractères se tord comme une martyre :

"*A Madame ma fille, la Reine catholique,*

"*Ma fille aimée, ma mie, ma docile Isabelle, j'ai bien reçu de vos nouvelles d'Espagne. Monsieur de Guise me les apporta. Certes! il ferait beau voir tous ces méchants hérétiques brûlant en une seule torche (ainsi en France comme vous faites là-bas). Hélas! mignonne, ici rien ne se peut. Ce n'est chez nous que perversion; et douleurs pour votre bonne mère. Vous savez les afflictions qu'il plaît au ciel de m'envoyer et qui sont des plus grandes qu'il envoya jamais à personne. Brûler les hérétiques! Ah! oui, beau bouquet de flammes, certes! grand feu de joie et qui plairait à Dieu. Mais quoi, fillette, en France rien ne se peut. Tout reste ici dans l'ombre, même l'Ombre royale. . . .*"

A l'ombre d'un visage pend une lèvre blanche. Sous un bonnet de tulle noir un front se penche, battu de rides mouvantes comme un clocher d'oiseaux, et plus ce front se penche et plus il paraît haut. L'œil mouillé de Catherine s'argente. La courbe dure et fine du long nez italien se profile, que tire, ainsi qu'un arc, le pli de la narine.

C'est l'instant où Catherine, boudeuse et pacifique, biffe d'un trait de plume sa phrase impolitique.

Or un autre visage s'est levé dans la salle. Derrière elle Catherine sent vivre une pâleur. Elle a cessé d'écrire en écoutant son cœur. Deux petites mains gantées lui tombent aux épaules, comme deux chauves-souris tuées d'un même coup de gaule. Et l'une des petites mains roulant jusqu'à son cœur, vient s'y crisper. . . .

Alors, du bout de sa plume d'oie, Catherine, pensivement, doucement, la caresse. Et *tous deux* songent et l'heure est pleine de paresse.

La main se déraidit, tremblante. . . . Par un doigt! voici le parchemin désigné par un doigt! "*Tout reste ici dans l'ombre, même l'Ombre royale.*"

Deux mains saisissent le cou de Catherine, et la reine levant son front terrible vient de crier : "Mon roi!" — Un cri bref du parquet révèle une fuite soudaine, et bientôt Henri III descend l'escalier vide.

VII

Il franchit l'antichambre obscure et désertée, se jette contre un mur les deux bras écartés et cherche le couloir tout le long du mur vide.

Plus rien : du vide.

Le roi chancelle ; il court, chancelle ; il court jusqu'à sa porte ouverte et veut passer, mais s'arrête, le poing sur la gorge et livide, devant une hallebarde somnolente et bercée.

Henri saisit la jambe du garde qu'il réveille, car — ô stupeur! — derrière la garde qu'il réveille, là! dans son lit! . . . quelqu'un, quelqu'un ou quelque chose, de semblable à lui-même (et peut-être lui-même), de noir et blanc, un homme, un roi ou quelque chose, un roi peut-être? Charles IX ou François? un fantôme couché dort du sommeil des morts.

— "Garde! Allons, toi! Qui donc est chez le roi de France? A qui cette pâleur? Ces loques sont à moi! Suis-je sorti, voyons, ou bien est-ce moi, là? Quelle est cette chose?" — "Hélas!" dit l'homme dans les transes, "hélas! mon cher seigneur, mais je . . . je ne sais pas."

— "Silence," dit une voix. Une voix dit: "Silence. . . ." Le roi tremble accroupi comme une grenouille au froid, et la hallebarde tombe et le garde se sauve.

— "Ce n'est rien, mon doux sire, c'est Chicot qui repose."

Et Chicot déguerpit en entraînant un drap.

VIII

Minuit? . . .

Minuit sonne à Saint-Germain-l'Auxerrois.

If I were asked to pick out which was the finest poem of all those written by the men we have been studying, I should unhesitatingly pick out that. To understand it thoroughly one must, of course, know one's French history. The poem is saturated with historical allusions; every little happening has its meaning. I have no space here to unravel all these suggestions, they can easily be followed by any one conversant with history, and may serve as a starting point for inquiry to any one who is not. The whole poem is so impregnated with the supernatural, so full of foreboding, that the real and the imagined blend, until one hardly knows what is fact, what reminiscence, and what presentiment.

Briefly, the story is of the secret return of the Duc de Guise to Paris, egged on thereto by Philip II of Spain. His return, you will remember, was followed by the "Day of the Barricades" in which Henri III was besieged in his own palace by the population of Paris. With his escape to Chartres, and the subsequent events of his reign, the poem does not deal.

Henri III is a series of scenes, and nothing is lacking, no little touch, to give the character of Henri, of Catherine, of the Duc de Guise. All the King's effeminacy is in the pale face and long pearls which his *mignons* see advancing down the corridor. How excellent in its vacillating impotence is his scene with Catherine, when he puts up his hand to strangle her, but "un cri bref du parquet révèle une fuite soudaine" and the King flees down the staircase! Then the finding of the fool in his bed and fearing for a moment that it is himself, that he is a ghost — he or that other; then, when the fool has been roused and routed, the sudden striking of midnight from the belfry of Saint-Germain-l'Auxerrois, the hour and the clock which had ushered in the Massacre of Saint Bartholomew. It is breathless, this end, worked up as it has been by one stroke after another, all through the poem.

But, to go back a moment to the beginning, notice how the tone is given by the first lines: "Les rideaux des croisées sont clos. Les meubles dorment;" and, a little farther on, "Trois petites flammes bleues dansent sur le foyer. . . . Plus rien. L'obscurité chasse les quatre murs." In this weird darkness, pierced every now and then by a spurt from the dying fire, the long procession of French Kings passes through the room and plunges into the great oak chest. They come, and come, some of them on horseback "poussé par la tempête silencieuse des Temps et des Temps et des Temps," in which the words fall like the hoof-beats of a galloping horse — until Henri III wakes with a cry to the twilight "rose, avec de la neige." It is sketched in with a word, that cold twilight. He enters the antechamber "all lit up with swords, and full of clashings," then — "Une hallebarde sonne," and we hear the butt of it ringing on the stone pavement as the guard comes to attention. But the poem is here, why point out what can escape no one.

After *Louis XI* came *Les Idylles Antiques* and *L'Amour Marin*, both in 1900. Fort is very charming in his Idylls. His antiquity is neither old nor new. It is neither conventional nor *pastiche*, it is just Nature, if I may so express it. Nature mas-

querading as Pan for the sake of convenience. One
short quotation must suffice us here :

PAN AUX CERISES

(Vision de Berger)

Io ! j'ai reconnu Pan à sa libre parure, à ses poils ! Il sautait
dans le soleil, cueillant d'un geste aisé, parfois, une cerise aux
arbres vermeils. Qu'il était pur ! Des gouttes d'eau perlaient
sur sa lisse toison comme des étoiles : on l'eût dit d'argent.

Et c'était sous l'azur de mon jeune printemps.

Or, ayant avisé dans l'air une cerise plus grosse et plus belle,
il la saisit, et puisa le noyau sous la pulpe sanglante. Je m'ap-
prochai. J'étais ravi . . . Lui m'ayant visé l'œil, je reçus le
noyau. J'allais tuer Pan de mon couteau ! Il étendit un bras,
fit une volte, et tout le Monde tourna.

Adorons Pan, le dieu du Monde !

Fort is excellent in his sailor poems. In them one
can smell the salt wind, and hear the waves lapping
on the beach. *L'Amour Marin* is probably the most
successful of them, but as it is a very long poem in
dialect I will give instead *Les Baisers*.

LES BAISERS

En se quittant, on n's'est rien dit. Et nous avons cru que
l'on ne s'aimait guère. Pendant qu'on s'quittait, on s'est tu
bien longtemps. C'était, comme on dit, comme de l'indifference.

On s'était bien embrassés pourtant, hier et avant, tu m'as
dit : cinq jours. Mais on s'était dit : ça n'dure pas longtemps,
cinq jours de baisers, c'est comme le beau temps.

Aujourd'hui mer bleutée et demain c'est l'orage. Y n'faut
pas trop demander à l'amour. Et puis, les marins, voyez-vous,
ça voyage. Un bateau baise le sable. . . . Que les baisers
sont courts !

And now we come to one of the most enchanting
of all Fort's books. *Paris Sentimental ou le Roman
de Nos Vingt Ans.* It is as full of youth as *Henri
III* was full of history. It is bubbling over with
adolescence. One poem in it I must print here :

PREMIER RENDEZ-VOUS

(Square Monge)

Ivresse du printemps ! et le gazon tourne autour de la statue
de Voltaire. — Ah ! vraiment, c'est d'un beau vert, c'est très
joli, le square Monge : herbe verte, grille et bancs verts, gardien
vert, c'est, quand j'y songe, un beau coin de l'univers. — Ivresse
du printemps ! et le gazon tourne autour de la statue de Voltaire.

Et c'est plein d'oiseaux dans les arbres pâles, où le ciel ouvre
ses fleurs bleues. — Les pigeons s'aiment d'amour tendre. Les
moineaux remuent leur queue. J'attends. . . . Oh ! je suis
heureux, dans ce délice de l'attendre. Je suis gai, fou, amoureux ! — et c'est plein d'oiseaux dans les arbres pâles, où le ciel
ouvre ses fleurs bleues.

Je monte sur les bancs couleurs d'espérance, ou bien je fais de l'équilibre . . . sur les arceaux du parterre, devant la statue de Voltaire. Vive tout! vive moi! vive la France! Il n'est rien que je n'espère. J'ai les ailes de l'espérance. — Je monte sur les bancs pour quitter la terre, ou bien je fais de l'équilibre.

Elle a dit: une heure; il n'est que midi! Aux amoureux l'heure est brève. — L'oiseau chante, le soleil rêve. Chaque fois qu'Adam rencontre Ève, il leur faut un paradis. Derrière la grille, au soleil, l'omnibus y pense engourdi. — Elle a dit: une heure; il n'est que midi! Aux amoureux l'heure est brève.

Devant la statue, un chat blanc, un jaune, — et le jaune, c'est une chatte! — roulent, s'éboulent sur le gazon chaud, se montrent les pattes, miaulent, se battent. Le soleil étire doucement ton sourire, ô mon doux Voltaire, ô bon faune. — Devant ta statue, un chat blanc, un jaune, roulent, s'éboulent, se montrent les pattes.

Les arbres s'enfeuillent au chant des oiseaux. Le bourgeon de mon cœur éclate! — Et je vacille rien qu'à voir les diamants de l'arrosoir envelopper l'herbe d'une bruine. Un arc-en-ciel part de l'échine du philosophe, et va trembler dans les branches d'un marronnier. — Les arbres s'enfeuillent au chant des oiseaux. Le bourgeon de mon cœur éclate!

L'azur est en feu: un chien flaire un chien sous le banc où dort le gardien. — Une petite fille saute à la corde, et sur son ombre, et d'autres et d'autres. Je vois leurs ombres, sur l'allée, ou s'élargir ou s'affiner. Et tout ça chante à qui mieux mieux: "Au petit feu! au grand feu! c'est pour éclairer le bon Dieu!"

— L'azur est en feu : un chien flaire un chien, sous le banc où dort le gardien.

Voici le marchand de coco musical, chargé de ses robinets d'or. — Ses robinets sont des serpents, d'où gicle son coco sonore dans les timbales des enfants. Rafraîchissons notre luxure : vite ! pour un sou de ta mixture, Laocoon étincelant. Je bois à toute la Nature, je bois à ton bronze bouillant, toi qui souris de l'aventure, ô vieux Voltaire, ô doux méchant. — Voici le marchand de coco musical. Ses robinets sont des serpents.

Ah ! printemps, quel feu monte de la terre ! quel feu descend du ciel, printemps ! — Devant la statue de Voltaire, j'attends ma nouvelle Manon. Et cependant qu'elle tarde, Voltaire, assis, est patient : je regarde ce qu'il regarde, une pâquerette dans le gazon. J'attends. — J'attends, ô ciel ! j'attends, ô terre ! sous toutes les flammes du printemps !

Deux heures. Éparpillons cette marguerite. "Un peu, beaucoup, passionnément . . ." — Passionnément, petite Manon, viens vite, accours, je t'en supplie. — Hé ! toi, tu souris d'un sourire à me rendre fort mécontent. Sale encyclopédiste ! — Oh ! . . . La voici sous toutes les flammes du printemps ! . . .

Et les arbres tournent et le gazon tourne autour de la statue de Voltaire. — Décidément, c'est d'un beau vert, c'est délicieux, le square Monge : herbe verte, grille et bancs verts, gardien vert, c'est, quand j'y songe, un beau coin de l'univers. — Je monte sur un banc couleur d'espérance. On doit me voir de toute la France !

Where is there a better presentation of youth and Spring! The young man balancing himself upon the wire arches which border the flower-beds, and, in the laughing egoism of his bubbling exuberance, declaring that surely from there he can be seen by all France, is delightful. I wish I had space for others of the poems in this volume, particularly *Sur le Pont au Change*, but I must leave them for my readers to find.

In 1903, *Hymnes du Feu* came out, and in 1906, *Coxcomb ou l'Homme Tout Nu Tombé du Paradis*. This last is a strange sort of ironical allegory. It cannot be taken to pieces, I leave it to those who wish to read it. It is one of his best things and well worth the trouble of getting the volume.

In 1905, Paul Fort founded the quarterly, *Vers et Prose*, which he has edited ever since. How he has found time for such an arduous task, with all his other writing, I do not know. The theory that we are harder workers, or greater hustlers, in America, does not seem to be borne out by the lives of Verhaeren, Gourmont, Régnier, and Fort. This description of Fort *chez lui* is not without interest, depicting as it does that most intimate thing about a man, the room in which he feels most at home :

"A little beyond the great bronze lion of the Place Denfert-Rochereau, in the Avenue d'Orléans — a little street, narrow, grey, and sad. On the second floor of one of the houses in this street lives Paul Fort, with his mother, his wife, and his daughter. The room in which Paul Fort works is small, rather sombre, furnished with a bed of walnut half-covered with a big eiderdown of violet serge, all puffed up; some chairs, a chest of drawers, and a wardrobe; and against the window, with its white curtains, a round table packed with papers, books, and reviews, which mount in zigzagging piles to within a short distance of the ceiling. On the walls, pictures — little paintings given by painter friends, family photographs. Paul Fort is there, dressed in black, and as usual, at whatever hour you see him, tightly cravatted with a large ribbon of black silk wound many times round his neck."

Paul Fort looks like the traditional poet, with long hair. He complains that he is taken for a musician on account of it. Possibly for D'Indy, he says, with a smile, D'Indy being bald.

Some years ago, Paul Fort was elected *Prince des Poètes*; a position which Verlaine, Mallarmé, and Léon Dierx held before him. The *Société des Poètes* elects the holder of this purely visionary office, its reason for being consisting in the honour of election to it. That Paul Fort should have received it, proves that even typography cannot keep a man for ever from his just rights. All his critics bewail the fact that, writing *Chansons Populaires*, still Paul Fort is not yet accepted by the people. Whether his

Chansons are really for the masses, those who know the French proletariat are the best judges. But I cannot help feeling that, judging by most proletariats, Paul Fort's irony and learning, his many overtones and subtle meanings, would do away with any success his robustness might win him. Whether the proletariat agrees or not, Paul Fort is a great poet, a very great poet.

It is interesting to us to have him say : "I have a great admiration for the English poets, for Keats first of all. They always present themselves in a poetic intoxication. Their poems do not begin, do not end. They make one think of outspread moonlight, which gives mystery and profoundness to nature and to the objects bathed in its radiance. I should like to realize, in French, a poetry like theirs, which would enable me to envelop more, to blur more, so to speak, the psychological subjects of my writings, which, on the other hand, would be obliged to keep a very French character."

It is this endeavour which gives to Paul Fort his qualities of Englishman and Frenchman, which I have spoken of several times.

I have not mentioned in detail all Paul Fort's books. I have spoken of eight, and there are eight others I have not mentioned. It is not possible to take more than a bird's-eye view of such a man as Paul Fort in a single chapter. Suffice it to say, that the eight volumes I have not mentioned, although full of beautiful things, do not perhaps show any distinctively new facet of his genius.

Since the outbreak of the war, Paul Fort has been writing poems on the war. These are issued in little, unbound parts, twice a month. It was from the first of these that I quoted, when I gave the description of his childhood in the shadow of the Cathedral at Rheims. In closing, I want to quote one more poem from the *Poèmes de France*, as he calls them. This is no longer the time for *Ballades*, as Fort naturally feels.

This poem is a new note. It is Paul Fort burnt in the fire of a great national calamity:

LE CHANT DES ANGLAIS

It's a long way to Tipperary.

Feu! Tommy . . . Le cœur gigue aux chocs de nos canons. Du calme, bon garçon. Ah! c'est rudement long, rudement long pour aller à Tipperary. Depuis la soif d'hier apaisée sans whisky, je canonne, on canonne. Ah! . . . c'est rudement bon.

Qui m'a jeté sa gourde? Eh! vieux Bob, tu es mort? Du calme, cher garçon. A bientôt Leicester . . . Square. . . . All right! il est mort pour sa vieille Angleterre. La gourde est vide: feu! Tommy, canonne encore! Nous nous battons si bien, all right! les morts ont tort.

Du calme, fier garçon. Ah! c'est rudement long, rudement long pour aller à Tipperary, là-bas, près de la jolie fille que je

connais. Elle me disait oui quand je lui disais non. Feu !
Tommy. Le cœur gigue aux chocs de nos canons.

Tommy, sache, Tommy, que l'amour a du bon. Oui, c'est
une lointaine et fine demoiselle, que l'on n'atteint jamais qu'en
rêve. O large bec ! Tu rêves et tout vient, l'âme et le corps
avec. Ici rien que la mort, elle est fichue donzelle.

La mort ! ah ! si j'avais tourné les yeux vers elle, la teutonne
m'eût pris le cou de son bras sec et fait goûter sa bouche en-
dentée de shrapnells, en m'étouffant le sein jusqu'à l'extrême
angoisse. Juste Seigneur ! l'amour n'a rien de plus cruel !

Mais la mort, on n'y pense pas, elle est en face. Du calme,
heureux garçon. La mort, la verrais-tu ? Flottant sur la bataille ainsi qu'un étendard, c'est un grand vieux squelette usé de
toute part : elle flotte à présent sur les casques pointus.

Feu ! Tommy . . . Quoi ! tu meurs aussi, garçon fidèle ?
Te voilà dans les bras de la fichue donzelle ? Relève-toi, garçon !
Ah ! c'est rudement long, rudement long pour aller à Tipperary.
Adieu, Leicester Square, adieu, Piccadilly !

Nous étions quinze, hurrah ! nous sommes trois qui bougent.
O canon, tes boulets sont teints de notre sang, notre sang qui
refait notre uniforme rouge : devant nous les Teutons sont ex-
sangues de peur, ils croient que nous chargeons ta gueule avec
nos cœurs.

Dansons ! dansons la gigue ! — Ah ! oui . . . quoique vain-
queurs, nous dansons notre gigue en plein ciel du Seigneur.

Nous, bons garçons, nous sommes à Tipperary. Bonjour, Kate, bonjour, Annie, bonjour, Nelly . . . Nos cœurs se trouvent bien, pourvu que sur la terre,

elle vive à jamais notre vieille Angleterre !

To take "Tipperary," and make such a terrible, tragic thing with it, this is Paul Fort's genius : to react to the stimuli about him, and so reacting to produce great art. More than any one, he has felt the common, and turned it into the uncommon.

The book is done. I have not attempted any very far-reaching criticism. My object has been to talk a little while about a few great figures in a generation which is already past the meridian. For eighty years or so, this great era for French poetry has lasted. But already before the war it was on the wane. The younger men : Jules Romains, André Spire, Guillaume Apollinaire, Guy-Charles Cros, Charles Vildrac, do not seem to have quite the same remarkable power. Foolish fads, a sure sign of disease, were creeping in. Now the war has ended a period. When France recovers herself from the exhaustion which must follow her supreme effort, it will be another generation of poets who will be writing ; they will sing their present, and our present will be their past. The six men we have studied are the last glorious flower of a time already over.

APPENDICES

APPENDIX A

Most of the following translations are in prose, for the reason that I have stated in the Preface, but the stanzas have been preserved in order to make comparison with the original easier for the reader.   In a few cases the stanzas have been suppressed, but only when the transition from one to another became awkward in the prose form.   The French fondness for parentheses has made it necessary to change the punctuation somewhat, but the original punctuation has been kept wherever practicable.   A few of the translations are in *vers libre*, because the feeling of those particular poems seemed to evaporate in prose ; and three of the translations are in metre, because the originals appeared to me to require such a rendering.   Opposite each translation is the number of the page in the text where the original poem may be found.

ÉMILE VERHAEREN

Page 8.　　　A fist of terror tortures the villages ;
　　　　　　In the distance, tall steeples
　　　　　　Send the echo of their alarm-bells
　　　　　　Rebounding from shore to shore.

Page 8.　　The wind sings, the wind babbles,
　　　　　　with chaffinch and grosbeak and sparrow,
　　　　　　the wind whistles, shines and sparkles

at the points of the tall reeds;
the wind knots itself together, and winds about itself
    and unwinds,
and then suddenly escapes to the bright orchards be-
    yond,
where the apple-trees, like white peacocks —
mother-of-pearl and sunlight —
outspread themselves.

Page 9.   And up above, September journeys
    With his sky of mother-of-pearl and gold,
    And hangs the shining blocks of his most beautiful
        clouds
    Over the meadows, the fields, and the villages.

Page 9.   Do you hear it, do you hear it,
    The little stream upon the pebbles?
    It flows, and runs, and slides;
    And, to the branches
    Which hang above it,
    Softly dedicates its smooth song.

Page 10.   I remember the village near the Escaut,
    From which one saw the great boats
    Pass like a dream plumed with wind
    And marvellous with sails.
    Evening in procession under the stars.

THE KITCHEN

Page 14. The threshold of the kitchen was old and split. The hearth shone like a red puddle, and its flames, incessantly gnawing at the back plate, had eaten into it an obscene subject in melted iron.

The fire rejoiced under the mantelpiece which stretched over it like the penthouse roof over a booth, and the bright ornaments of wood, of copper, of lacquer upon it sparked less to the eyes than the writhing coals.

Rays escaped from it like a spray of emeralds, and here — there — everywhere — gave fillips of brilliance to the glass jugs and glazed platters. To see the sparks fall upon every raised surface, one would have said — into such particles did the fire crumble itself — that the sun had been winnowed through a leaded window.

LONDON

Page 18. And this London of brass and bronze, my soul, where iron plates clash under sheds, where sails go forth without Notre Dame for star — go forth, away, toward unknown hazards. Sooty, smoky stations, where gas weeps its distant silver melancholies to roads of lightning; where bored animals yawn at the hour which, immensely mournful, tolls from Westminster. And these embankments, infinite with fatal lanterns — Fates whose spindles plunge into darkness — and these drowned sailors, under the petals of mud flowers where the flame throws its light. And these shawls and these gestures of drunken women, and these alcohols of golden letters up to the roofs, and all at once death in the midst of these crowds.

O my soul of the evening, this black London which drags through you !

THE WINDMILL

Page 19. The windmill turns in the depths of the evening, very slowly it turns, against a sad and melancholy sky. It turns, and turns, and its wine-coloured sail is infinitely sad, and feeble, and heavy, and tired.

Since dawn its arms — pleading, reproachful — have stretched out and fallen ; and now again they fall, far off in the darkening air and absolute silence of extinguished nature.

Sick with winter, the day drowses to sleep upon the villages ; the clouds are weary of their gloomy travels ; and along the copses where shadows are gathering, the wheel-tracks fade away to a dead horizon. Some cabins of beech logs squat miserably in a circle about a colourless pond ; a copper lamp hangs from the ceiling and throws a patina of fire over wall and window. And in the immense plain, by the side of the sleeping stream — wretched, miserable hovels ! — they fix, with the poor eyes of their ragged window-panes, the old windmill which turns, and — weary — turns and dies.

THE DEAD

Page 21. In its dress of the colour of gall and poison, the corpse of my reason trails upon the Thames.

Bronze bridges, where wagons clank with interminable noises of hinges, and sails of dark boats, let their shadows fall upon it. With no movement of hands over its clock face, a great belfry, masked with red, gazes at it as though at some one immensely sad and dead.

My reason is dead from too much knowledge, from a too great desire to shape the motive of every being and every thing, and place it upon a black granite pedestal. It died atrociously, of a clever poisoning ; it died also of a mad dream of an absurd and red empire. On the illuminated evening of a festival, when it felt this triumph float, like eagles, over its head, its nerves gave way. It died when it could no more feel ardour and aching desires. And it killed itself, infinitely exhausted.

All down the length of mournful walls, the length of iron factories where hammers boom like thunder, it trails to the funeral.

There are wharves and barracks, always wharves with lanterns — slow and motionless spinners of the dim gold of their lights. There are the drearinesses of stones, a brick house, a black jail, whose windows, like dull eyelids, open to the evening fog. There are great insane dockyards, full of dismantled ships and yards quartered against a sky of crucifixions.

In its dress of dead jewels, which celebrates the hour of purple at the horizon, the corpse of my reason trails upon the Thames.

It goes toward the perils in the depths of shadow and fog, to the long hollow sound of the tolling of heavy bells breaking their wings at the corners of towers. Leaving unsatisfied behind it the immense city of life, it goes toward the black unknown, to sleep in the graves of evening, far away, where the slow and powerful waves, opening their endless caverns, swallow the dead forever.

Page 25.   In a wide flash of lightning through the mists, an avenue suddenly opens; and Saint George, fermenting with gold, with plumes and froth at his bridleless horse's white breast, descends. The diamond trappings make of his fall the triumphal road for Heaven's pity to come to Earth.

THE RAIN

Page 28.   Long like threads without end, the long rain
Interminably, across the grey day,
Streaks the green window-panes with its long grey
      threads,
Endlessly, the rain,
The long rain,
The rain.

Since yesterday evening it has ravelled itself so,
Out of the rotten rags hanging

From the solemn and black sky.
It stretches itself, patiently — slowly —
Upon the roads,
Since yesterday evening — upon the roads and lanes,
Continually.

Along the miles
Which go from the fields to the suburbs,
By ways interminably winding,
Pass the teams with arching hoods —
Toiling, sweating, smoking —
Like a funeral train seen in profile;
In the straight ruts,
Parallel for such a distance that at night they seem
    to join the heavens,
The water drips for hours;
And the trees weep, and the houses,
Soaked as they are by the long rain,
Tenaciously, indefinitely.

Through their rotten dikes
The rivers burst over the meadows
Where the drowned grain floats;
The wind slaps alders and walnut trees.
Ominously, half-submerged in water,
The great, black oxen bellow to the tortured heavens;
Evening comes with its shadows,
And the plains and the coppices are clogged with them,
And always there is the rain,
The long rain,
Fine and dense like soot.

The long rain,
The rain — and its identical threads
And its systematic nails
Weave the shroud of destitution
Mesh by mesh,
For the houses and the enclosures
Of the grey old villages;
Linens and rosaries of rags
Which ravel out
All down the upright beams;
Blue pigeon-houses glued to the roof;
Windows whose dilapidated panes
Have a plaster of brown paper;
Dwellings where the symmetrical gutters
Form into crosses above the stone gables;
Windmills planted, uniform and dull,
Each on its hill, like horns;
Belfries and neighbouring chapels,
The rain,
The long rain,
Assassinates them during the Winter.

The rain
The long rain, with its long grey threads,
With its hair of water, and its wrinkles,
The long rain
Of old countries,
Eternal and torpid.

THE MILLER

Page 31.   He was being buried, the old miller of the black mill, buried in Winter, on an evening of rough cold and bitter North wind, in a ground of cinders and hemlock plants.

The daylight darted its deceiving brilliance at the grave-digger's shovel. A dog wandered about near the grave, and barked at the brightness.

At each dig the shovel changed like a mirror, shone, took hold, and buried itself in the disturbed earth. The sun went down beneath suspicious shadows.

Against a background of sky, the grave-digger, like an enormous insect, seemed to fight with fear. The shovel trembled in his hands, the ground opened in spite of him, and nothing filled up the hole which, like the night, widened in front of him.

In the village yonder, no one had lent two sheets to the dead.

In the village yonder, no one had said a prayer.

In the village yonder, no one had rung the passing bell for the dead.

In the village yonder, no one had wanted to nail the coffin.

And the houses and cottages along the roads facing
the cemetery, all had their shutters closed so as to see
nothing.

The grave-digger felt himself alone with this dead
man who had no shroud, for whom every one felt
hate and fear in their blood.

Upon his hill, gloomy with evening, the old miller
of the black mill had been used to live in harmony
with space and distance, and the mad flight of tempests streaming from the flapping mane of the North
winds; for long he had listened to what the dark and
golden mouths of the stars reveal to those who are
attentive to the eternal; the grey desert of austere
heather had ringed his eyes with the mystery by which
things make souls aware of them, and speak to them
and counsel them; the great currents which flow
through everything that lives had entered his mind
with such power, that, in his isolated and profound
soul, this simple peasant had felt the movement and
fermentation of the world.

The oldest man did not know how long it was that
he had been hiding yonder, far from the village, watching the flight of birds and their journeyings, and the
signs of flame in the clouds.

He awed by the silence of which he had noiselessly
woven his existence; he awed still further by the
golden eyes of his windmill, shining suddenly at
night.

No one would have known of his agony and death, were it not for the four wings which he turned, like eternal supplications, to the unknown; were it not that one morning they were absolutely rigid, black and immovable like a cross above a destiny.

The grave-digger saw the surging shadows increase like crowds, and the village and its shut windows fade into the distance and disappear.

The universal disquiet peopled the solitude with cries; in black and brown veils the wind passed by as though it were some one; all the vagueness of hostile horizons became fixed in feverish rustlings, until the moment when, with wild eyes, throwing his shovel no matter where, with the multiple arms of night in menaces behind him, like a thief he fled.

Then came silence, absolute, all about. In the riven earth the hole appeared gigantic, nothing moved any more; and, alone, the insatiable plains in their Northern immensity of shadow absorbed the dead man, whose life had been rendered limitless and exalted to the infinite, by their mystery.

THE BURNING HAYRICKS

Page 35. The plain, in the dark evening distance, is all alight, and the alarm-bells break and jangle to the four walls of the horizon.

z

— A hayrick burns ! —

By way of the roads, the crowd — by way of the villages, the crowd surges; and in the yards the watch-dogs howl.

— A hayrick burns ! —

The flame roars, and breaks, and pounds, tears itself into tatters which it waves, or, sinuous and tailed, unrolls itself to streaming hair — eager, slow — then suddenly calms and lets go, and dodges and disappears — or leaps up again : and now, bright, of mud and gold, it veers in a plume over the black sky.

— When suddenly in the distance another hayrick catches fire ! —

It is enormous — like a red, shaken bundle of sulphurous serpents. The glare ! — it passes over acres of land, and farms, and villages, where, from window-pane to window-pane, a red clot moves.

— A hayrick burns ! —

The fields? They become limitless with terrors; the foliage of the woods lifts itself up in light over the marshes and the ploughed lands; rearing stallions whinny at the terror; enormous flights of birds become dazed and fall into the flames — and stifled cries rise from the ground; and it is death, death brandished and flung up again by the lifted arms of the conflagration.

And the silence after fear — when suddenly, over there, formidably, in the weary evening, a new fire fills the deeps of the twilight.

— A hayrick burns! —

At the cross-roads, haggard men make bewildered gestures, children cry, and old men lift their withered arms to the flames waving like banners. While farther off, obstinately silent, madmen, with stupor in their eyes — look on.

— A hayrick burns! —

The air is red, the sky seems to have died, ominously, under the shut eyes of the stars. The wind drives gold pebbles before it in a tearing of veils. The fire becomes a clamour howling in flames to the echoes, to the distance, to the other shore, where suddenly the far side of the river lights up like a dream. The whole plain? It is a live coal, an illusion, blood and gold — and the tempest sweeps on the passing death of the heavens so violently that at the confines of the terror the entire sky seems to have disappeared.

THE STOCK EXCHANGE

Page 39. The enormous street and its quadrangular houses border the crowd and dike it with their granite, eyed with windows and porches, in whose panes aureoled evenings shine farewell.

Like an upright torso of stone and metal, containing in its unclean mystery the beating and panting heart of the world, the monument of gold stands in the darkness.

About it, black banks lift their pediments supported by the arms of bronze Hercules, whose great weary muscles seem to be holding strong-boxes up to victory.

The square, from which it erects its battleground, sucks in the fever and the tumult of each wave of passion towards its occult lover — the square and its open spaces, and its walls, and its numberless gasjets, which make the clusters of shadows and lights upon the sidewalks stir.

How many dreams, like red fires, intermingle their flames and their eddies from the top to the bottom of the mad palace! Monstrous and culpable gain tightens itself into knots, and its desire sows and propagates itself, going out to inflame neighbouring vanities from door to door, through the town. Heavy counters grumble like a storm, gross profusions become jealous and rage, and tempests of failures, suddenly, with brutal blows, beat and overturn the great monumental men of the town.

At a given moment of the afternoon, the fever increases still more, and penetrates the building, and ferments in the walls. One almost believes one sees it quickening itself at the motionless flame-flowered lamps, running from banister to banister, assembling itself, and bursting out and crackling, upon the landings and the marble of the stairways.

At the mirage of a pale hope, a rekindled fury mounts through the funnel of noise and smoke from those fighting by theft below. Dry tongues, piercing looks, contradictory gestures, and brains crossed by whirlwinds of millions, exchange their fear and their terror there. Haste simulates audacity, and audacities surpass themselves; fingers scratch the insanity of their anguish upon slates; cynically, a discount which breaks a people at the other end of the world, illuminates it; chimeras are winged with light; luck flees or over-abounds; deals concluded, deals broken off, struggle and clash together in disputes; the air burns — and paradoxical figures, in flat packages, in heavy bundles, are thrown back, and jolted, and shaken, and worried in these tumults until their weary sums, masses against masses, are broken.

On those days when catastrophes happen, Death scrolls them over with suicides, and failures crumble to ruins which flame in exalted obsequies. But the same evening, in the pale hours, wills revive in fever, and the sly fury takes hold again as before.

People betray, smile, gnaw, and encompass other deaths. Hate hums like a machine about those whom it assassinates. Men of needy fortune are robbed with authority. Honour is mixed with swindling to lure even nations into the universal madness, the hunt for the burning and infamous gold.

Oh, gold! In the distance, like towers in the clouds, like towers upon the steps of illusion! Enormous gold! Like towers in the distance, with millions of arms stretched towards it, with gestures and calls in the night, and the muttering of the universal prayer, from end to end of the horizons of the world!

In the distance, cubes of gold upon triangles of gold, and all about, celebrated fortunes mounting upon the scaffoldings of algebras.

Gold! — to eat and drink gold! — and, even more ferocious than the rage for gold, the faith in the mysterious gamble and its dark and hazardous chances, and the certainty of its arbitrary designs to restore the old destiny. Play, terrible axis, where future passion will turn desperately about adventure for the sole pleasure of anomaly, for the sole need of bestiality and frenzy, over there, where laws of terror cross with supreme disorders!

Like an upright torso of stone and metal, containing in its unclean mystery the beating and panting heart of the world, the monument of gold stands in the darkness.

GET YOU GONE

Page 46.   Get you gone, get you gone,
The entire inn is for those who come.

It belongs to us, it belongs to us,
For very nearly three hundred years.
It belongs to us, it belongs to us,
From the outer door with its heavy bolts
Up to the very chimney tops.

Get you gone, get you gone,
The entire inn is for those who come.

We know it well, we know it well,
Every decay and every crack.
But it is we alone who pretend
To put new plaster instead of the old
From the ground-sills up to the edge of the roof.

Get you gone, get you gone,
The entire inn is for those who come.

We venerate those who are dead,
Lying in their coffins of oak;
We envy those already dead

Unconscious of the cries of hate
Which leap and bound from plain to plain.

Get you gone, get you gone,
The entire inn is for those who come.

It is our right, it is our right,
To put an Eagle on our sign;
It is our right, it is our right,
To own, according to the law,
More than we need of barley and rye.

Get you gone, get you gone,
Gestures and words mean nothing now.
Get you gone, get you gone,
And understand,
It is our hunger makes our right!

ALBERT SAMAIN

Page 73. My soul is an Infanta in robes of state, whose exile, eternal, monarchical, is reflected in the great, empty mirrors of some old Escurial, like a galley forgotten at its anchorage.

Two Scotch greyhounds, with melancholy eyes, stretched out magnificently at the feet of her armchair, hunt, when it pleases her, symbolic animals in the forest of Dreams and Enchantment.

Her favourite page, who is called "It-was-Once,"
reads bewitching poems to her softly, while immovable,
a tulip in her fingers, she listens to their mystery
dying within her.

The park which surrounds her spreads out its foliage, its marbles, its basins, its balustrades; and she
intoxicates herself gravely upon the illustrious dreams
which noble horizons hold for us.

She is there, resigned and gentle, and without surprise; knowing too much to struggle where all is
fatality; and feeling, despite some inborn disdain,
sensible to pity, as the wave is to the breeze.

She is there, resigned, and gentle in her sobs, more
sombre only when she evokes the dream of some
Armada, shadowed by the eternal falsehood, and so
many beautiful hopes asleep under the waters.

In the heavy purple evenings when her pride sighs,
Van Dyck portraits, with their long, pure fingers,
pale in black velvet against the tarnishing gold of the
walls, with their airs of greatness dead, make her
dream of empire.

The old, golden illusions have dissipated her
mourning, and in the visions which cheat her lassitude,
suddenly a ray — of glory, of sunlight — lights up
within her all the rubies of her pride.

But she calms these fevers with a sad smile; and dreading the crowd with its iron tumults, she hearkens to life — in the distance — like the sea . . . and the secret deepens upon her lips.

No quiver troubles the pale water of her eyes, where sits the veiled spirit of dead cities; and through the apartments, with their silently opening doors, she wanders, enchanting herself with mysterious words.

The ineffectual waters of fountains in the distance fall — fall — and pale at the casement, a tulip in her fingers, she is there, reflected in the mirrors of old days, like a galley forgotten at its anchorage.

My Soul is an Infanta in robes of state.

SUMMER HOURS

Page 75.   Bring golden crystals,
And glasses the colour of dreams;
That our love may be prolonged
In exasperated perfumes.

Roses! Roses still!
I adore them, even to pain.
They have the melancholy attraction
Of things which give death.

The golden summer streams into the goblets;
The juice of the peaches which you are cutting
Spouts over your snowy breast.

The park is dark, like a gulf . . .
And in my stormy heart
Is a misery of sweetness which suffers.

MUSIC ON THE WATER

Page 76.   Oh! Listen to the symphony;
Nothing is so sweet as an agony
In music, which indefinitely
Comes from a vaporous distance.

The night is drunk with lassitude
And our hearts, freed from the rude
Monotonous effort of living, are wooed
To fade and die in a dreamy trance.

Let us slide between the water and sky,
Let us slide under the far-off, high
Moon; my whole soul, the world passed by,
Has sought a refuge in your eyes.

I watch their pupils in the moon,
Under the wailing string-notes swoon,
Like supernatural flowers in tune
To beams of graceful melodies.

Oh! Listen to the symphony;
Nothing is so sweet as the agony
Of lip to lip united by
Music prolonged indefinitely.

OCTOBER

Page 77.   October is sweet. — Pilgrim Winter goes forward
to the sky where, startled, the last swallow is flying.
Let us dream . . . the fire springs up and the North
wind croons. Let us dream . . . the fire sleeps
under its ermine cinders.

The transparent, rose-coloured lampshade shines.
The window is black under the monotonous downpour.
Oh! the sweet "remember" in the chamber of
Autumn, where from dead pier glasses the soul dif-
fuses itself.

The town is far away. Nothing — save a muffled
sound of carriages which dies, sadly, in the thick
folds of the curtains . . . Let us fashion exquisite
dreams upon miniatures.

In mauve distances of a faded sweetness my soul
loses itself, and the beribboned hour strikes a hundred
years from the superannuated mantel-clock.

NOCTURNE

Page 78.   Summer Night. — Under the sky of lapis-lazuli, the enchanted park bathes in its soft shadows. The flowers dream, love perfumes itself at their corollas. Quietly the moon mounts into the pale sky.

There is a fête at Bergamo, this evening, at the Lanzoli palace. Entwined couples descend from gondolas. The ball opens, starred with pink candelabra. Flutes and horns, — the orchestra is conducted by Lulli.

Madrigals, among the flowered dresses, offer their sublimated insipidities with cloying sweetness. And over the gold glazing of the transparent floors, gossips of the Regency, exquisitely elderly, detail the advised languor of gavottes to the perfumed rhythm of dying fans.

THE FORTUNATE ISLE

Page 79.   Tell me, Pretty Band,
My soul is melancholy,
Tell me, I supplicate you,
     Where it is.
Is it in Venice, in Florence?
Is it in the country of Hope?
Is it in the Ile-de-France?
     Who knows?

Come, you will see shepherdesses,
And sylvan marchionesses,
The white sheep of china tables,
    And more,
Birds which sing and birds which nest,
Names like Lindor and Angèle,
And roses at the margins of
    The wells.

Come, you will see Lucindas,
Agneses, and Rosalindas,
Festooned with pearls brought from the Indies,
    Holding
A parroquet on the forefinger,
With a ruffle for a collar,
And a great fan of ostrich feathers
    Hanging.

Irises and fair Estelles,
In hats of floating, filmy lace,
Dream near the silver, fine cascades
    Which weep.
And softly closing their great wings,
The butterflies in love with them
Become at once unfaithful to
    The flowers.

United in a close embrace
Lovers wander free from fear
About the windings of the secret
    Labyrinth.

Over the diaphanous garden hovers
A half-silence, no rumour lingers
But dies and leaves the strolling lovers
    In peace.

It is that very Day Divine,
Drawn by dreams over the grass,
That grass which seems to be a little
    Faded.
Loves there are quite fulfilled,
Amber and emerald eyes are stilled,
Proposals without haste are frilled
    Over an avowal.

Evening falls . . . The hour is soft,
And draws away with even feet
Hardly resting on the sweet
    Moss.
An indecisive light persists
And pensive twilight wreathes its mists,
Opens its eyes like amethysts
    Moistened.

Swans sail about in troupes;
We lunch upon the grass in groups,
Glasses clink against the glasses
    Of finest gold.
Sèvres are the plates from which we eat;
And madrigals, so arch, so sweet,
Sugar the singing lips, a treat
    Endless and old.

Afternoon denies those joys;
Daylight intoxication cloys,
It fades into an infinite
    Lassitude.
Smoke from cottage chimneys rises
In the darkening sky, surprises
Glow of stars, with silver light.
    Dreams.

Lovers whisper what they please,
Women's eyes no longer tease
But are faithful, and one sees
    Their souls.
Two and two, like angels roaming
In some painted Missal's gloaming,
Wistful kisses given, taken,
    Couples pass.

To the sound of music slow,
Lovers pace there to and fro,
Steps lag slower, careless, so
    They go.
Upon the earth the heavens float,
A solitary evening note
Tinkles from the Angelus
    Over Cytherea.

A DEAD CITY

Page 82.   Vague, lost in the depths of monotonous sands, the city of other days, without towers or ramparts, sleeps the last sleep of old Babylons, under the white winding-sheet of her sparse marbles.

Formerly she reigned ; upon her strong walls Victory extended her two iron wings. All the people of Asia besieged her hundred gates; and her great stairways descended toward the sea . . .

Empty now and forever silent, stone by stone, she dies, under the reverent moon, close to her old river, exhausted like herself.

And alone, in the midst of disaster, an elephant of bronze, still upright upon the summit of a broken doorway, tragically lifts its trunk to the stars.

THE CORONATION

Page 83.   . With the bronze voices of its twin towers, Notre-Dame announced the apotheosis ready of fulfilment. In the distance great cannon boomed; and flags bellied out, shivering, under the pride of the festival.

The Emperor bowed himself, bare-headed and with joined hands, and in the glare of torches the Pope appeared, holding in his fingers, which glittered with rings, the Crown bearing the Latin cross on its apex.

2 A

"My son!" said the Pontiff . . . then the organ was hushed. Over every bowed forehead ran a shiver, like the sudden beating of an immense wing;

And nothing could be heard, O triumphant Cæsar, in the nave where an august silence hovered, but an old woman, on her knees, weeping for her child.

AFFECTION

Page 84. I adore the indecisive — sounds, frail colours, everything which trembles, undulates, shimmers, and glistens, hair and eyes, water, leaves, silk, and the spirituality of slender forms.

Rhymes rubbing up against each other like turtledoves; smoke where dreams turn in spirals; the twilit room, where Her profile fades into darkness, and the caress of Her supernatural hands.

The heavenly hour of coaxing lips, the soul inclined as under a weight of delight, the soul which dies like a faded rose,

And some heart of chaste shadow, perfumed with mystery, where a mystic and solitary love, like the ruby flame of a hanging lamp, watches night and day.

Page 85. I dream of soft verses and intimate branchings and entwinings,
Of verses which brush against the soul like wings.

Of pale-hued verses whose fluid meaning streams wide,
As under the water streams Ophelia's hair.

Of silent verses, without rhythm and without plot,
Where the noiseless rhyme slips past like an oar.

Of verses of an ancient stuff, exhausted,
Impalpable like sound and cloud.

Of verses of Autumn evenings, enchanting the hours
With the feminine rite of minor syllables.

Of verses of evenings of love, enervated with verbena,
In which the soul — barely — exquisitely — feels a
        a caress.

And which, the whole length of nerves bathed in caress-
        ing waves,
Die forever in feline swoonings,
Like a perfume dissolved in a closed warmness.

Viols of gold and *pianissim' amorose.*

I dream of soft verses dying like roses.

GETTING READY THE REPAST

Page 88.   Quit your needle and your linen, my girl, the master
will soon be here.   Put the clear, flowered china, and
the bright glass, on the oak table with its new cloth
with the shining folds.   In the cup with the handle

which curves like a swan's neck, upon vine leaves, arrange your chosen fruits — peaches with their virgin velvet still upon them, heavy blue grapes mixed with grapes of gold ; and see that all the baskets are filled with nicely-cut bread. Then shut the doors and drive out the bees . . .

The sun burns outside, and the wall cooks. Close the shutters and make it almost dark, so that the room, plunged in shadow, is all perfumed with the fruits on the table. Now go and draw fresh water in the court, and above all, be careful that the pitcher, when you bring it back, keeps a light vapour, iced and slowly melting, for a long time upon its sides.

THE BUBBLE

Page 88.   In the court where the fowls are clucking, Bathyles, bending over a basin, puffs into a straw. With a great noise the soapy water froths, and boils, and overflows. The child, exhausting himself to no purpose, feels a salt bitterness on his lips. Happily, at last, there is the outline of a bubble. Conducted with art, it lengthens, widens, and finally rounds itself into a sparkling globe. The child continues to blow, and the bubble keeps on growing. It has the hundred colours of the prism and of dawn, and in its thin crystal sides are reflected the trees, the house, the road, and the horse. Ready to take flight, marvellous, it shines ! The child holds his breath, and the bubble oscillates, and gently rises — pale green and transparent pink — like a frail shining prodigy, into the air !

It rises . . . And suddenly, his soul still dazzled,
Bathyles seeks the vanished glory in vain.

PANNYRE OF THE GOLDEN HEELS

Page 89.   In the noisy room a silence falls . . . Pannyre of
the golden heels comes forward to dance. She is
entirely hidden in a veil of a thousand folds. With
a long, silver trill the flute first invites her; she starts
forward, intersects her steps, and with a slow movement of the arms, gives a bizarre rhythm to the sympathetic material, which stretches, undulates, bellies
and hollows, and at last spreads itself in a great whirlwind . . . And Pannyre becomes flower, flame,
butterfly! Every one is silent; eyes follow her in
ecstasy. Bit by bit she takes fire in the fury of the
dance. Always she turns: quick! quicker still!
The flame, in the glare of the golden torches, reels dis-
tractedly! . . . Then, sharply, in the middle of the
room, she stops; and the veil, twining about her in a
spiral, suspended in its course, calms its long folds, and
glued to her pointed breasts and polished sides, shows,
in a divine flash, as through silky and flowing water,
Pannyre standing naked.

WATTEAU

Page 92.   Above the great, dark woods, the shepherd's star
comes out . . . Groups upon the grass in the mist
. . . Pizzicati of violins . . . Hands linger in
hands, the sky on which the lovers gaze leaves a rose-
coloured reflection in the water; and in the misty
clearing which approaching night idealizes, between

Estelle and Cydalise, passes the enamoured shade of Watteau.

Watteau, ideal painter of the *Charming Fête*, your frail art was tender and gentle as a sigh, and you gave an unknown soul to Desire, placing it at the feet of Melancholy.

Your exquisite shepherds held canes of gold in their fingers; your shepherdesses, not without a somewhat haughty manner, rambled under the shade where fountains sang, in their dresses with the straight pleat behind.

Roses died in the warm, bluish air; hearts opened in the shade of the quiet garden, and lips, taking kisses from lips, united wistful love with the sweetness of things.

Pilgrims go to the Country of Ideals. . . . The golden galley abandons the shore; and the maiden at the prow, pensive, listens to the sound of a flute dying away in the distance of the crystal evening.

Oh! To depart with them on an evening of mystery! O Master, to live one evening in your enchanted dream! The sea is rose-coloured . . . A Summer breeze sighs, and when the ship approaches a silver shore

The moon rises softly over Cytherea.

A fan, waving unceasingly to the intimate rhythm of avowals, lifts the hair from the forehead with each movement. The shadow is soft . . . Everything rests. Agnes smiles; Leander places his violin upon his cloak; and over the scented dresses and over the hands of the lovers, along the soft branches, floats the divine soul of Watteau.

VERSAILLES

I

Page 94. O Versailles, why does the thought of you obsess me on this faded afternoon? The vehemence of Summer is passing, and the worn-out season is coming towards us.

I should like to see once more, for a whole calm day, your green-blue waters strewn with red leaves; and breathe again, on a gentle, golden evening, your beauty which is more touching at the decline of the year.

Here are your coned yews, and your fat-cheeked Tritons, your patterned gardens where Louis comes no more, and your pomp which proclaims plumes and helmets.

Like a great lily you are dying, noble and sad, without sound; the old water slips past the mouldy lips of your basins as softly as a sob in the night.

II

Page 94. Grand manner. Urbanity of ancient customs. High ceremonial. Endless reverences. Créqui, Fronsac, beautiful names glistening with satin. Ducal hands in old valenciennes lace.

Royal hands upon spinets. Anthems of bishops before Monseigneur the Dauphin. Gestures of the minuet and hearts of fine porcelain, and those graces which were called Austrian.

Princesses of the blood, whose state soul the centuries have steeped to the purest of castes. Great lords spangled with wit. Marquises of Sèvres china.

An entire world, gallant, lively, brave, exquisite and silly, with its slender sword at the angle for drawing, and, above all, the scorn of death, like a flower, at the lips.

III

Page 95. My steps have stirred up buried enchantments. O mirror of old Saxe in which the Past is reflected . . . Here the Queen, listening to Zémire and dreaming, fanned herself because the nights were warm.

O visions: panniers, powder and patches; and then, light as a perfume, beautiful as a smile, it is the air of old France which everything here breathes; and always this penetrating smell of box . . .

But what most seizes and crushes my heart, in the light of a long evening which gilds its agony, is the Great Trianon, solitary and kingly,

And its deserted stone stairway, where Autumn so gently, dreamily, lets fall his red hair upon the divinely sad water of the great canal.

IV

Page 96. The grove of Vertumnus is abandoned by the Graces. This shade which creeps from marble to marble, moaning, and steadies itself with a beautiful, feeble arm, is, alas! the mourning Genius of old races.

O Palace, supreme horizon of the terraces! Something of your beauty runs in our blood; and it is this which gives you an indescribable accent when a sublime sunset lights up your windows.

Glories of which you were for so many days the scene, souls glittering under the chandeliers. Golden evenings. Versailles . . . But already the sombre night is closing in.

And suddenly my heart tightens; for I hear, like a sinister battering ram striking against the walls of time, always the great, dull sound of black waters in the darkness.

LANDSCAPES

I

Page 96.   The air is of triple lightness. Under a sky of triple purity, the old market town, crumbling within its black walls, smiles, this clear winter morning, under its pebbles, at its familiar mountains which dream in the blue sky.

A flagstone set in the pavement speaks, after two thousand years, in obscure Latin of ancient funerals. Cæsar passed this way to gain his battles. A Spring bird sings upon an old wall.

Noisy, in the lacy shade of a tree, the sculptured fountain in its marble basin flings up four silver threads to sparkle in the sunshine.

And while, through a crowd of urchins, the yellow diligence turns into the principal street, the Signador's tower tosses out the hour, dreaming.

II

Page 97.   Pale and adroit, the watchmaker works quietly; lazily, with wide-open doors, the shops sleep; and the frankness of good-mornings is exchanged from one sidewalk to the other, as in old times.

Notary's sign and doctor's plate . . . A boy is watering donkeys at a well; and conducted by a nun, in symmetric lines, the small children are going to say their catechism.

All of a sudden, a ray of sunshine flung like an arrow starts a fresh, clear voice singing in a lane as dark as though it were a corridor.

Little brooks stream in a crowd from the mountain, and everywhere there is a noise of rushing water which flows from dawn with its forehead of silver until evening with its eyes of gold.

THE KITCHEN

Page 98. In the kitchen, where the scent of thyme floats, the return from market is like an evening after a day of booty. Pell-mell with the heavy meats, are heaped up leeks, radishes, garlands of onions, great violet cabbages, the red pumpkin, the glossy tomato, and the pale lemon. Like a great kite, the enormous and flat skate lies, dug into by a knife, with a scarlet wound. A hare with red fur, and with eyes like burst grapes, sprawls on the pavement. From a heap of oysters emptied out of a basket covered with sea-weed, comes the smell of the open and the freshness of waves. Quails, partridges with soft, slate-coloured stomachs, hang their broken necks, the beaks all covered with blood. It is a butcher's stall, vibrating with green fruits, vegetables, mother-of-pearl, clear silver, scales and feathers. A chunk of salmon bleeds, and, still alive, a great bronze lobster, bought at the port and flung by chance with the provisions, moves a broken feeler as he dies.

PROVINCIAL NOCTURNE

Page 99. The little, noiseless town sleeps soundly in the night.

In the old branching street lamps, the feeble gas is dying; but suddenly the moon comes out, and along the whole line of white houses the windows shine with silver.

The warm night fans itself all along the chestnut trees . . . the unhastening night, in which light is still floating. In the old parts of the town all is black and deserted. Lean on the old stone bridge, my soul, and breathe the good smell of the river.

The silence is so great that my heart shivers. Only the noise of my feet resounds on the pavement. The silence makes my heart tremble, and midnight strikes.

Along the great walls of a convent, leaves rustle in the wind. Schoolgirls . . . Orphans . . . Blue ribbons on tippets . . . It is the garden of the Ursulines.

Through the barred gate a breeze passes as gently as a sigh. And that star of quiet flames, over there, beyond the hornbeam hedges, seems a night-light of sapphire.

Oh! under the slate roofs, whitened by the moon, virgins, and their pure sleep in clear rooms, and their little round necks knotted with scapulars, and their sinless bodies in the whiteness of the beds!

Here one monotonous hour is followed by another monotonous hour, and peaceful innocence sleeps at the edge of life . . .

Infinitely sad and deserted under the electric moonlight, the historic square solemnly lines up its old houses of Parliament.

At the corner, a window is still lit up. A lamp is above, watching while everything sleeps. Every now and then, behind the thin stuff which dims the light, the shadow of a woman glides furtively.

The window opens a little; and the woman, poignant admission, wrings her beautiful, naked arms in the blue air . . .

O secret ardours of provincial nights! Hearts which burn! Disordered hair spread out! Beautiful breasts heavy with desire, kneaded by pale hands. Great beseeching appeals, and never heard!

I evoke you, O you, unknown mistresses, whose flesh is consumed like a wasted torch, who weep hopelessly over your beautiful bodies, and made for love

and by love devoured, you will be laid some evening
as virgins in the grave!

And my pensive soul, at the corner of the square,
stares always over at the window where the shadow
passes.

The frail curtain shakes in the wind . . . The
lamp goes out . . . One o'clock strikes. No one,
no one, no one.

FIRST ELEGY

To Albert Samain

Page 102. My dear Samain, it is to you that I write still.
This is the first time I send to death these lines which,
to-morrow, in Heaven, some old servitor of an eternal
hamlet will bring to you. Smile at me so that I
shall not weep. Say to me: "I am not as ill as you
think." Open my door again, dear friend. Cross
my threshold, and say to me as you enter: "Why
are you in mourning?" Come in further. You are
in Orthez. There is Bonheur. Put your hat on
that chair. You are thirsty? Here is blue water
from the well, and wine. My mother will come down
and say to you: "Samain . . ." And my dog will
lean his muzzle on your hand.

I talk. You smile with a serious smile. Time does
not exist. And you let me go on talking. Evening

comes. We walk in the yellow light which makes the end of the day like Autumn. We walk along the mountain stream. A hoarse pigeon complains softly in a blue-green poplar. I chatter. You still smile. Bonheur is silent. See the road, dark at Summer's end, see the shadow kneeling near the four o'clocks which deck the black thresholds where the blue smoke comes.

Your death changes nothing. The shade which you loved, in which you lived, in which you suffered, in which you sang, it is we who leave it, and you who keep it. Your light was born of this darkness which brings us to our knees on beautiful Summer evenings, when, under the black creepers, scenting God who passes and gives life to the grain, watch-dogs bark.

I do not regret your death. Others will put the laurel which is your right over the wrinkles of your forehead. For I, knowing you, I should fear to wound you. The glory of those who die uncrowned should not be hid from the sixteen-year-old children who will follow your bier, weeping over your lyre.

I do not regret your death. Your life is there. As the voice of the wind which rocks the lilacs does not die, but returns after many years to those same lilacs which we had thought faded, so your songs, my dear Samain, will come again to soothe those children with whom our thoughts are already teeming.

Like some antique shepherd whose flock weeps upon the bare hill, I should seek in vain upon your grave for something which I can take away. The salt would be eaten by the mountain sheep, and the wine would be drunk by those who have plundered you.

I dream of you. The day fades like that day when I saw you in my old country parlour. I dream of you. I dream of my native mountains. I dream of this Versailles where you took me, where we recited poems, sadly, and step by step. I dream of your friend, and I dream of your mother. I dream of those sheep who, waiting for death on the shores of the blue lake, bleat over their little bells.

I dream of you. I dream of the pure emptiness of the heavens. I dream of the endless water, of the brightness of fires. I dream of the dew which sparkles on the vines. I dream of you. I dream of myself. I dream of God.

REMY DE GOURMONT

Page 112. I have seen the portrait. The moon, pale and green, swam through the room; I had just waked up, and indistinct and ophidian visions still haunted me. Suspiciously, with feverish eyes, I looked about me. Was I in my room and in my bed? Perhaps. There, over the chimney, the mirror slowly changed its tint; its moon-green, its green of transparent water under willow trees, suddenly brightened and became more golden. One would have said that in the centre of the light, as it is also on the face of the moon, shadows were thrown which had the appearance of human features, while about the vague face a luminous undulation wound, like blond hair undone and floating.

Page 112. A church with flying buttresses, short and heavy, first attracted the inexperienced attention, and fixed it by the splendour of its beribboned Madonna. When the setting sun, shining into the oval niche, bathed it in light, the rubies and peridots of her tiara, the lepidolites and the topazes, starry aureole, shimmered with the brilliance of so many stars, and the face with the diamond eyes shone with ecstasy.

DREAM FIGURE

SEQUENCE

Page 123. The dearly beloved with the clear eyes appeared under the moon, under the ephemeral moon, mother of beautiful dreams. The misty blue light powdered her star-blossomed forehead with an ethereal dust, and her light hair floated in the air behind her springing steps : the chimera slept in the depths of her eyes. On the bare, delicate skin of her neck, the starry smiles of a rosary of pearls arranged in rows the reflections of their pale lightnings. About her wrists were identical bracelets, and her head bore the

2 B

crown, incrusted with the seven mystical stones, whose flames pierce the heart like knives, under the ephemeral moon, mother of beautiful dreams.

Page 126.   Hypocritical flower,
                 Flower of silence.

Page 126.   Rose with the black eyes, mirror of your nothing-ness, rose with the black eyes, cause us to believe in mystery, hypocritical flower, flower of silence . . .

Rose, colour of silver, censor of our dreams, rose, colour of silver, take our hearts and make smoke of them, hypocritical flower, flower of silence . . .

Wine-coloured rose, flower of arbours and cellars, wine-coloured rose, mad alcohols gambol in your breath; whisper to us the horror of love, hypocritical flower, flower of silence.

Page 127.   Rose of silk paper. Rose the colour of dawn, the colour of time, the colour of nothing. Flesh-coloured rose. Rose of the virginal heart. Rose, the colour of evening. Blue rose, iris-coloured rose. Carbuncle rose, rose blossomed on the black forehead of the dragon.

Page 127.   Transparent rose, colour of clear springs spouting up among grasses, transparent rose, Hylas is dead of having loved your eyes, hypocritical flower, flower of silence.

Papal rose, rose watered by the hands which bless the world, papal rose, your golden heart is of copper, and the tears which fall in pearls upon your worthless petals are the tears of Christ, hypocritical flower, flower of silence.
Hypocritical flower,
Flower of silence.

Page 128. I prefer you to the most gallant hearts, dead hearts, hearts of other days . . .
Jonquils, of which the pure eyelashes of so many blond girls are made . . .
Aconite, flower helmeted with poison, warrior of the raven's wing . . .
Campanulas, little enamoured bells that the Spring tinkles . . .
Four-o'clock who knocked at my door, it was midnight, I opened my door to the Four-o'clock, and her eyes bloomed in the darkness . . .
Lavender, little serious one, perfume of virtue . . . shirts by the dozen in oaken wardrobes, lavender not too mischievous and so tender . . .
Alyssum, whose beautiful soul entirely evaporates in song . . .

Page 128. Birch, shiver of the bather in the ocean of wild grasses, while the wind plays with your pale hair . . .
Mountain-ash, fringed parasol, coral seeds upon the golden necks of gypsies . . .

Larch, lady of sad thoughts, parable leaning upon the ruin of a wall, the silver spiders have spun their webs in your ears . . .

Horse-chestnut, court lady in crinoline, lady in a dress embroidered with trefoils and feathers, lady, useless and beautiful.

ASCENSION

Page 130. An evening in the deserted heather with my Beloved smiling and weary . . . O Sun, like a picked flower your heavy head dies and falls, pale, to the horizon. Ah, if I were with my weary Beloved, one evening in the deserted heather !

Among meadow-sweet and reeds, the tree-frogs cried their love songs. Beetles climbed up the horse-tails. Blue jays made the frail branches bend. One heard the love cries of the tree-frogs among the meadow-sweet.

Up above, at the threshold of a half-open door, a dog wails to the new-risen and green moon which gives a little joy to the blind sky ; a cow about to be milked moves and lows, a dog wails to the new-risen and green moon, up above, at the threshold of a half-open door.

While we climb to the curve of the summit with restless and smiling souls, Vision, remaining halfway up, sits thoughtfully, her head in her hands ; and we mount to the summit, we climb smiling, with restless souls.

Page 131. Somewhere in the mists there is an island, and on the island a castle, and in the castle a great hall lit by a small lamp, and in the great hall are people who wait. For what do they wait? They do not know. They wait for some one to knock at the door, they wait for the lamp to go out, they await Fear, they await Death. They speak; yes, they say words which trouble the silence for a moment, then they listen again, leaving their sentences unfinished, their gestures interrupted. They listen, they wait. It will not come perhaps? Oh, it will come! It always comes. It is late, perhaps it will not come until to-morrow. And the people assembled in the great hall, under the little lamp, smile and hope. Some one knocks. And that is all; the whole of a life, the whole of life.

DEDICATION

Page 132. O travellers, who journey dreaming, dreaming perhaps of rose-coloured distances, while the dust and sunlight of arid spaces have burnt your bare arms and your wavering souls, O travellers, who journey dreaming, dreaming perhaps of rose-coloured distances!

Here is the road which leads to the mountain, here is the clear spring where balsams grow, here is the wood full of shadow and anemones, here are pines, here is peace, here are the lofty summits, here is the road which leads to the mountain, here is the clear spring where balsams grow!

O travellers, who journey dreaming, follow the voice which calls you to the heavens: the foliage of the trees is sweet as honey, and women with pure hearts become more beautiful there. O travellers, who journey dreaming, follow the voice which calls you to the heavens.

AGATHA

Page 133.   Jewel found among Sicilian stones, Agatha, virgin sold to the love-dealers, Agatha, victorious over necklaces and rings, of the seven magic ubies and the three moonstones, Agatha, rejoiced by the fire of red irons as an almond-tree by the gentle rains of Autumn, Agatha, embalmed by a young angel with purple vestments, Agatha, stone and iron, Agatha, gold and silver, Agatha of the order of Malta, Saint Agatha, put fire into our blood.

COLETTE

Page 134.   Grievous beauty hidden in prayer, Colette, severe to your heart and more severe to your flesh, Colette, prisoner in bitter cloisters where the necklaces of love are chains of iron, Colette who lay down upon the ground to die, Colette who after her death remained fresh as a stone, Saint Colette, cause our hearts to become as austere as stones.

JEANNE

Page 134.   Shepherdess born in Lorraine, Jeanne who tended sheep in a coarse cotton dress, and who wept at the

miseries of the people of France, and who conducted
the King to Rheims amid lances, Jeanne who was a
bow, a cross, a sword, a heart, and a lance, Jeanne
whom the people loved as they do father and mother,
Jeanne, wounded and taken, and thrown into a
dungeon by the English, Jeanne, burnt at Rouen
by the English, Jeanne, like to an angel in anger,
Jeanne d'Arc, put much anger into our hearts.

URSULA

Page 135.   Griffin of the North, sacred beast come in the blue
light of a boreal dream, Ursula, snow-flake drunk by
the lips of Jesus, Ursula, red star to the purple tulip,
Ursula, sister of so many innocent hearts, whose
bloody head smoulders like a carbuncle in the circle
of the arch, Ursula, ship, sail, oar and tempest,
Ursula, flown away upon the back of a white bird,
Saint Ursula, bear our hearts away to the snows.

HER HAIR

Page 136.   Simone, there is a great mystery in the forest of
your hair.

You savour of hay, you savour of stones against
which animals have leaned; you savour of leather,
you savour of grain when it has just been winnowed;
you savour of wood, you savour of bread which is
brought in the morning; you savour of flowers which
have sprung up along an abandoned wall; you savour
of brambles, you savour of ivy washed by the rain;
you savour of rushes and bracken which is mown

at the fall of night; you savour of holly, you savour of moss, you savour of red and dying grass which seeds itself in the shade of hedges; you savour of nettles and broom, you savour of clover, you savour of milk; you savour of fennel and anise; you savour of nuts; you savour of fruits which are very ripe and being picked; you savour of the willow and the linden when their leaves are full of flowers; you savour of honey, you savour of life which walks the fields; you savour of the ground and the river; you savour of love, you savour of fire.

Simone, there is a great mystery in the forest of your hair.

THE HOLLY

Page 137. Simone, the sunshine laughs upon the holly leaves: April has come back to play with us.

Upon his shoulders he carries baskets of flowers which he gives to the hawthorns, to the chestnuts, and to the willows;

He sows them one by one in the grass of the fields, upon the banks of brooks, ponds, and ditches;

He keeps the jonquils for the water, the periwinkles for the woods, in those places which are overhung by branches;

He throws violets into the shade under briars, where his naked foot fearlessly hides them and thrusts them in.

To all the fields he gives Easter daisies, and primroses which have necklaces of little bells.

In the forests, all along the cool paths, he lets fall lilies-of-the-valley with anemones.

He plants irises upon the roofs of houses, and in our garden, Simone, where it is so pleasant,

He will scatter columbines and pansies, hyacinths, and the good smell of wallflowers.

THE FOG

Page 138.   Simone, put on your cloak and your great, black sabots, we will go as in a boat through the fog.

We will go to islands of beauty where the women are beautiful like trees and naked like souls; we will go to islands where men are gentle like lions, with long, red hair. Come, the uncreated world awaits our dream for its laws, its joys, for its gods who make the seed blossom, and the wind which makes the leaves shine and rustle. Come, the innocent world will soon rise from a grave.

Simone, put on your cloak and your great, black sabots, we will go as in a boat through the fog.

We will go to islands where there are mountains from which can be seen peaceful stretches of country, with happy animals cropping the grass, shepherds who look like willow-trees, and sheaves being lifted into carts with forks. It is still sunlight, and the sheep stop near the stable, before the gate of the garden which smells of burnet, tarragon, and thyme.

Simone, put on your cloak and your great, black sabots, and we will go as in a boat through the fog.

THE DEAD LEAVES

Page 140.   Simone, let us go to the wood; the leaves have fallen; they cover the moss, the stones, and the paths.

Simone, do you like the sound of steps upon dead leaves?

They have such soft colours, such grave tints, they are such frail waifs upon the earth.

Simone, do you like the sound of steps upon dead leaves?

They have such a mournful look at twilight, they cry so tenderly when the wind tumbles them about.

Simone, do you like the sound of steps upon dead leaves?

When they are crushed under foot, they lament like souls, they make a noise of wings or of women's dresses.

Simone, do you like the sound of steps upon dead leaves?

Come : some day we shall be poor dead leaves.
Come : the night is already falling and the wind bears us away.

Simone, do you like the sound of steps upon dead leaves?

THE RIVER

Page 141. Simone, the river sings an ingenuous tune, come, we will go among the rushes and the water-hemlocks ; it is noon : the men have quitted their carts, and I — I shall see your naked foot in the clear water.

The river is the mother of fishes and flowers, of trees, of birds, of scents, of colours ;

She gives drink to the birds who have eaten their grain and who are about to fly to a distant country ;

She gives drink to the blue flies with green stomachs, and the water-spiders who row like galley-slaves ;

The river is the mother of the fish : she gives them worms, grass, air, and ozone;

She gives them love; she gives them wings to follow the shadows of their females to the ends of the earth.

The river is the mother of flowers, of rainbows, of everything which is made of water and a little sunshine.

She nourishes the French grass and the hay, and the meadow-sweet which has the perfume of honey, and the mullens

Which have leaves as soft as the down of birds; she nourishes the corn, the clover, and the reeds;

She nourishes the hemp, she nourishes the flax, she nourishes the oats, the barley, and the buckwheat;

She nourishes the rye, the osiers and the appletrees; she nourishes the willows and the great poplars.

The river is the mother of forests : from her bed the beautiful oaks have drawn the pure water of their veins.

The river fertilizes the sky: when the rain falls
it is the river drawn up into the sky and falling back;

The river is a very powerful and very pure mother,
the river is the mother of all nature.

Simone, the river sings an ingenuous tune, come,
we will go among the rushes and the water-hemlocks,
it is noon: the men have quitted their carts, and I —
I shall see your naked foot in the clear water.

THE ORCHARD

Page 143.   Simone, let us go to the orchard, with a wicker
basket. As we go into the orchard we will say to
our apple-trees: This is the season of apples. Let
us go to the orchard, Simone, let us go to the orchard.

The apple-trees are full of wasps, for the apples
are very ripe: there is a great murmuring about the
old *doux-aux-vêpes.* The apple-trees are full of
apples, let us go to the orchard, Simone, let us go to
the orchard.

We will pick the *calville,* the *pigeonnet,* and the
pippin, and also cider-apples which are a little taste-
less. This is the season of apples, let us go to the
orchard, Simone, let us go to the orchard.

You will have the smell of apples on your dress
and on your hands, and your hair will be full of the

sweet perfume of Autumn. The apple-trees are full
of apples, let us go to the orchard, Simone, let us go
to the orchard.

Simone, you will be my orchard and my apple-
tree of the *doux-aux-vêpes*; Simone, drive the wasps
away from your heart and my orchard. This is
the season of apples, let us go to the orchard, Simone,
let us go to the orchard.

AUTUMN SONG

Page 144.   Come, my Dear, come, it is Autumn, damp and
monotonous Autumn, but the leaves of the cherry-
trees and the ripe fruit of the sweet-briars are red
like kisses. Come, my Dear, come, it is Autumn.

Come, my Dear, come, the rude Autumn draws
his mantle closer about him and shivers, but the
sunshine is pleasant; in the air which is as soft as
your heart, the mist cradles its languor. Come, my
Dear, come, it is Autumn.

Come, my Dear, the Autumn wind sobs like a
person. And in the gaping thickets the brambles
writhe their perverse arms, but the oaks are always
green. Come, my Dear, come, it is Autumn.

Come, my Dear, the Autumn wind scolds harshly
and lectures us, words whistle down the paths, but

the gentle sound of wood-pigeons' wings can be heard in the brush. Come, my Dear, come, it is Autumn.

Come, my Dear, the melancholy Autumn abandons itself to the arms of Winter, but the grass of Summer still grows, and the last heather is sweet, and one thinks one sees the blossoming of the moss. Come, my Dear, come, it is Autumn.

Come, my Dear, come, it is Autumn, the poplars shiver, all bare, but their foliage is not dead; puffing out its gold-coloured dress, it dances, it dances, it still dances. Come, my Dear, come, it is Autumn.

HENRI DE RÉGNIER

Page 158.   I dreamt that these verses should be like those flowers which the hands of master carvers twine about golden vases of cunning dimensions.

Page 164.   The water of the springs where, in the evening, falls the universal death of roses, was happy at the sight of us combing our tawny hair.

A little of this water — our mirrors!

The fountains were loud in the woods of Moonlight and Night; crystal in which is reflected and isolated some star fled from the sky . . .

The water in our amphoræ is dried up.

The stairways curve their balustrades . . .
Oh, cold feet upon pavements!
The doors and the high chambers for the naked
sleep of Psyches . . .

The oil is coagulated at the bottom of the lamps!

MAD AUTUMN

Page 165. Mad Autumn exhausts its roses in garlands, pale
like lips and smiles; and the misery is to have lived
among roses, masks, vanities, and deliriums!

From new leather bottles, laughing Ægypans drank
old wine in which the fire of Summer still lives; vines
puffed out the clear amber of their maturity, their
bunches fell into the water, grape by grape.

Roses decorated cups, ivy-twined staffs, and the
skirts of youthful dresses; in the shade, the souls
of fountains wept; the vine-branches about the
staffs seemed the blood of flaming torches.

Mad Autumn exhausts itself in supreme garlands,
red-haired satyrs prowl through the woods, empty
masks are hung in garlands, and the wind laughs
through the holes of their voiceless mouths.

THE RIM OF THE MEDAL

Page 166. One evening, at the meeting of the roads in the forest — one evening, in the wind, with my shadow — one evening, weary of the cinders of altars and years, uncertain of the predestined hours, I sat down.

The roads led toward days, and I could still go with them, and always toward places, waters, and dreams, always, until the day when Death, with magical and patient hands, should have closed my eyes with the seal of her peaceful and golden flower.

Roads of tall oaks and solitude, your rough stone is difficult to weariness, your pebbles hard for tired feet, and at each step I should see the wounds of my past still bleeding; and your haughty oaks mutter in the harsh wind, and I am tired.

Road of clear birches which shed their leaves and tremble, pale like the shame of your pale travellers who lose their way in your sticky mud-holes, and go together and turn away so as not to see one another face to face; road of mud and oozing water, the wind whispers its lamentations to your leaves, the great silver marshes of moons and hoar-frost stagnate in the twilight at the ends of your tracks, and Dulness takes those by the hand who would follow you.

Road of smooth ash trees and of thin sands, where the wind effaces the footsteps and desires one to

2 C

forget and one goes as it goes, from tree to tree, your honey flowers have the colour of the gold of the sands, your curve is such that one can hardly see where one turns; the town to which you lead is kind to strangers and my steps upon the thresholds of its doors would be pleasant, had they not remained along another life where my weeping Hopes watch dead Shadows.

I will not go toward your oaks, nor beside your birches and ash trees, nor toward your sunshine, your towns, and your waters, O roads! I hear the steps of my bleeding past coming, the steps that I believed dead, alas! but which come again, and seem to precede me in your echoes, O roads; you, the easy — you, the shameful — you, the disdainful — and I listen to the wind, companion of my vain wanderings, who walks and weeps under the oaks.

O my soul, evening hangs sadly over yesterday,
O my soul, evening hangs gloomily over to-morrow,
O my soul, evening hangs solemnly over you!

SOME ONE DREAMS OF DAWN AND SHADOW

Page 169. "I thought I saw my Sorrow standing under the willows. I thought I saw her — said she softly — standing near the gentle brook of my thoughts, the same which, one whole evening, flowed past with the current, roses floating upon them, waifs from the bouquet of wounded hours. Time passes with passed waters; she thought with my thoughts so long that the bluish woods were mauve, then darker, and black.''

I thought I saw my Sorrow — said he — and I did see her — said he softly — she was naked, sitting in the most silent grotto of my inmost thoughts; she was there, the gloomy dream of frozen waters, the anxiety of anxious stalactites, the weight of rocks as heavy as time, the pain of porphyries red like blood; she was there, silent, sitting in the depth of my silence. And naked as a person is who thinks to himself.

Page 170. Ripe with shadows and dreams, in their skins from which the golden juice is oozing, the fruits of the past hang and fall, one by one, and one again, in the orchard of dream and shadow.

The soft twilight fades, and revives from time to time on a pale ray of sunshine through the trees, and the moment comes when, one by one, tree by tree, the wind touches the beautiful fruits which swing and knock their warm, pale golds, and still tremble when the wind has passed and the darkness is quiet, and fall, one by one, and one again.

Sorrow has ripened her fruits of shadow in the quiet orchards of our dreams, where the past sleeps, starts, and sleeps again, to the sound of ripe fruits falling through the forgetfulness of death, one by one, and one again.

THE FAUN WITH THE MIRROR

Page 172. Sorrow, I have built your house, and the trees
mingle their chequering with the stains of your
marbles. Sorrow, I have built your green and black
palace, where the yew of mourning mingles with the
myrtles of hope; in the crystal panes of your windows are reflected the gardens, with balustrades and
waters whose exactness frames the sky; the dismal
echo converses with solitude who seeks herself among
the cypresses; farther off is silence and all the forest,
the rude life, and the prowling wind, the lush grass
on which is printed, according to what thing passes,
an animal shoe in place of a divine foot; farther off
is the Satyr; and still farther, the God of the Woods
and the Nymph, who, naked, inhabits the solitary
fountains where, near the Thessalian waters, the
Centaur nicks the pebbles in kicking; and then, grey
sands after red sands, the monsters of Desire, the
monsters of the Flesh, and beyond the arid beach is
the Sea. Sorrow, I have built your house, and the
trees have mottled the crystals of your basins like a
marble; the white swan sees its black shadow in the
water, as pale Joy sees in the lake of my memory her
silver wings dimmed by a twilight through which
her naked face, recoiling from her, makes signs to her
across the forever that she is dead; and I, who have
come in without shutting the door, I am afraid in the
darkness of some hand on the key; and I walk from
room to room, and I have veiled my dreams not to see
myself in them any more; but, from beyond, I still

feel shadows dogging my footsteps; and the crystal
which tinkles, and the watered silk which my per-
petually-weary hand crumples, warn my anguish, for
I hear in the hypocritical, sleeping chandelier the
sound of silver water laughing in golden flowers, and
the dripping of antique fountains where Narcissus
drank, lips pressed to his own lips, for which the spring
laughed at the anxious drinker; and I cursed my
mouth, and I cursed my eyes, for having seen the
warm skin and touched the cold water, and when
my fingers again wrinkle the stiff stuff, I hear, out of
my gossiping past which will not be still, the leaves
and the wind of the old forest; and I walk among
the solitary rooms where some one speaks with a
pretence of being silent, for my life has the eyes of a
sister who is not dead, and I am afraid, when I enter,
of seeing from the threshold of the door some laughing
and ghostly monster come from the shadow with the
smell of the woods on his naked hide, some Faun who
still has mud, and grass, and leaves, sticking to his resonant shoes, and of seeing him, in the silent room, dancing upon the polished floor and laughing to himself in
the mirrors!

THE VASE

Page 175.   My heavy hammer rang in the light air; I saw the
river and the orchard, the field, and as far as the
woods, beneath the sky growing bluer hour by hour,
then rose and mauve in the twilight; then I stood up
straight and stretched myself, happy in the task
of the hours, numb with having crouched from dawn

till twilight before the block of marble upon which I
cut out the sides of the vase, still in its shell, that my
ponderous hammer struck, stressing the clear morning and the good day, happy at being resonant in the
light air.

The vase took shape in the worked stone. Slender
and pure, it had grown larger, still unformed in its
slenderness, and I waited, with idle and unquiet
hands, for days, turning my head to the left, to the
right, at the slightest sound, without polishing the
belly farther or lifting the hammer. The water ran
from the spring as though breathless. In the silence,
I heard the fruits of the orchard trees falling, one by
one, from branch to branch; I breathed a heralding
perfume of distant flowers on the wind; often I
thought that some one spoke low, and one day that I
dreamed — not sleeping — I heard, beyond the fields
and the river, the playing of flutes.

Still another day, between the ochre and gold
leaves of the woods, I saw a faun with shaggy yellow
legs dancing; I caught sight of him also, another
time, coming out of the wood, along the road, and
sitting down upon a stump to take a butterfly from
one of his horns.

Another time, a centaur crossed the river swim-
ming, the water streamed from his man's skin and
his horse's coat; he advanced a few steps into the
reeds, snuffed the wind, whinneyed, and crossed back

over the water; the next day I saw the prints of his hoofs stamped in the grass.

Naked women passed carrying baskets and sheaves, very far off, quite at the other end of the plain. One morning I found three at the spring, and one of them spoke to me. She was naked. She said to me: "Carve the stone after the form of my body in your thoughts, and make my bright face smile in the marble block; listen all round you to the hours danced by my sisters, whose circle winds itself, interlaced, and revolves and sings and unwinds."

And I felt her warm mouth upon my cheek.

Then the vast orchard, and the woods, and the plain, shivered to a strange noise, and the spring ran faster, with a laugh in its waters; the three Nymphs standing near the three reeds took one another by the hand and danced; red-haired fauns came out of the wood in troupes, and voices sang beyond the trees of the orchard, with flutes awake in the light air. The ground echoed to the gallop of centaurs; they came from the depths of the resonant horizon, and one saw lame satyrs, stung by bees, sitting on the rushing cruppers, holding twisted staves and big-bellied leather bottles; hairy mouths and vermillion lips kissed each other, and the immense and frenzied circle — heavy hoofs, light feet, fleeces, cruppers, tunics — turned wildly about me, who, grave while it went on, carved on the rounded sides of the vase the whirl of the forces of life.

From the perfume sent out by the ripe earth, an intoxication mounted through my thoughts, and in the smell of fruits and crushed grapes, in the shock of hoofs and the stamping of heels, in the fallow odour of goats and stallions, under the breeze of the circle and the hail of laughter, I carved upon the marble what I heard humming; and amidst the hot flesh and the warm exhalations, neighings of muzzles or murmurings of lips, I felt, loving or savage, upon my hands, the breath of nostrils or the kisses of mouths.

Twilight came and I turned my head.

My intoxication was dead with the accomplished task; and upon its pedestal, at last, from foot to handles, the great vase stood up naked in the silence, and carved in a spiral about its living marble, the dispersed circle, of which a feeble wind brought the echo of the vanished noise, turned, with its goats, its gods, its naked women, its rearing centaurs, and its nimble fauns, silently round the side, while alone forever in the gloomy night, I cursed the dawn and wept toward the darkness.

FOR THE GATE OF THE WARRIORS

Page 179.   High gate! Never fear the darkness, leave open your door of hard bronze and your door of iron. They have thrown your keys into the cistern. Be forever cursed if fear closes you; and, as with a two-edged knife, cut the fist from every hand which would shut you; for under your sombre arch which resounded to their footsteps, men have passed who do not draw back, and Victory, still ready and panting, walked in the midst of them, naked in her golden wings, and guided them with the calm gesture of her sword; and her ardent purple kiss upon their lips bled, and the trumpets thrilled to the roses of their mouths, murmur of copper and of savage bees! Drunken swarm of war in hives of armour, go and pluck death upon the flower of ripe flesh; and if you come back to your native town, may one be able to trace when they shall have passed, Victory, under your wings, the mark of bright blood from their red soles on the marble stones of my threshold.

FOR THE GATE OF THE MERCHANTS

Page 180.   Be blessed, black portal, which we saluted in entering! The strong coffers balanced on the backs of asses; to display them in the courtyards we brought what one fashions by night, what one embroiders by day, the bright pendant, and the woven stuff. The oldest among us carried a caduceus,* he was the scrupulous master of barters and traffics; and the humpbacked gourd and strange pearls were mingled together in our dusty hands; and each one, purveyor of provisions or merchant of perfumes, emptied his baskets and swelled his wallet; for every

---

* Mercury's wand. Mercury was the god of commerce, hence of merchants.

buyer gives way to the gesture which catches him
by the hem of his robe or the tail of his cloak. The
smallest ones climbed on high stools, and the gentlest
as well as the most crafty counted and recounted their
piles of gold as they left; and each one, — that
the highwaymen on the watch for coin should not
wait for him in the shadow of the hedges in the
deserted road, O Gate! that a god should give us
rapid steps — each one, without looking at the one
who follows him, nails a copper piece upon your
stone sill.

FOR THE GATE OF THE COMEDIANS

Page 181.   The chariot stops at the angle of my wall. The
evening is fine, the sky is blue, the grain is ripe;
about the fountain the Nymph turns and dances;
the Faun laughs; mysterious Summer brings back,
at its hour, the wandering troop, and the old chariot,
and those whose acting, by means of masks and
paint, impersonates upon the trestle on which their
naked feet rest, the popular fable or the ingenuous
myth, and the divine, human, and monstrous story
which, in the mirror of the fountain, at the bottom
of deep grottoes, with bounds and cries and laughs,
the silvery Dryad and the yellow Satyr take up again,
from age to age, in the shade of the great woods.
Come! the moment is propitious and the crowd is
silent; already expectation smiles in the bright
eyes of children and gentle old men, and through
my gate, which, for you, will open wide, hospitable
and gay and heavy with garlands, I see you who

come, a rose in your hand, with your bright cloaks and your painted faces, and, smiling, each one before entering puts her foot up on the stone and laces her buskin.

FOR THE GATE WHICH GOES DOWN TO THE SEA

Page 182.   I, the Keeper of the poop, and the Watcher at the prow, who have known the buffet of waves on my cheek, the wind shaking out her hair across the foam, the clear water of the amphora and the ashes of the urn, and, silent brilliance or vermillion flame, the torch which starts up or the lamp which watches, the stair of the palace or the threshold of the ruin, and the welcome of the eyes of dawn, and the exile of the eyes of darkness, and the love which smiles and the love which weeps, and the cloak without holes which the wind shreds to tatters, and the ripe fruit bleeding, and the head cut off at the stroke of the bill-hook or the flight of the sword, and, vagrant of winds and courses and waves, of the marine race and the shock of gallops, I who keep always the noise and the murmur of the shepherd's horn and the rower's song, here am I, returned from great, distant countries of stone and of water, and always alone in my destiny and naked, still standing upright at the impetuous prow which snorts in the foam; and I shall enter burnt with joy and the sun, rearing keel and spreading yard, with the great pale gold and bright silver birds. I shall enter by the Gate which opens on the Sea!

ODELETTE I

Page 184. A little reed has sufficed me to make the tall grass rustle, and the whole meadow, and the gentle willows, and the singing brook as well; a little reed has sufficed me to make the forest sing.

Those who pass have heard it in the depths of the evening, in their thoughts, in the silence and in the wind, clear or lost, near or far . . . Those who pass listening to their thoughts in the depths of themselves will hear it still, and hear it always singing.

It has sufficed me, this little reed gathered at the spring where Love comes sometimes to mirror his grave, weeping face, to make those who pass weep, and to make the grass tremble and the water rustle, and I have made the whole forest sing in the breath of a reed.

ODE III

Page 185. I have known you, dear naked Shade, with your hair heavy with sunlight and pale gold, with your smiling mouth and your sweet flesh. From my most distant days beyond, you have come, at the ends of old roads of corn and mosses, along meadows, beside woods, when I followed the path and the brook, happy in the clear brook and the fresh pathway, and in my hands, between my fingers, the flower gathered in the thick grass was all damp with dew and trembling with the gold of a resting bee. At the

April season when the reeds sang of themselves at
the slightest breeze, near waters and fountains, I
knew you, once, sitting upon the threshold of the
porch of Life and of Dream and of the Year — you,
who, from the threshold, plaited coronals and
watched the coming of dawn.

I have seen you again, dear naked Shade, with
your hair reddened with ruddy gold, solemn with all
the weight of its Autumn; the old East wind weeps
in the hedges, heavy with wandering, and with trailing wing; the vine loosens itself from the trunk as
it unwinds, and the earth crumbles from the slope
which holds it; Joy is brief, and the hour passes, and
each one walks toward another which draws back,
and the flower of dawn is fruit at twilight, and the
golden fruit of evening is ashes in the night.

I saw you again, you were naked, as at the dawn
when I came by the road of the corn, I who return to
you by the stubble road, with the trembling evening,
and the steps of Autumn, to the echoes of my life
when Spring was laughing. What will you put in
the hands which return holds out to you? For I
have lost the obolus, and the ring, and the key, and
the flower crown of hope, from which I felt the rose
and the laurel fall, petal by petal; the opal is shat-
tered in the unset ring, and again my voice hesitates
to pray to you, for forever standing, finger on mouth,
as though to listen to the echo of time which flies,
your obstinate silence, patient and austere, watches
the darkness come and weeps to the night.

Page 190. I pretended that Gods had spoken to me; this one streaming with seaweed and water, this other weighed down with bunches of grapes and corn, this other winged, wild and beautiful in his stature of naked flesh, and this one always veiled, and this other again, who picks heartsease and hemlock, singing, and who winds two twisting serpents about his golden staff, others still . . .

Then I said: Here are flutes and baskets, let us eat fruits; let us listen to the singing of the bees and the humble sound of green osiers being plaited or reeds being cut.

Again I said: Listen, listen, there is some one behind the echo, standing upright amid the universal life, who carries the double bow and the double torch, and who is ourselves divinely . . .

Invisible face! I have engraved you upon medals of silver, mellow like the pale dawn; of gold, blazing like the sun; of bronze, dark like night; I have them of every metal, those which sing clear like joy, those which toll heavily like glory, like love, like death; and I have made the most beautiful of fine clay, dry and fragile.

One by one, you counted them, smiling, and you said: He is clever; and you passed on, smiling.

Not one of you saw that my hands trembled with tenderness, that the whole great terrestrial dream lived in me to live in them, that I engraved upon the sacred metals my Gods, and that they were the living face of what we have felt in roses, in water, in wind, in the forest and the sea, in everything, in our own flesh, and that they are divinely ourselves.

THE SPINNER

Page 192.   Spinner! The shadow is warm and bluish. A bee buzzes heavily in the sleeping sunlight, and your wheel mingles with this golden and winged humming which slows up little by little, and sleeps. It is late. It is evening. The grapes hang on the trellis, their clusters are ripe for the swarm which sucks at them, but to gather them to-morrow, before dawn comes and the cock wakes up, I must still round with my palm and fashion with my thumb in the obedient and soft clay this amphora which swells between my indistinct hands, while my labour hears all about it your wheel imitating the harsh buzzing of some invisible wasp loose in the night.

MARINE ODE

Page 193.   I hear the sea murmur in the distance when the wind in the pines, often, brings its harsh and bitter sound, which stuns, coos, or whistles, through the pines, red against the clear sky . . .

Sometimes its sinuous, supple voice seems to creep into the ear, then to recoil even more softly into the depths of the twilight, and then it is silent for days as though sleeping with the wind, and I forget it . . . but one morning it begins again with the surge and the tide, louder, more despairing, and I hear it.

It is a sound of water which suffers and scolds and laments behind the trees without our seeing it, calm or foaming, according to whether the sunset bleeds or blushes, dies blazing, or fades coolly away . . .

Without this great murmur which grows or ceases, and rolls or rocks my hours, each one, and my thoughts — without it, this crude and cracked country, swelled and humped up here and there by a yellow hillock where roses grow with sparse, sickly, hanging flowers — without it, this bitter and morose place, where I can only see a forlorn horizon of solitude and silence, would be too sad for my thought.

For I am alone, you see.   All of Life still calls me to its past which laughs and cries by a thousand eloquent mouths, behind me, over there, with hands stretched out, standing upright and naked; and I, lying upon the ground which is so hard to my bleeding nails, I have only a little clay to carve my quivering dream and make its fragile form eternal — nothing else to fashion my melodious medals, in the ochrous glaze of which I know how to make the full face of shadow or the profile of light, Sorrow smile or Beauty weep . . .

But in my soul afar, love mutters or coos like the
sea, over there, behind the red pines.

BATTLE SCENE

Page 195. He is booted in leather and cuirassed with bronze.
He stands upright in the smoke, and over his hip
floats the knot of the white scarf from which his
sword hangs. His glove is crumpled up by the gesture of his hand.

His foot rests upon the hillock where in the black
ground the flaming grenade opens a red gash, and the
flash of the cannon empurples his rude and fresh
Burgundian face with the horsehair wig.

All about him, everywhere, confused and micro-
scopic, the fight goes on, hesitates, shifts, holds its
ground — skirmishes, mêlée and carnage and noble
deed.

And the naïve painter who enlarged his size, was
no doubt praised, in those days, for having made his
hero, all by himself, larger than the battle.

THE MONKEY

Page 196. With her paroquet, her dog, and her negress, who
holds out her dressing-gown and dries the water of
the bath on her body which, whiter under the black
hand, bends its suppleness where the throat rises,

2 D

She has caused to be painted also, to show her tenderness, for libertine humour, or jesting caprice, the life-like portrait of her African monkey, who crunches a nutmeg and scratches his buttock.

Very grave, nearly a man and slyly a monkey, hairy, bald, attentive, he picks his nut, and looks all about, sitting up;

And his bare, snub-nosed face in which the eyes move sneeringly, contracts in a grimace, and wrinkles up his green and yellow turban in which a red plume quivers.

THE AMATEUR

Page 197.　　In his calm manor, between the Tille and the Ouche, in the country of Burgundy where the vine flourishes, he has lived tranquil like a ripened grape. For him wine has flowed from uncorked bottles.

Friend of nature and particular of palate, he courted his muse, and left in writing, poems, madrigals, epistles, pot-pourri, and dusty parchments to bear witness to his stock.

If he walked in the street in Dijon in his horse-hair periwig, leaning on his malacca cane, the Élite of the town and the members of Parliament

Saluted Monsieur le Chevalier from a distance, less for his name, his fields, his vine, and his plantation, than for having received three letters from Voltaire.

THE PORCELAIN CLOCK

Page 198. The garden laughs to the river and the river sighs with the eternal regret of his bank which he is leaving, the wistaria hangs down and leans toward him, the lilac is reflected and the jasmine is mirrored there.

The bindweed darts forward and the ivy stretches out; a new-sprouted bud is a flower to-day; heliotrope perfumes the darkness, and each night another lily half opens for dawn to admire it;

And in the house, bright with tapestries, a flowered porcelain clock outlines its rockwork where Love decorates himself with garlands,

And the whole fresh nosegay with which the garden honours itself, survives in the old Saxe where time for offering has grafted the silver flower of its clear tone.

SALUTATION TO VERSAILLES

Page 199.   Whose soul is sad and who brings to Autumn his
heart still glowing with the ashes of Summer, he is
the sceptreless Prince and the uncrowned King of
your solitude and your beauty.

For what he seeks in you, O gardens of silence, under
your sombre shade where the sound of his footsteps
pursues in vain the echo which always outruns it,
what he seeks in your shade, O gardens, is not

The secret murmur of the illustrious fame with
which the century has filled your always beautiful
groves, nor some vain glory leaning upon a balustrade,
nor some young grace beside the clear waters;

He does not ask to have pass or return the immortal
hero or the famous living man whose proud life,
striking and disdainful, was the star and the sun of
this august place.

What he desires is calm, is solitude, the perspective
of alley and stairway, the *rond-point*, the *parterre*, and
the effect of the pyramidal yew next to the clipped
box;

The taciturn grandeur and the monotonous peace
of this melancholy and unrivalled spot, and this
perfume of evening and this smell of Autumn which
breathes out of the shade at the end of the day.

THE FACADE

Page 200.   Glorious, monumental and monotonous, the stone
façade wastes its crumbling cornice and its weary
garland in the passing wind, opposite the yellow park
over which Autumn is leaning.

On the marble medallion with which Pallas crowns
it, the double letter still twines and interlaces; Hercules wearies himself supporting the balcony; the
fleur de lys drop their petals for Time to harvest.

Reflected in its deserted basins, the old Palace
watches naked Solitude and the sleeping Past crouch
in black and green bronze;

But the sun, flaming in the golden window-panes,
seems each evening to light again within it the spark
of its benumbed Glory.

THE GREEN BASIN

Page 201.   Her bronze, which was flesh, lifts her up in the
green water, Goddess once so sorrowful at being
a statue; the moss little by little is covering her
naked shoulder, and the silent urn hangs heavily
from her stiffened hand;

The stagnant water perfidiously mirrors the shadow
that everything in it has become, and its fluid mirror,
in which a nude is stretched out, imitates inversely
a sky which it parodies.

The grass, perpetually green, is like a blue-green basin. It is the same square of equivocal greenness with which marble or box frames grass or water.

And watch, in the emerald-green water and the emerald grass, turn by turn, move about in rival golds, the dead yellow leaf and the prowling carp.

THE NYMPH

Page 202. The calm, sleeping water in its slumbering trouble, overflows and rests in the porphyry basin and in the weeping fountain, and its greenish-blue pallors reflect the cypress and reflect the rose.

The God and the Goddess stand opposite each other, smiling; one holds the sceptre and the bow, the other the urn and the flowers, and in the alley between, joining his shadow to theirs, Love stands upright and naked, and interposes himself.

The grass slope borders the clear canal; the yew mirrors its mass, the holly its green cone, and the obelisk alternates with the pyramid;

A Dragon faces his enemy the Hydra, and both of them, from the clammy holes of their wet mouths, spit out a silver jet upon the sleeping Nymph.

THE PAVILION

Page 203. The basket, the shepherd's pouch, and the ribbon knotting the double flute and the straight shepherd's crook; the oval medallion where the narrow moulding frames a grey profile in the whiter panel;

The hurrying mantel-clock and the tall clock with slow steps, where Time, turn by turn, contradicts itself and limps; the weary mirror which seems a moist and shining water; the half-open door, and the fluttering curtain;

Some one who has gone, some one who will come, Memory sleeping with Recollection, an approach which delays and dates from an absence;

A window open upon the bitter smell of box, and upon roses from which the wind swings the crystal chandelier above the shining wood floor.

SEPTEMBER

Page 206. Before the harsh wind exiles the birds, disperses the leaves and dries up the reeds where I used to cut my arrows and my flutes, I wish, sitting on this sill which is framed by the wild vine, to see again, with my eyes already half closed over the days which, one by one, we have loved, the face which the Year flying, month by month, turns away smiling from the shadow which was I.

September, September, gatherer of fruits, stripper
of hemp, in the clear mornings, in the red evenings,
you appeared to me, upright and beautiful, against
the gold of the forest leaves, beside the water, in
your dress of mist and silk, with your hair reddening
with gold, copper, blood, and amber. September,
with the fat goatskin bottle loaded on your shoulder,
hanging heavily and oozing at its vermilion seams
about which the last bees buzz.

September! The new wine ferments, and foams
from the cask into the pitchers; the cellar smells
sweet, the granary sags; the sheaf of Summer gives
way to the wine-stock of Autumn; the grindstone
glistens with the olives which it crushes. You,
Lord of the wine-presses, of hay-ricks and of hives,
O September, sung by all the fountains, listen to the
voice of the poem. The evening is cold, the shadow
lengthens from the forest, and the sun goes down
behind the great oaks.

FRANCIS JAMMES

Page 219. I went to Monsieur Lay's, the teacher's. My
alphabet was like the flowers. I remember the
stove and the log of wood that each village child
brought when the sky is a white beehive, and when
on waking up one says: "It has been snowing!"

I remember also the gaiety of my apron, on ripe
Summer days when I left school somewhat earlier.

A little, little fellow, I still had Heaven within my eyes like a drop of water through which one can see God.

Page 220. . . . The sight of the monkey being shot is always with me, you understand.

Page 220. Water, foliage, air, sand, roots, flowers, grass-hoppers, earthworms, kingfishers, mist falling upon a radish field, vine tendrils on the weaver's roof: O gentle genii, who have made me their slave! You amused me. I so little, you so great!

Page 222. Oh, Father of my Father, you were there, before my soul which was not born, and the advice-boats slipped by with the wind in the Colonial night.

Page 222. . . . At the foot of a blue guava tree, amid the cries of the Ocean and the beach birds.

YOU WROTE . . .

Page 222. You wrote that you hunted wood-pigeons in the Guava woods, and, a little before your death, the doctor who took care of you wrote about your sober life.

"He lives," said he, "like a native, in his woods." You are the father of my father. Your old correspondence is in my drawer and your life is pungent.

You left Orthez as a doctor of medicine, to make your fortune far away. Your letters were brought by a sailor, by Captain Folat.

You were ruined by earthquakes in the country where rain-water is caught in tubs and drunk, heavy, unhealthy, bitter . . . And all that, you wrote.

And you bought an apothecary's shop. You wrote: "The capital has nothing like it." And you said: "My life has made me a real Creole."

You are buried there, I think, in Guava. And I am writing in the place where you were born: your old correspondence is very sad and grave. It is in my chest of drawers, locked up.

Page 226. Oh, Jammes, your house is like your face. A beard of ivy climbs up it, a pine-tree shades it, eternally young and spirited like your heart.

THE HOUSE WOULD BE FULL OF ROSES . . .

Page 227. The house would be full of roses and wasps. In the afternoon one would hear the ringing of vespers; and the transparent-stone-coloured grapes would seem to sleep in the sunshine under the slow shadow. How I should love you there! I give you my whole heart which is twenty-four years old, and my mocking spirit, my pride, and my poetry of white roses; and yet I do not know you, you do not exist. I only know that if you were living, and if you were at the bottom of this meadow, as I am, we would kiss each other, laughing, under the white bees, near the cool brook, under the thick leaves. We should hear nothing but the heat of the sunshine. You would have the shadow of the hazels on your ear, then we would join our mouths and stop laughing, to tell our love which cannot be told; and I should find upon the red of your lips, the taste of white grapes, of red roses, and of wasps.

THE DINING ROOM

Page 228. There is a cupboard, not very shiny, which has heard the voices of my great-aunts, which has heard the voice of my grandfather, which has heard the voice of my father. The cupboard is faithful to these memories. One is wrong in thinking that it only knows how to be silent, for I talk with it.

There is also a wooden cuckoo-clock. I do not know why it has no voice any more. I do not like to ask it. Perhaps, indeed, it is broken — the voice which was in its spring — for good, like that of a dead person.

There is also an old sideboard which smells of wax, preserves, meat, bread, and ripe pears. It is a faithful servant which knows that it ought not to steal anything from us.

Many men and women have come to my house who do not believe in these little souls. And I smile when a visitor, thinking that I am the only living thing, says to me as he comes in : " How are you, Monsieur Jammes ? "

I WRITE IN AN OLD KIOSK . . .

Page 230. I write in an old kiosk, so bushy that it is damp, and like a Chinaman, I listen to the water of the pool and the voice of a bird — there, near the water -(sh !)

fall. I am going to light my pipe. This is it. I level the ashes. Then memory gently descends in poetic inspiration.

"*I have come too late into too old a world,*" and I am bored, I am bored at not being present at a circle of little girls with great wide hats.

"Cora, you will get the bottom of your pantalets dirty if you touch that wretched dog." That is what little girls of fashion would have said on an evening of the olden time.

They would have looked at me, smiling, as I slowly smoked my pipe, and my little niece would have said, gravely : "He is going in to write verses now."

And her little companions, without understanding, would have stopped the charming chatter of their circle for a moment, believing that verses were going *to be seen* — perhaps.

"He has been to Touggourt, my dear," the circle of older scholars would have said. And Nancy would have announced: "There are savages and dromedaries."

Then, I should have seen issue upon the road the caracoling of the donkeys of many gentlemen and many ladies coming back, in the evening, from a ride.

My heart, my heart, is it only in death that you will find again this immense love for those whom you have not known in those tender and deceased days?

THE USEFUL CALENDAR

Page 233. In the month of March (the Ram ♈), one sows clover, carrots, cabbages, and lucerne. One stops harrowing, and one puts manure at the foot of the trees, and one prepares the beds. One finishes the pruning of the vines, and after having ventilated them, one puts the poles in place.

It is the end of Winter rations for the beasts. Heifers with beautiful eyes, and whose mothers lick them, are no longer led to the fields, but are given fresh nourishment. The days increase by one hour and fifty minutes. The evenings are sweet, and, at twilight, straggling goatherds puff their cheeks out

over flutes. Goats pass in front of the good dog,
who wags his tail and is their guardian.

Page 233.   At last the beautiful PALM SUNDAY comes. When
I was a child, they attached some cakes to me, and I
went to vespers, docile and sad. My mother said:
"In my country there were olives . . . Jesus wept in
an olive garden . . . They went, with great pomp,
to seek for him . . . In Jerusalem, people wept,
calling his name . . . He was gentle like the sky,
and his little ass-foal trotted joyously over the strewn
palms. Embittered beggars sobbed for joy as they
followed him, because they had faith . . . Bad
women became good, seeing him pass with his halo,
so beautiful that one believed it to be the sun. He
had a smile and hair of honey. He raised the
dead . . . They crucified him . . ." I remember
this childhood and the vespers, and I weep, my throat
convulsed at being no more the very little boy in these
old months of March, at being no more in the old
village church where I carried the incense in the procession and where I listened to the priest repeating the
PASSION.

Page 234.   You will find it pleasant, in the month of March,
to walk over the black violets with your mistress. In
the shade you will find the milk-blue periwinkles, beloved of Jean-Jacques, the sad, passionate man.

In the woods you will find lungwort, with its violet
and wine-coloured flower, the leaves verdigris, spotted

with white, hairy and very rough; there is a holy legend about it. The lady's smock to which the saffron butterfly comes; the light crowfoot and the black hellebore; the hyacinth which one crushes easily, and which, crushed, has sticky brightnesses; the evil-smelling jonquil, the anemone, and the narcissus which makes one think of the snows of Swiss mountain sides; then the ground-ivy, good for asthmatics.

THESE ARE THE LABOURS . . .

Page 235. These are the labours of man which are great : the one which puts the milk into the wooden jars; the one which picks the sharp and upright ears of corn; the one which watches the cows close to the fresh alders; the one which bleeds the forest birches; the one which plaits osiers near quick brooks; the one which repairs old shoes near a dim chimney-corner, with its old mangy cat, a sleeping blackbird, and happy children; the one which weaves and makes a returning noise, when, at midnight, the crickets sing piercingly; the one which makes bread; the one which makes wine; the one which sows garlic and cabbage in the garden; and the one which gathers warm eggs.

THE VILLAGE AT NOON . . .

Page 236. The village at noon. The golden fly buzzes between the horns of the oxen. We will wander, if you like, if you like, in the monotonous country.

Hear the cock . . . Hear the bell . . . Hear the peacock . . . Hear, over there, over there, the donkey . . . The black swallow soars. The poplars in the distance roll out like a ribbon.

The well eaten up with moss! Listen to its pulley, grating, grating again, for the girl with the golden hair holds the old black bucket from which the silver falls like rain.

The young girl walks away with a step which makes the pitcher lean sideways on her golden head, her head like a hive, which mingles with the sunshine under the flowers of a peach-tree.

And in the town, see how the black roofs shoot blue flakes at the blue sky; and the lazy trees at the quivering horizon scarcely sway.

LISTEN, IN THE GARDEN . . .

Page 239.   Listen, in the garden which smells of chervil, listen to the bullfinch singing in the peach-tree.

His song is like clear water in which the air bathes itself, trembling.

My heart is sad unto death, even though many have been, and one is, mad about it.

The first is dead. The second is dead; — and I don't know where another is.

There is still one, however, who is as lovely as the moon . . .

I am going to see her this afternoon. We will take a walk in a town . . .

Will it be in the bright quarter of rich villas, of strange gardens?

Roses and laurels, railings, shut gates, have an air of knowing something.

Ah, if I were rich, that is where I should live with Amaryllia.

I call her Amaryllia. How silly! No, it is not silly. I am a poet.

Do you imagine it is amusing to be a poet at twenty-eight?

In my purse I have ten francs and two sous for my powder. It is annoying.

I conclude from that that Amaryllia loves me, and loves me for myself alone.

Neither the *Mercure* nor *l'Ermitage* pay me wages.

She is really very nice, Amaryllia, and as intelligent
as I.

Fifty francs are lacking to our happiness.   One
cannot have everything — and the heart.

Perhaps if Rothschild said to her : "Come along . . ."
She would answer him :

"No, you shall not have my little dress, because I
love another . . ."

And if Rothschild said to her : "What is the name
of this . . . of this . . . of this . . . poet ? "

She would say to him : "It is Francis Jammes."
But the sad thing about all that would be :

That I do not think that Rothschild would know
who that poet was.

PRAYER TO GO TO PARADISE WITH THE DONKEYS

Page 242.   When the time for going to you will have come, O
my God, let it be on a day when the countryside is
dusty with a festival.   I wish, just as I do here, to
choose the road and go as I please to Paradise, where
there are stars in broad daylight.   I will take my stick
and I will go along the high road, and I will say to the
donkeys, my friends : "I am Francis Jammes and I
am going to Paradise, because there is no hell in the

country of the Good God." I will say to them:
"Come, gentle friends of the blue sky, poor, dear
animals, who, with a sudden movement of the ears,
drive away silver flies, blows, and bees . . ."

Grant that I appear before you in the midst of these
animals that I love so much, because they hang their
heads gently, and when they stop put their little feet
together in a very sweet and pitiful way. I shall ar-
rive followed by their millions of ears, followed by
those who carry baskets on their flanks, by those who
draw acrobats' carts or carts of feather-dusters
and tin ware, by those who have dented cans on their
backs, she-asses full like gourds, with halting steps,
and those on whom they put little pantaloons because
of the blue and running sores which the obstinate flies
make, sticking in circles. My God, grant that I come
to you with these asses. Grant that angels conduct us
in peace to tufted streams, where glossy cherry-trees
quiver like the laughing flesh of young girls, and grant
that, leaning over your divine waters in this place of
souls, I become like the donkeys who mirror their
humble and gentle poverty in the clearness of eternal
love.

Page 243.   It is a watch-dog barking to the moonlight as its
shadow moves over the roses.

Page 243.   We awaited it at that red hour when noon-day balances its blue wings over country belfries.

AMSTERDAM

Page 145. The pointed houses have the appearance of leaning over. One would say that they were falling. The masts of the ships, confused against the sky, are bent over like dry branches in the midst of green, of red, of rust, of smoked herrings, of sheepskins, and of coal.

Robinson Crusoe passed through Amsterdam (at least I believe he did), coming back from the shady and green island of fresh cocoanuts. What an emotion he must have had when he saw the enormous doors of the town, with their heavy knockers, shining.

Did he look curiously at the entresols where clerks were writing in account books? Did he feel like weeping when he thought of his dear parrot, of his heavy parasol, which sheltered him in the sorrowful and clement island?

"Blessed be thou, O Eternal One," he cried to himself, before the chests brightly painted with tulips. But his heart, saddened by the joy of return, regretted his goat, who remained all alone among the vines of the island, and was dead perhaps.

And I thought of this in front of the big warehouses where one dreams of Jews touching the scales with bony fingers encircled by green rings. See! Amsterdam sleeps under the eyelids of the snow in a perfume of fog and acrid charcoal.

Yesterday evening the lit white globes of the cheap saloons from which you hear the wheezing entreaties of heavy women, hung like fruits which resemble gourds. Blue, red, green, the posters glittered. The sharp prickling of sugared beer has rasped my tongue and made my nose itch.

And in the Jewish quarters where the residue is, one smelt the raw cold odour of fish. On the sticky pavements was orange peel. A bloated head opened its eyes wide, and onions were shaken from a disputing arm.

Rebecca, at little tables you sold perspiring bonbons, wretchedly arranged.

One would have said that the sky, like a dirty sea, emptied clouds of waves into the canals. A smoke which one does not see, the commercial calm, rose from the wealthy roofs in imposing layers, and one breathed India in the comfort of the houses.

Ah, I should like to have been a great merchant, of those who used to go from Amsterdam to China, confiding the administration of their houses to faithful proxies. Like Robinson, I would have signed my power of attorney pompously before a notary.

Then, my integrity would have made my fortune. My business would have flourished like a moonbeam upon the imposing prow of my barrelled ship. In my cabin I should have received the nobles of Bombay, who would have tempted my buxom wife.

Smiling under his great parasol, a negro with gold earrings come from the Great Mogul to trade! His wild tales would have enchanted my slender eldest daughter, to whom he would have offered a dress with rubies, spun by his slaves.

I should have had the portraits of my family painted by some clever painter whose lot had been unfortunate: my beautiful and portly wife with fair, pink cheeks, my sons whose beauty would have charmed the town, and the varying and pure grace of my daughters.

So that to-day, instead of being myself, I should have been some one else, and I should have visited the imposing house of these past centuries, and, dreaming, I should have let my soul float before these simple words: there lived Francis Jammes.

MADAME DE WARENS

Page 248.   Madame de Warens, you watched the storm wrinkling the gloomy trees of the melancholy *Charmettes,* or else you played shrilly upon the spinet, O sensible woman whom Jean-Jacques lectured!

It was an evening like this, perhaps . . . The sky was blasted by black thunder . . . A smell of branches cut before the rain rose mournfully from the box borders . . .

And I saw again, pouting, at your knees, in his little coat, the boy poet and philosopher . . . But what was the matter with him? . . . Why, weeping to the rose-coloured sunsets, did he look at the swinging of the magpies' nests?

Oh! how often he implored you, from the bottom of his soul, to put a curb upon those exaggerated spendings which you indulged in with that frivolity which is, alas! the characteristic of the majority of women.

But you, witty as well as gentle and tender, you said to him: "Look at him! the little philosopher!" Or else you pursued him with some pink drug with which you would powder his wig, laughing.

Peaceful sanctuaries! Peaceful years! Peaceful retreats! Fresh alder whistles blew among the beeches . . . Yellow honeysuckle framed the window . . . Sometimes one received the visit of a priest . . .

Madame de Warens, you had a fancy for this boy with the slightly mischievous face, lacking in repartee, but not at all stupid, and above all, clever at copying music according to the rules.

Ah ! how you should have wept, inconstant woman, when, abandoning him, he was obliged to go back, alone, with his poor little bundle on his shoulders, through the fir-trees of the waterfalls.

Page 250. I want no other joy, when Summer returns, than that of the past year. I will sit down under the sleeping grape vines. In the depth of the woods there is a singing of fresh water, and there I shall hear, I shall feel, I shall see, everything which the forest hears, feels, and sees.

I want no other joy when Autumn returns, than that of yellow leaves scraping the hillsides where it thunders, than the rumbling sound of new wine in the casks, than heavy skies, than cows jangling their bells, than beggars asking an alms.

I want no other joy when Winter returns, than that of iron skies, than the smoke-wreaths of cranes grating in the air, than firebrands singing like the sea, and than the lamp behind the green squares of window-glass in the shop where the bread is bitter.

When Spring returns, I want no other joy than that of the piercing wind, than the flowering of leafless peach-trees, than muddy and green paths, than the violet, and the bird, singing like a storm-swollen brook gorging itself.

Page 252. Like a smoking and woolly flock, the sky travelled under the rainy wind. The rain glistened on the blue slates. Near the gate an ox-cart squeaked. A cock pecked a cock. And on the old wooden bench, Jean de Noarrieu yawned.

One heard the servant moving about. The hearth, dim and red, blazed up brighter under the shining kettle. Near the black chest, greasy with age, it lit up the smooth-bellied gourd, and the sheep-dog stretched himself, yawning.

Twelve o'clock struck. The fat in the saucepan spurted up. And Lucie carefully broke two hen's eggs, with brown shells, against the tall andiron, and one saw, puffing up beside the white fat, the eggs which sputtered and leapt about.

Page 252. On the dresser are beautiful plates upon which are painted birds ornamented with aigrettes, yellow fruits and violet flowers. The silver in the wicker basket jingles brightly as Lucie touches it. She changes the plate and smiles at her master.

Page 253. And blossoming Easter came. Halleluia! Oh! sweet festival! Harmoniums grumbled in the hearts of the churches. Halleluia! Gilded was the green

of the shining meadows.   Crickets chirped.   Halleluia! Lilacs glistened in the blue night.

On a blessed and soft evening, Halleluia! — of a
sudden one heard the lilacs slowly questioning the
stars. It was, it was, it was, Halleluia! the nightingale, the moon streamed, the nightingale in flowers.
Halleluia!

Be born again, Nature. Oh! See the wild cherry-
tree all white in the garden. Halleluia! The heart
bursts open . . .

Page 253.   They cross the frail bridge over the torrent of a
little, old, whirling mill, all compounded of moss and
silver laughter; a torrent as pretty as though it were
in a novel, full of water-cress and quivering sunlight
and pebbles rolling over pebbles.

It leaps back.   They see and they hear the sparkling
shiver with which the running water twinkles.   The
wheel, covered with transparent moss, streams and
glitters, as in the Spring some emerald and silver val-
ley glitters in a blue cleft of the laughing Bigorres.

Page 254.   It was the July dog-days: the tops of the ears of the
Indian corn were silver, and their stamens were drying
up. The circular sweep of the scythe, with its rake
attached, with which one levels the corn, sounded in
the quivering sunshine.

The scythe, which makes a sharp wailing noise, shaved the corn and the white bindweed, the purple loosestrife and the winged thistle. In the fields, the heat made the hollow, sharp, round, and breaking straw crackle. And exploded the grating cicada.

Its cry took fire, suddenly, like powder, going on from tree to tree, and at the hour of the siesta when nothing is moving, the whole blue plain, curved about the reddish-brown corn, made the whistling that a child makes through his teeth to excite a dog on the road.

Except for this excruciating sound, everything was still.

Page 255.   Outside, the night cups the clear moon. The trees have a denser shade, a shade so dense that one would say that they had the shadow of the day in them, and that this shadow had retired into them to sleep until morning.

What silence of love, only interrupted by the chirping of a toad under one of the stone steps ! . . . The moon is rising through the catalpa tree. One can distinguish its continents, eaten into by light, where dreams are sleeping.

The garden prays. One feels the hearts of the peaches beating in the silence of God. They are

downed like the lustre of the shining cheeks of those
dancers, who, in Laruns, display themselves like
flowers in slow, lazy dances.

The fruits weigh more at night. Night seems to
lean on the fruits. They bend to each other like Jean
and Lucie. One loves, trembling. Kisses end more
slowly, like those round wrinkles which the wind
starts and stills on the water.

One by one, the stars rise. And Jean sees them
sparkle, white, yellow, and pure, in the centre of the
dark windows. To the Southward, swollen storm
clouds creep slowly along, sometimes passing over the
moon, then leaving her bare.

Page 257.   How exactly parallel all the shops are! All little
towns are alike. Right: Grocery. Left: Dye Shop.
Right: Police Station. Left: Apothecary Shop.
Right: Inn. Left: Leather Worker's. Right:
Lawyer. Left: Doctor. Then ten or twelve middle-
class houses, with gardens full of blue foliage and
hollyhocks and the shining and rose-coloured heat
of light. Over there? That is the Town Hall and
its lightning-rod, and the four-cornered square, with
elms and chains . . .

Page 257.   How beautiful the night is over the little town!
Elevenbluehours! Againsttheshadowof themoonlight,
the tulip-tree of this garden is even softer than the line
of silver-blue hills in the distance.   Bright moonlight!

It is so beautiful and bright, one wonders why one does not live at night, like the hares. No one in the street. A cricket chirps. A cat coughs, probably he has the croup. I should like not to go to bed, to stretch out in a field, and swim in this blue light.

Page 261. The peace of the fields extends all about the chapel. And at the dusty crossroads, in the midst of oats, mint, chicory and agrimony, stands a great Christ of hollow wood, in which the bees have made their nest. And one can see these busy creatures, full of honey, go and come like black letters written upon the sky.

With what shall one nourish one's God if not with honey? Sometimes the road-mender, breaking stones, raises his head and sees the Christ, the only friend he has on this road where midday throbs. To break the stones, the workman kneels in the shadow of this Christ whose flank is crimson. And then all the honey sings in the sunshine.

The poet looks and meditates. He tells himself, before the slow quivering of the fields, that each blade is one of the wise colony of God's people, each grain of which, to be vivified, waits for water to be sent forth from the grottoes of Heaven. He tells himself that henceforward this grain will grow in the precious azure which everything deepens, and that in the image of the Son of God, he too born in a grotto, it will nourish those who are hungry. And the ear, which in its turn will be born of this grain, will be shaped like a belfry at dawn.

THE CHILD READS THE ALMANAC . . .

Page 262. The child is reading the almanac, close to her basket of eggs. And apart from the Saints, and the weather it will be, she can contemplate the beautiful signs of the heavens: *The Goat, The Bull, The Ram, The Fishes,* et cætera.

Thus this little peasant girl can believe that, above her in the constellations, there are the same markets, with donkeys, bulls, rams, goats, and fishes.

It is the market of Heaven about which she is reading, no doubt. And when the page turns at the sign of *The Scales,* she says to herself that in Heaven, as in the grocer's shop, they weigh coffee, salt, and consciences.

Page 262. . . . rang gaily
For a farmer's daughter was being married.

DENIS

Page 263. How light the wind is! It lifts up the vine . . . Stay so, my Dear, in this soft wakefulness . . . I looked at your arms a little while ago, when you were haymaking . . . They know, innocently, how to fold themselves to your heart. What emotion is it which, when I touch your eyes, prevents me from thinking of anything but them? What sentiment is it which, if I hear you singing, makes me feel that it is my voice which you have borrowed? When your heart rests upon mine, what is it which makes me confuse us in the same sweetness?

LUCIE

What lovely words you know how to say to me! Alas! I do not know how to answer in poetry, but I love you just the same. If I do not know how to return your love in charming verses, be very sure that I know how to take all the emotion which you want to give me, and that I am yours with simplicity. Blessed be work if it forces my arms to take the curves which you desire, and which will enfold you . . . Poetry is the soul of life. I cultivate it, and you make it flower. Denis, I am nothing but the poor servant who listens to the wise word with faith.

TO MARY OF NAZARETH, MOTHER OF GOD

Page 264.   In dedicating this work to You, to You also I dedicate my daughter Bernadette, whose patron saint saw You in my native country, which is the mountainous Bigorre.

The old botanists also dedicated their herbals to You, and they painted You on the first page, standing, Your son in Your arms, all surrounded by lilacs, blue rays, roses, gloxinias, weigelias, peonies, guelder-roses, lilies, and the thousand flowers which will come no more, because they are no longer gathered for You by robust visionaries, who got up in the morning with the forget-me-nots, and went to sleep with the closing of the nasturtiums.

You are the Mother of all men and of God. You were born in Nazareth as simply as my Bernadette in Orthez. They have told the truth. They have not invented an extraordinary origin for You. I hold You in my heart as a certainty. Possibly I am unintelligent, but the incense of all created flowers rises from the earth for You, and You change it into love, like this climbing rose which flings itself toward the top of the cedars.

You see that I do not know any more what I am writing, but my thoughts cling to You after the manner of this flowering vine, and I dedicate this poor work to You as a servant might her pot of mignonette, and it trembles in my uplifted hands.

Page 266.   In this way the verses of which I make use are thoroughly classic, simply and solely freed by common sense.

After a great battle in which I took part, I look and realize that we are only slightly divided.

Becomes too sonorous and too easy and slack, the pure alexandrine, formerly so beautiful, is just repetition.

Vers libre does not give a clear enough sense of where the stanza begins and ends.

But wanting all liberties, it has at least gained some. They open the way.

Few as they are, they are quite enough. Lines shall be equal and not assonanced.

As the male bird in turn answers the female, the male rhyme follows a female rhyme.

Although lines be thus bound together, I accept the rhyming of plurals with singulars.

Again like the bird, who takes his rhythm from heaven, here and there the rhyme may pause at the cæsura.

Sometimes the hiatus comes just in time to recall him who is a poet to the simplest speech.

Now that the mute *e* is slipping out of speech, I do not wish it to count in my verse any more.

The syllables to be counted are only those which the reader habitually pronounces.

Having established this brief but definite Art of Poetry, my inspiration once more opens its door.

Page 267.   The wind streamed over the blue silk of the grain and wrinkled it, and the rattle of the crickets trembled like the bell of a little railroad station. The line of the horizon slept, stretched over the ears of wheat,

2 F

and the leaves of the stubble rose and fell like mast pennants for grasshoppers. Sometimes one saw in the sky a cloud like a grove of shadows lifted up from the hill, and while it slid along, the hill shone, darkened, and shone again.

PAUL FORT

THE GREAT INTOXICATION

Page 274. On blue Summer nights when the cicadas sing, God spills a cup of stars over France. The wind brings a taste of the Summer sky to my lips. I want to drink from this freshly silvered space.

For me, the evening air is the edge of the cold cup from which, with half-shut eyes and voracious mouth, I drink the starry freshness which falls from the clouds, as though it were the squeezed juice of a pomegranate.

Lying upon a grassplot where the grass is still hot from having flaunted itself in the day air, oh! this evening, with what love would I empty the immense blue cup in which the firmament moves!

Am I Bacchus or Pan? I am intoxicated with space, and I quench my fever in the freshness of nights. With my mouth open to the sky in which the stars shiver, oh! that the sky would flow into me! that I might melt into it!

Byron and Lamartine, Hugo, Shelley, are dead, intoxicated with space and the starry heavens. Space is always there; limitless it flows; scarcely drunk, it sweeps me along, and I am still thirsty.

THE SKY IS GAY, 'TIS PLEASANT MAY

Page 275. Over the hedge the sea is sparkling, the sea sparkles like a shell. One wants to fish in it. The sky is gay, 'tis pleasant May.

The sea over the hedge is soft, it is soft like the hand of a child. One wants to caress it. The sky is gay, 'tis pleasant May.

The glittering needles which sew the sea to the hedge move in the quick hands of the breeze. The sky is gay, 'tis pleasant May.

Upon the hedge the sea exhibits its frivolous butter-flies. Little vessels about to sail. The sky is gay, 'tis pleasant May.

The hedge — it is depths, with golden beetles. The breezes are more mischievous. The sky is gay, 'tis pleasant May.

As soft as a tear upon a cheek, the sea is a tear on the hedge which softly descends to the harbour. But one scarcely wishes to weep.

"A boy has fallen into the harbour!" — "Dead in the sea, 'tis a pleasant death." But one scarcely wishes to weep. The sky is gay, 'tis pleasant May!

Page 277. . . . It came into the world for me, real, great, immense, and dreamed at the same time.

It came into the world for me, divined by my eyes, on a Spring morning, to the twittering of swallows. My little hands believed they took it from the blue sky! It was faithful to me, being born again each dawn, all inhabited by Saints, by Kings, and by Heroes, and by Angels half in flight, like a tree of birds.

Great plaything of my soul, O French forest of stones; and my immense rattles, your towers; you remained the sole Pastime of my spirit, with the three high porches in a flaming triangle, and above them the Rose, where one saw the fluttering of pigeons pecking at the fleeting reflections.

Then, my Cathedral, when I was at last old enough to join a kite to the wings of your angels, and make your walls ring with my cries, and pursuing my cries with streaming hair, to surround your old walls with the hundred games of childhood . . .

Page 278. Monstrous General Baron von Plattenberg, if to you I owe this love song to my Church, I give you in return, even if it immortalizes you, the poet's slap in the face, and the scaffold of the Word — but I have a magazine of hate consecrated to all the Germans whom I have chanced to meet.

JOACHIM

Page 282. Night glides thick and cold through Paris. Two shadows in the darkness, two thin little shadows, move chillily, then slide into the night.

"Sweet Sire, I have sworn. We go to-night."
"Very well, follow me, follow me."

Little lanes in the midst of little lanes, two thin little shadows move in the cold, — then stop.

There, before a half-buried hovel, a voice, a little bitter-sweet voice, tart, a little voice drenched with sobs:

"I am neither lion, nor wolf, nor fox, I am a man, Croy! Knock at this door, Croy! Here, — good. Call: Dame Simone des Chaînes!"

"Dame Simone des Chaînes!"

"Good. Listen, listen! . . . Ask if some one did not die yesterday at her house."

"Dame Simone, did some one die here yesterday?"

"Alas, sweet Sir! You know it then? My son Joachim, my son, last night."

"I am neither lion, nor wolf, nor fox, I am a man. Croy, come back, hold me up! Joachim! . . . Croy! I am neither lion, nor wolf, nor fox, I am all

three, Croy, I am a man. Goodbye, little crea-
ture . . . Joachim! Joachim! Come now, let us
go. Dame Simone was . . . Dame Simone was . . .
I am a man, Croy, I am weeping for a little crea-
ture . . . Joachim! Alas! . . . my little child . . ."

Night glides thick and cold through Paris, two thin
little shadows push, slide, move. Oh! what a little
tart voice, tart . . . Oh, its little anguished cries!

THE MIRACULOUS CATCH

Page 283.   The news was so charming, — an uncle dead so a
propos! — my sweet little Louis XI wished very
much to celebrate it, but intimately, in agreeable
society.

Master Tristan, all imagination, counselled an out-
door party, and, as he winked with his sly red eyes : —
"Understood," said the king, "you are nothing but
a rascal."

The next morning, under the blue heavens, gay and
contented, my sweet little Louis XI, Tristan l'Ermite,
and their madcap mistresses, Simone des Chaînes
and Perrette de Trésor, were come to tease the gudgeon of the Seine, at the reedy foot of the Tour de
Nesle.

Master Olivier, virgin, kept watch on the bank,
crushing the grass with his long strides. He stared
gloomily into the air : the fall of Buridan occupied his
mind.

Simone des Chaînes, heart and soul bound to the heart and soul of her dearly-loved King, like a water-lily bending over an old nenuphar, leaned her snow-white neck, her milk-white forehead, and her little white velvet nose, over the shrivelled shoulder of her lover; and, from time to time, the gracious King Louis of France asked her for a worm. Then it was with such a great charm that she drew one out of a little green box; it was with such a disturbing charm that she presented it, all wriggling, to the King, that Louis could not resist kissing her ear (not that of the worm but that of Simone des Chaînes), even whispering lovingly these words: "Sweetheart, you shall assist at the States General."

.   .   .   .

Master Olivier, virgin, kept watch on the bank, crushing the grass with his long strides. He stared gloomily into the air: the fall of Buridan occupied his mind.

With an inattentive eye, as though he were a riverside flower, he watched a certain Master Villon running through the reeds after dragonflies, and who, sometimes, turned eyes full of anarchy toward those *bourgeois* fishing over there, with their friends. Master Olivier, virgin, was absent minded . . . He scarcely saw Master Villon, in the reeds, taking off his clothes. He scarcely murmured, as one murmurs in a dream: "Really, this naked gentleman is not unknown to me."

And Tristan caught nothing. And the King caught
nothing. The worms spun out, spun out . . . And
François Villon, taking to mid-stream, whispered to
the fishes as he floated: "Hurrah for liberty! Don't
let yourselves be taken."

.   .   .   .

"Hush!" cried the King, "or I shall lose this
turbot."

"A turbot, my Lord, is a sea fish . . ." timidly
risked the tender Simone. "I sold them, with my
mother, at the great Saint-Honoré Market, in the
time of my virginity." — "A sea fish? Hey, that is
certainly why I have missed him!" replied the King,
not at all disconcerted.

"Past days do not return," hummed Perrette, ad-
justing her stockings. "Yes, youth is only once,"
struck up Tristan, with conviction. Then the timid,
the tender Simone cooed, to an air then little known:
"It is twenty years since I lost my mother . . ."
Nothing more was needed. Tristan burst into tears,
— while the King, all the time fishing the wind,
sang at the top of his voice: "No, my friends, no, I
do not want to be anything! . . ."

And Tristan caught nothing. And the King
caught nothing. The worms spun out, spun out . . .
And the intelligent gudgeon, flapping their gills,
applauded. — (Undoubtedly, "applauded" is only a
metaphor. But does one really know what goes on
in the water?)

At the reedy foot of the Tour de Nesle, the boon companions, the King and the hangman, sang in chorus, like birds. And the gudgeon waltzed, waltzed agreeably round the corks.

Master Olivier, virgin, kept watch on the bank . . .

Suddenly Perrette burst out laughing in her skirt! My sweet little Louis XI, throwing up his line with spirit, had hooked a kingfisher. — Tristan said : "A forfeit!" Simone : "Fish flying!" and Master Olivier stopped short in the middle of a stride.

"By my soul! I believe I've been mistaken," said François Villon to himself as he swam under water. "To fish for a bird instead of a gudgeon . . . This bourgeois is not devoid of lyrism."

And the gudgeon waltzed, waltzed agreeably round the corks.

THE GIRL WHO DIED IN LOVING

Page 292.   This girl is dead, is dead while she loved.

They have laid her in the earth, in the earth, at break of day.

They have laid her there alone, alone in her fine array.

They have laid her there alone, alone within her coffin.

They have returned gaily, gaily with the light.

They have sung gaily, gaily: " To each his turn.

This girl is dead, is dead while she loved."

They have gone to the fields, to the fields as every day . . .

Page 293.   No, I must love, must trail my pain, to weep against the stone here, see, where I inscribed her name between a rock-rose, and this heart-coloured pink. I am benumbed ! — I am going plant-hunting by moonlight, seeking under the moss for the herb which restores youth.

THE ROUND

Page 296.   If all the girls in the world wished to take hands, they could make a circle all round the sea.

If all the boys in the world wished to be sailors, they could make a nice bridge over the waves with their ships.

Then one could make a round all round the world, if all the people in the world wished to take hands.

THE WEDDING

Page 296.   Ah, what joy, the flute and the bagpipe trouble our hearts with their enchanting strains. Here come the lads and girls, and all the old people, to the sound of the instruments.

Gai, gai, let us be married, ribbons and white starched caps, *gai, gai*, let us be married, and this pretty couple likewise.

What pleasure, when in the decorated church, bells and little bells call them, every one — three hundred little bells for the eyes of the bride, a great deep bell for the heart of the husband.

Gai, gai, let us be married, ribbons and white starched caps, *gai, gai*, let us be married, and this pretty couple likewise.

The bell at last holds our tongues silent. Ah! what pain when it is for us no more . . . Weep upon your prayerbooks, old men. Who knows? Soon the bell may be for you?

Gai, gai, let us be married, ribbons and white starched caps, *gai, gai*, let us be married, and this pretty couple likewise.

At last that is all, and the bell is silent. Come and dance to the happiness of the married couple. Hurrah for the lad and the girl and the festival. Ah! what joy when it is not for us.

Gai, gai, let us be married, ribbons and white starched caps, *gai, gai,* let us be married, and this pretty couple likewise.

What pleasure, the flute and the bagpipe make the old young again for a moment. See the lads and the young girls dancing. Ah, what joy to the sound of the instruments!

AND YOU YOU YOU

Page 298. And *you, you, you,* it is the fisherman dying, and *you, you, yu,* and the whole sea on top of him.

And *you, you, you,* it is the shepherdess weeping, and *you, you, ya,* love is lost to her.

And *you, you, you,* it is the sea there bleating, and *you, you, yon,* or it is the sheep there?

And *you, you, you,* pleasures are in Heaven, and *you, you, you,* beneath them are the clouds.

LIFE

Page 298. At the first sound of bells: "It is Jesus in his cradle . . ."

The bells have redoubled: "O *gué,* my lover!"

And then all at once it is the passing bell.

THE WHALES

Page 298. In the days when one still went after whales, so far, Sailor, it made our maidens weep, on every road there was a Jesus on the cross, there were Marquises covered with lace, there was the Holy Virgin and there was the King!

In the days when one still went after whales, so far, Sailor, it made our maidens weep, there were seamen who had faith, and great Lords who spat upon it, there was the Holy Virgin and there was the King!

Ah, well, now everybody is contented, it is not a thing to say, Sailor, but we are contented! There are no great Lords, nor Jesus any more; there is the republic, and there is the president, and there are no more whales.

THE TWO CLOWNS

Page 299. "Synthetic Clown-Clown, hip, hip, turn!"

"Six pirouettes, blue white white blue — behold the Sky! Six pirouettes, blue green green blue — behold the Sea! Six pirouettes, green yellow yellow green — behold the Desert! Six pirouettes, gold yellow yellow gold — behold the Sun!"

"Bravo, bravo, a little bravo, gentlemen. Analytic Clown-Clown, yours, turn!"

"Very well. Gentlemen, let us decompose ourselves, follow me carefully: Violet, two pirouettes, Indigo, three pirouettes, Blue, five pirouettes, Green, two pirouettes, Yellow, three pirouettes, Orange, five pirouettes, Red, ten pirouettes. Total: thirty pirouettes. Attention, Gentlemen, keep your eyes on the rainbow . . . Two, three, five, two, three, five, ten, rrrrrrran!"

"Stop, Analytic, stop, enough! He will burst . . . God . . . Ah!"

Synthetic writhed, then in the sawdust of the ring, with a profound finger, inscribed this sombre epitaph:

Here lies

ANALYTIC

this clown supposed to be wise

— very mad

and dead of rage

at having been unable to turn in a tempest.

SENLIS. EARLY MORNING

Page 301.   I go out. Has the town vanished this morning? Where has it flown to? By what wind, to what island? I find it, but dare not stretch out my hands. Senlis is as vaporous as muslin. I, to tear Senlis? Take care. Where is it? Roofs and walls are a transparent network of fog. Notre-Dame surrenders to the air her throat of lace, her slender neck, her delicate moon-coloured breast where the unreal hour strikes which only the angels remark, so stifled is the echo in the pillow of the sky made of the softly spread feathers of their wings on which God rests his forehead inclined toward Senlis.

HORIZONS

Page 302.   In the direction of Paris, but toward Nemours the white, a bullfinch sang in the branches this morning.

In the direction of Orleans, flown toward Nemours, the lark sang above the wheat at high noon.

In the direction of Flanders, in the golden twilight, far from Nemours the magpie has hidden his treasure.

In the evening, crying toward the East, toward Germany and Russia, the flock of crows has quitted this countryside.

But in my beautiful garden, sheltered by Nemours, Philomel has sung all through the starry night.

Page 303.   "And when he climbed up the ladder with his people, what did they throw at them, tell me? Chickens?" "Not so." "Radishes? Butter?" "You are wrong." "Lambs? Oxen?" "Rather!" "Strawberries and cream? Melons? Salsify? Fi! you are

joking!" "They threw melted iron in their eyes;
on their noses, under their noses, flaming torches
(like opened roses, good to inhale); and all over
their bodies a joyous pell-mell of furniture, paving
stones, slates, cannon-balls, spit, gnawed bones,
varying filths, little nails, big nails, anvils, hammers,
saucepans, wines, papboats of iron, plates, forks,
stoves, spoons, ink, boiling grease and oil, how do
I know? Tombstones, well-curbs, partition walls,
gutters, roofs, belfries, bells, little bells which tinkled
gracefully on heads."

"What else did they throw at them — and no
lie?"

"Ah! many objects very bruising, cutting, sharp-
ened, whetted, ball-shaped, socket-shaped, granulated,
horned, toothed, beaked, of earth, of sheet-iron, of
freestone, of iron, of steel, curved, bristled, twisted,
confused, everything that was badly used up, moss-
grown, rusted, frayed, in thongs, in wedges, hollow,
sieved, cross-shaped, screw-shaped, hooked, ringing,
grating, whistling and snoring, going humph, ouf,
louf, pouf, bring, sring, tringle, balaam, bottom, betting, batar, arara, raraboum, bul, bul, breloc, relic, relaps, mil, bomb, marl, broug, batacl, mirobol, pic,
poc, quett, strict, pac, diex, mec, pett, sec, sic, soïf,
flic, faïm, bric, broc, brrrrrr . . . , which battered in
skulls, enlarged noses, banged ears, widened mouths,
made fly teeth, fingers, elbows, arms, chins, cheek-
bones, and married eyes disdaining an omelette of
one, boned shoulders, brutalized chests, discouraged
hearts, thrust into bellies, pried first into one buttock
then another, pulled out false bowels, made wool of

thighs, billiard-balls of knee-pans, and enlarged feet, or cut a man into five, six, seven, — really."

"Indeed, and still, what did they throw at them? Corpses, insults, mobs and arrows?"

"Better than that! (shiver with me) — houses. And it wanted only a little more, and they would have thrown the whole town at them over the town!"

HENRY III

I

Page 305. The curtains of the windows are closed. The furniture sleeps. Sometimes the royal bed gives a long moan. It is the wood which complains, it is the soul of the old oak. Listen . . . Indeed, it scarcely moans. Listen. The dark fireplace comes to life and shines. Three little blue flames dance on the hearth, tossing great farewells to the fleur-de-lised walls.

Nothing more. Darkness pursues the four walls.

All at once a burst from the hearth brings them back. The bed, all shivering, gives a human wail; and Philippe de Valois detaches himself from a wall. Quickly he opens a chest, plunges into it and shuts it.

Louis XI, wary, slides hypocritically along; about his black hood a white mouse turns, and here, the shield of Brittany on their sleeves, devouring each other with their eyes, are Louis XII and Charles VIII. They open the chest, plunge into it and shut it.

2 G

The little blackguard, François II, goes to the fireplace and vomits. The bed, heaving up its sheets,
seems a phantom in pain. How short reigns are in
the chamber of Kings! Did you see the great wooden
coffer yawn?

Nothing more. Darkness pursues the four walls.

All at once a burst from the hearth brings them
back, and in front of Henri II limps François the first.
They dream, with bent heads, of Diane de Poitiers,
then plunge in together and shut the lid.

It is Charles V who raises it with his sceptre, and
the Wise King is red with a reflection from the faggots.
He jumps. Does the purple hinder jumping? He
rolls in his purple and lets go the truncheon. The
hand of justice flies from lock to lock (cric! crac!)
turning the keys.

For here is Jean le Bon.

Round-shouldered, covered with melodious and
melancholy chains, he has a wicked smile, and the
blue eyes of Christ. The madman Charles VI whips
him rhythmically from helmet to feet with the lilies
of France, and Charles VII, the drunkard, gathering
up the petals, bows his face. But he staggers. He
has drunk too much. Three sepulchral drops make
the chest resound.

The Valois Kings are in an uproar. The bed trembles. The eleven Valois Kings call another. There, and in the mirrors, see, the coffer yawns. Does Death exercise itself in metamorphoses? At each yawn the horns of Satyrs lift the lid and quickly draw back.

Then great silence . . .

At last, coming out of the half-shadow, a white face rises as the moon rises. And the bed sees Charles IX with the black eyes pass. Houp! the chest breathes him in, and everything vanishes. In the depths of the infinite a mouse nibbles.

II

The curtains of the windows are closed. The furniture sleeps. Sometimes the royal bed gives a long moan. It is the wood which complains, it is the soul of the old oak, or perhaps, with torches, would one see a man there? And wait! the dark fireplace comes to life and shines; three little blue flames stretch out their reflections which mow the harvest of the fleur-de-lised walls. The ceiling lights up and seems to grow higher; the bed, still in shadow, is swallowed up under its dome.

The room, where everything wavers, is a prey to phantoms.

A last glimmer strikes out on the chest the circle which is escaping from its half-opened abyss.

A quick gleam strikes out on the sides of the chest the circle which turns upon its wood in a tumult.

The reflection of the mirrors isolates and makes jut out the lascivious, bounding circle of twelve great Satyrs surrounding a frightened goat with their desires, — while in these mirrors, thirty times repeated, a Hercules of bronze whirls his mass about.

He has the grimacing smile of the Béarnais. He, truly! The very image!

The darkness is hot. A cry is smouldering . . .

In silence, at a gallop, urged by the silent tempest of Ages and Ages and Ages, in silence, to the gallop of his iron horse, Charlemagne traverses the room in a flash. Henri de Guise follows him on his tall, black horse, but having gone the wrong way, loses himself in a mirror. And afterwards, here is Catherine, her great and beautiful face — horrible to see!

Now from his stupor Henri tears a cry, a cry such as is heard at night in the depths of plains, that cry of the solitudes which swells and passes by and trails away, discouraging life in the heart of the traveller; and it is at this moment that at the window which is shining to the West, the iron of a halberd, caught in the fluttering stuff, lifts up an easy curtain.

Outside the day is dying, rose-coloured, with snow.

III

The King, dressed in black, has leaped out of bed; he goes to the mirrors to question his face, shrinks before his pallor, and, all trembling, puts on his hat. Then his black hat isolates his pallor. "Will you come to arouse a stupefied blood" (says he), "O Liquor! . . ." The cup falls at his feet. Softly opening the door, he listens to the antechamber, all lit with swords and full of clashings.

Gloves. Ebony cane. And he is gone.

"The King, Gentlemen. The King!" A halberd resounds. Voices, whisperings, noises of chairs. The twilight glimmer sparklingly underlines the gilded beams. The antechamber is confused, full of the shadows of vassals bending toward a passage where a white point is advancing.

Behind, the royal bed is crouched under its dome, quite at the end of a passage where a white point is advancing.

"The King!" Second echo. — A halberd resounds.

What oval whiteness, at the height of a face, agitates two long pearls such as the moon might have wept? Face and long pearls, Henri III appears. And the subject shadows, all the shadows, bow down.

Has a flight of dead leaves fallen here?

"You who risk an eye, look: does the twilight still underline the gilded beams?"

"Yes, but the King?"

"The King, my son? . . . He has gone by."

"Quélus, my good friend, that smacks of prodigy."

"Maugiron, Saint-Mégrin, listen to the marvel: this evening the Ghost of the King wanders about the palace, masked with moonlight and two tears in its ears."

"Is it going to find Catherine again in her clouds? It is going up the staircase."

"It is at the second story!"

A halberd resounds. Voices, whisperings, noises of chairs. Outside the day dies, rose-coloured, with snow.

IV

While the King hurries up the empty staircase, Chicot happens in, swinging his lighted lantern! They surround the Fool, who chuckles, and slips away, and reappears, lifting up his lantern and swinging it like a censer at the bottom of the staircase.

"Go on, Gentlemen, I am searching for a King," says he.

The antechamber is dark with great whitish corners, where already torches are springing into flame under many hands. One of them throws out a flame of snow and carmine. Quickly the hands spread out. —

One sees the whole room. — Agile, at tl : ends of arms, swords take fire, and joining thems..ves by twos, people the air with sparks; some blades hum, others are all clashings, and the shad·ws of bodies make the walls move, and the feet of *Iignons* rustle on the flagstones.

"Chicot," Quélus cries out, "the Ghost of the King wanders. What are you doing there, Chicot? Do you want to wander? Armed witl ·our candle, you will see it go up."

"No, I see it come down."

"Who then?"

"Henri de Guise."

"The Devil! He is in Spain . . . (Yours, Monsieur, touched!)"

"Pardon, my dear Sir, he is coming down the staircase."

"Chicot, take care of yourself! . . ." "It's damned true, Gentlemen, *I saw him.*"

The swords drop back on the flagstones.

Meanwhile the King hurries up the empty staircase, alone, to his mother Catherine's apartments in the clouds, and does not feel, sliding by, the limpid cuirass of Monseigneur de Guise, who draws back on the landing. The Duke is very much in the flesh, however. His heart beats strongly. But not enough to make the cold metal which Monseigneur hides with his hat jingle as he bows.

At the very bottom, the staircase blazes. The Duke comes down. He comes down step by step like a discreet phantom. They crowd about, they see him. The Duke is returning from Spain like a discreet phantom, and he even returns by the bed-chamber of the Queen!

"Unbelievable," says Maugiron.
"This Guise is a great fellow," says Saint-Mégrin.
"Way for my Lord the Duke!"

The limpid cuirass draws away the swords. Everything slips away. Everything is extinguished.

V

Meanwhile Henri III, half-lying on the railing at the top of the staircase, has seen everything this time. In his throat is a sob like a dove's, then he stands up.

A wall opens slightly for the King.

VI

Here, nothing but a lamp lighting up a hand.

Everything — except this lamp and save the parchment, where this hand, plump, old, starched, guides the goose-quill or seeks the ink-stand, — everything here is in shadow. The hand, by chance withdrawing a little, leaves the writing. Then this is what the flame, which writhes above the characters like a martyr, might read:

"*To Madame my daughter, the Catholic Queen,*

"*My beloved daughter, my dearest, my docile Isabel, I have just received news of you from Spain. Monsieur de Guise brought it to me. Indeed, it would be beautiful to see all the wicked heretics burning in a single torch (in France also, as you do there). Alas, Darling, nothing can be done here. With us there is only perversion, and suffering for your good mother. You know the afflictions which it pleases Heaven to send me, and which are the greatest ever sent to any one. To burn heretics! Ah! yes, beautiful bouquet of flames, indeed! A great bonfire, and one which would be acceptable to God. But what of that, little daughter, in France nothing can be done. Everything here remains in shadow, even the Royal Shadow . . .*"

A white lip hangs from the shadow of a face. Under a bonnet of black tulle, a forehead bends over, scored with moving wrinkles like a belfry of birds, and the more this forehead bends over the higher it appears. Catherine's wet eyes grow silver. The stern and delicate curve of the long Italian nose which the fold of the nostril pulls back like a bow, is in profile.

It is the moment when Catherine, pouting and pacific, crosses out the impolitic phrase with a stroke of her pen.

Now another face has risen up in the room. Behind her, Catherine feels the presence of a pallor. She has ceased to write, listening to her heart. Two little gloved hands fall on her shoulders, like two bats killed by the same blow of a stick. And one of the little hands circling down to her heart, clenches itself there . . .

Then, with the end of her goose-quill, Catherine pensively, gently, caresses it. And *both* dream, and the moment is full of indolence.

The hand relaxes, trembling . . . By one finger! — see the parchment designated by one finger! "*Everything here remains in shadow, even the Royal Shadow.*"

Two hands seize Catherine's neck, and the Queen, lifting up her terrible forehead, cries: "My King!" A quick squeak of the wood floor reveals a sudden flight, and soon Henri III descends the empty staircase.

VII

He crosses the dark and deserted antechamber, throws himself against a wall with both arms spread out, and searches for the passage down the whole length of the empty wall.

Nothing more : emptiness.

The King totters; he hurries, totters; he hurries to his open door and starts to go in, but stops, his hand at his throat and livid, before a sleepy and swaying halberd.

Henri seizes the leg of the guard whom he wakes, for — O Stupor! — behind the guard whom he wakes, there! in his bed! . . . some one, some one or something, like himself (and perhaps himself), black and white, a man, a King or something, a King perhaps? Charles IX or François? A prone phantom sleeps the sleep of the dead.

"Guard! Come, you! Who is in the rooms of the King of France? To whom does that pallor belong? Those are my clothes. Let me see, did I go out, or is it I, there? What is that thing?" "Alas!" said the man in alarm, "alas! my dear Sire, but I . . . I do not know."

"Silence," said a voice. A voice said: "Silence . . ." The King shakes, all crouched down like a frog in the cold, and the halberd falls and the guard escapes.

"It is nothing, my sweet Sire, it is Chicot, resting."

And Chicot decamps dragging a sheet after him.

VIII

Midnight?

Midnight chimes from Saint-Germain-l'Auxerrois.

PAN AND THE CHERRIES

(A Shepherd's Vision)

Page 317.   Io! I recognized Pan by his unconstrained attire, and his shaggy hair! He leapt in the sunshine, sometimes with an easy gesture picking a cherry from the crimson trees. How unpolluted he was! Drops of water trickled over his glossy fleece like stars: one would have said it was of silver.

And it was under the blue sky of my young Springtime.

Presently, having caught sight of a bigger, more beautiful cherry in the air, he seized it, and squeezed the stone from the bleeding pulp. I approached. I was overjoyed . . . He having aimed at my eye, I received the stone. I started to kill Pan with my knife. He stretched out an arm, made a sudden side-leap, and the whole World turned round.

Come and worship Pan, the god of the World!

THE KISSES

Page 317. When we went away from each other, we didn't say anything. And we thought we didn't love each other much. When we went away from each other, we didn't say anything for a long time. It was, as they say, like indifference.

We kissed each other well, however, yesterday and before, you said to me : "Five days." But we said to each other : "That doesn't last long, five days of kisses, it is like fair weather."

To-day blue sea and to-morrow it is a storm. You mustn't ask too much of love. And besides, sailors, do you see, it goes. A boat kisses the sand . . . How short kisses are!

FIRST APPOINTMENT

(Square Monge)

Page 318. Intoxication of Spring! and the greensward turns round the statue of Voltaire. — Ah! really, it is a beautiful green, it is very pretty, the Square Monge : green grass, railing and benches green, green policeman, it is, when I come to think of it, a beautiful corner of the Universe. — Intoxication of Spring! and the greensward turns round the statue of Voltaire.

The pale trees where the sky opens its blue flowers are full of birds. The pigeons make love tenderly.

The sparrows wag their tails. I am waiting . . .
Oh! I am happy, in the deliciousness of waiting. I
am gay, mad, in love — and the pale trees where the
sky opens its blue flowers are full of birds.

I climb up on the benches the colour of hope, or else
I balance . . . on the hoops of the flower bed, before
the statue of Voltaire. Hurrah for everything!
Hurrah for myself! Hurrah for France! There is
nothing I do not hope. I have the wings of hope. I
climb up on the benches to leave the earth, or else
I do a little balancing.

She said: one o'clock; it is only noon! Time is
short to lovers. The birds sing, the sunshine dreams.
Every time that Adam meets Eve they must have a
paradise. Behind the railing, in the sun, the torpid
or .ibus thinks of it. She said: one o'clock; it is
o .y noon! Time is short to lovers.

Before the statue, a white cat, a yellow one — and
the yellow one is a female! — roll, tumble upon the
hot grass, show their paws, miau, fight together.
The sun gently widens your smile, O my gentle Voltaire. O good faun. — Before your statue, a white
cat, a yellow one, roll, tumble, show their paws.

The trees put out leaves to the song of the birds.
My heart's bud bursts open! And I shake for nothing
but having seen the diamonds of the watering-pot
cover the grass with mist. A rainbow springs from

the spine of the philosopher and goes quivering into the branches of a horse-chestnut tree. The trees put out leaves to the song of the birds. My heart's bud bursts open!

The azure is on fire: under the bench where the policeman is sleeping, a dog scents a dog. A little girl skips rope over her shadow, and others, and others. I see their shadows on the walk grow bigger or shrink. And all these things sing, one better than another: "Little fire! Big fire! so that it lights the good God!" The azure is on fire: under the bench where the policeman is sleeping, a dog scents a dog.

Here is the musical cocoa-vender, loaded with his golden taps. His taps are serpents from which his tinkling cocoa spurts into the cups of the children. Cool our lust: quick! for a sou of your mixture, glittering Laocoon. I drink to all Nature, I drink to your boiling bronze, you who smile at adventures, O old Voltaire, O gentle, wicked man. — Here is the vender of musical cocoa. His taps are serpents.

Ah, Spring, what fire rises from the earth! what fire falls from the sky, Spring. — Before the statue of Voltaire, I am waiting for my new Manon. And while she delays, Voltaire, seated, is patient: I look at what he is looking at, an Easter daisy in the grass. I am waiting. — I am waiting, O Sky! I am waiting, O Earth! under all the flames of Spring!

Two o'clock. Let us pull this daisy to pieces. "A
little, very much, passionately . . ." Passionately,
little Manon, come quickly, run, I implore you. Hey!
you — you smile in a way to make me exceedingly
annoyed. Dirty encyclopedist! Oh! . . . Here she
is under all the flames of Spring!

And the trees turn and the greensward turns round
the statue of Voltaire. — Decidedly, it is a beautiful green, it is delicious, the Square Monge: green
grass, railing and benches green, green policeman, it is,
when I come to think of it, a beautiful corner of the
Universe. — I climb up on a bench the colour of hope.
One should be able to see me from the whole of France.

THE SONG OF THE ENGLISH

Page 324.   *It's a long way to Tipperary.*

Fire! Tommy . . . My heart capers to the banging of our cannon. Be calm, old fellow. Ah! it is
a long way, a long way to Tipperary. Since yesterday's thirst quenched without a drop of whiskey, I
shoot, every one shoots. Ah! . . . it's fine.

Who threw me his bottle? Ah, old Bob, you're
dead? Be calm, dear boy. Soon Leicester . . .
Square . . . All right! He died for old England.
The bottle is empty. Fire! Tommy, shoot some
more! We are all fighting very well, all right, the
dead are wrong.

Quiet, old boy. Ah, it is a long way, a long way to Tipperary, over there, near the pretty girl I know. She said yes when I said no. Fire, Tommy. My heart capers to the banging of our cannon.

Tommy, understand, Tommy, love has points. Yes, it's a delicate, distant lady that one never reaches except in dreams. O big mug! You dream and everything comes; the soul and the body with it. Here there is nothing but death, she is an infernal woman.

Death! Ah! if I had looked her way, the German would have taken my neck under her withered arm, and made me taste her mouth with shrapnel for teeth, suffocating my chest to torture. Good God, love hasn't anything crueller than that.

But death, one doesn't think about it, it is in front. Calm, lucky chap. Do you want to see death? She is a great, old, worn-out skeleton, floating over the battle like a standard: just now she is floating over the pointed helmets.

Fire! Tommy . . . What, you are dying too, faithful fellow? You are in the arms of the infernal woman? Get up, old man! Ah, it is a long way, a long way to Tipperary. Goodbye, Leicester Square, Goodbye, Piccadilly!

We were fifteen, hurrah, there are three of us moving. O cannon, your balls are tinged with our blood, our blood which makes our uniforms red again : in front of us the Germans are bleeding fear, they believe that we load your jaws with our hearts.

Dance, dance the jig ! Ah, yes . . . though victors we dance our jig in God's open sky. We, good boys, we are at Tipperary. Hullo, Kate; hullo, Annie; hullo, Nellie . . . Our hearts are comfortable, provided that, on earth,

our old England lives forever !

APPENDIX B

BIBLIOGRAPHY

ÉMILE VERHAEREN

LES FLAMANDES, poèmes. Bruxelles, Hochsteyn, 1883. (Réimpr. dans *Poèmes*. Paris, Société du Mercure de France, 1895.)

LES CONTES DE MINUIT, prose. Bruxelles (Collection de la " Jeune Belgique "), Franck, 1885.

JOSEPH HEYMANS, PEINTRE, critique. Bruxelles, "Société Nouvelle," 1885.

LES MOINES, poèmes. Paris, Lemerre, 1886. (Réimpr. dans *Poèmes*. Paris, Société du Mercure de France, 1895.)

FERNAND KHNOPFF, critique. Bruxelles, "Société Nouvelle," 1887.

LES SOIRS, poèmes. Bruxelles, Deman, 1887. (Réimpr. dans *Poèmes, nouvelle série*. Paris, Société du Mercure de France, 1896.)

LES DÉBÂCLES, poèmes. Bruxelles, Deman, 1888. (Réimpr. dans *Poèmes, nouvelle série*. Paris, Société du Mercure de France, 1896.)

LES FLAMBEAUX NOIRS, poèmes. Bruxelles, Deman, 1890. (Réimpr. dans *Poèmes, nouvelle série*. Paris, Société du Mercure de France, 1896.)

AU BORD DE LA ROUTE, poèmes. (Liége, extrait de *La Wallonie*.) Bruxelles, Vaillant-Carmanne, 1891. (Réimpr. dans *Poèmes*. Paris, Société du Mercure de France, 1895.)

LES APPARUS DANS MES CHEMINS, poèmes. Bruxelles, Lacomblez, 1891. (Réimpr. dans *Poèmes, IIIe série*. Paris, Société du Mercure de France, 1899.)

LES CAMPAGNES HALLUCINÉES, poèmes. Couverture et ornementation de Théo van Rysselberghe. Bruxelles, Deman, 1893. (Réimpr. à la suite des *Villes Tentaculaires*. Paris, Société du Mercure de France, 1904.)

ALMANACH, poèmes. Illustré par Théo van Rysselberghe. Bruxelles, Dietrich, 1895.

LES VILLAGES ILLUSOIRES, poèmes illustrés de quatre dessins de Georges Minne. Bruxelles, Deman, 1895. (Réimpr. dans *Poèmes, IIIe série*. Paris, Société du Mercure de France, 1899.)

POÈMES (*I^e série*). (*Les Bords de la Route. Les Flamandes. Les Moines.* augmentés de plusieurs poèmes.) Paris, Société du Mercure de France, 1895. (Réimpr. augmentés de nouveaux poèmes. Paris, Société du Mercure de France, 1900.)

LES VILLES TENTACULAIRES, poèmes. Couverture et ornementation de Théo van Rysselberghe. Bruxelles, Deman, 1895. (Réimpr.: *Les Villes Tentaculaires* précédées des *Campagnes Hallucinées*. Paris, Société du Mercure de France, 1904.)

POÈMES (*nouvelle série*). (*Les Soirs. Les Débâcles. Les Flambeaux Noirs.*) Paris, Société du Mercure de France, 1896.

LES HEURES CLAIRES, poèmes. Couverture et ornementation de Théo van Rysselberghe. Bruxelles, Deman, 1896. (Réimpr.: *Les Heures Claires*, etc. Paris, Société du Mercure de France, 1909.)

ÉMILE VERHAEREN, 1883–1896, portrait par Théo van Rysselberghe. (An anthology, "pour les amis du Poète.") (Bruxelles, Deman, 1897.)

LES AUBES, drame lyrique en 4 actes. Couverture et ornementation de Théo van Rysselberghe. Bruxelles, Deman, 1898.

LES VISAGES DE LA VIE, poèmes. Couverture et ornemen-

tation de Théo van Rysselberghe. Bruxelles, Deman, 1899.
(Réimpr.: *Les Visages de la Vie*. Paris, Société du Mercure de France, 1908.)

POÈMES (*3e série*). (*Les Visages Illusoires*. *Les Apparus dans mes Chemins*. *Les Vignes de ma Muraille*.) Paris, Société du Mercure de France (1899).

LE CLOÎTRE, drame en 4 actes, en prose et en vers. Couverture et ornementation de Théo van Rysselberghe. Bruxelles, Deman, 1900. (Réimpr. dans *Deux Drames*. Paris, Société du Mercure de France, 1909.)

PETITES LÉGENDES, poèmes. Couverture et ornementation de Théo van Rysselberghe. Bruxelles, Deman, 1900.

PHILIPPE II, tragédie en trois actes. Paris, Société du Mercure de France, 1901. (Réimpr. dans *Deux Drames*. Paris, Société du Mercure de France, 1909.)

LES FORCES TUMULTUEUSES, poèmes. Paris, Société du Mercure de France, 1902.

LES VILLES TENTACULAIRES, précédées des *Campagnes Hallucinées*, poèmes. Paris, Société du Mercure de France, 1904.

TOUTE LA FLANDRE: LES TENDRESSES PREMIÈRES, poèmes. Couverture et ornementation de Théo van Rysselberghe. Bruxelles, Deman, 1904.

LES HEURES D'APRÈS-MIDI, poèmes. Couverture et ornementation de Théo van Rysselberghe. Bruxelles, Deman, 1905. (Réimpr.: *Les Heures Claires*. Paris, Société du Mercure de France, 1909.)

REMBRANDT (Collection "Les Grands Artistes, leur Vie, leur Œuvre"), biographie critique illustrée de 24 reproductions hors texte. Paris, Laurens, 1905.

IMAGES JAPONAISES, texte d'É., V. . . . illustrations de Kwassou. Tokio, 1906.

LA MULTIPLE SPLENDEUR, poèmes. Paris, Société du Mercure de France, 1906.

TOUTE LA FLANDRE: LA GUIRLANDE DES DUNES, poèmes.

Couverture et ornementation de Théo van Rysselberghe.
Bruxelles, Deman, 1907.

Les Lettres Françaises en Belgique. Bruxelles, Lamertin,
1907.

Les Visages de la Vie (*Les Visages de la Vie. Les Douze
Mois*), poèmes, nouvelle édition. Paris, Société du Mercure de France, 1908.

Toute la Flandre : Les Héros. Couverture et ornementation de Théo van Rysselberghe. Bruxelles, Deman, 1908.

James Ensor, monographie. Bruxelles, E. van Oest, 1908.

Toute la Flandre : Les Villes a Pignons. Bruxelles, Deman, 1909.

Helena's Heimkehr. Leipzig, Insel-Verlag, 1909. (Translation by Stefan Zweig from ms. of *Hélène de Sparte*.)

Les Rhythmes Souverains, poèmes. Paris, Société du Mercure de France, 1910.

Pierre-Paul Rubens, critique. Bruxelles, G. van Oest & Cie.,
1910.

Les Heures du Soir, poèmes. Leipzig, Insel-Verlag, 1911.

Hélène de Sparte, tragédie en 4 actes. Paris, "Nouvelle
Revue Française," 1912.

Toute la Flandre : Les Plaines. Bruxelles, Deman, 1911.

Les Blés Mouvants, poèmes. Paris, Crès, 1912. (Réimpr. :
Les Blés Mouvants. Paris, Société du Mercure de France,
1913.)

La Belgique Sanclante. Paris, Édition de la "Nouvelle
Revue Française," 1915.

Albert Samain

Au Jardin de l'Infante, poèmes. Paris, Société du Mercure
de France, 1893. (Réimpr. : augmentée d'une partie
inédite : *L'Urne Penchée*. Paris, Société du Mercure de
France, 1897.)

Aux Flancs du Vase, poèmes. Paris, Société du Mercure de France, 1898. (Réimpr.: *Aux Flancs du Vase, suivi de Polyphème et des Poèmes Inachevés.* Paris, Société du Mercure de France, 1901.)

Le Chariot d'Or (*Le Chariot d'Or. Symphonie Héroïque*), poèmes. Paris, Société du Mercure de France, 1901.

Contes (*Xanthis. Divine. Bontemps. Hyalis, Rovère et Angisèle*). Paris, Société du Mercure de France, 1902.

Polyphème, deux actes en vers. ᐧParis, Société du Mercure de France, 1906.

Remy de Gourmont

Merlette, roman. Paris, Plon et Nourrit, 1886.

Sixtine, *Roman de la Vie Cérébrale.* Paris, Savine, 1890.

Le Latin Mystique: *Les Poètes de l'Antiphonaire et la Symbolique au Moyen Age. Préface de J.-K. Huysmans.* Paris, Société du Mercure de France, 1892.

Litanies de la Rose, poèmes. Paris, Société du Mercure de France, 1892. (Réimpr. dans *Le Pèlerin du Silence.* Paris, Société du Mercure de France, 1896.)

Lilith. Paris, des Presses des "Essais d'Art Libre," 1892. (Réimpr.: *Lilith, suivi de Théodat.* Paris, Société du Mercure de France, 1906.)

Le Fantôme, avec 2 lithographies originales de Henry de Groux. Paris, Société du Mercure de France, 1893. (Réimpr. dans *Le Pèlerin du Silence.* Paris, Société du Mercure de France, 1896.)

Théodat, poème dramatique en prose. Paris, Société du Mercure de France, 1893.

L'Idéalisme, avec un dessin de Filiger. Paris, Société du Mercure de France, 1893.

Fleurs de Jadis, poèmes. Édition elzévirienne. Sans nom d'auteur ni d'édit. (Monnoyer imprim., 1893.) (Réimpr.

dans *Le Pèlerin du Silence*. Paris, Société du Mercure de France, 1896.)

HISTOIRES MAGIQUES, contenant une lithographie de Henry de Groux. Paris, Société du Mercure de France, 1894.

HIÉROGLYPHES, poèmes. Manuscrit autographique de 19 feuillets, avec une lithographie originale de Henry de Groux en frontispice. Paris, Société du Mercure de France, 1894. (Réimpr. dans *Divertissements*. Paris, Société du Mercure de France, 1914.)

HISTOIRE TRAGIQUE DE LA PRINCESSE PHÉNISSA, expliquée en quatre épisodes. Paris, Société du Mercure de France, 1894. (Réimpr. dans *Le Pèlerin du Silence*. Paris, Société du Mercure de France, 1896.)

PROSES MOROSES (tirage à petit nombre). Paris, Société du Mercure de France, 1894. (There is a second edition of this book, undated.)

LE CHÂTEAU SINGULIER, orné de 32 vignettes en rouge et en bleu: tirage à petit nombre. Paris, Société du Mercure de France, 1894. (Réimpr. dans *Le Pèlerin du Silence*. Paris, Société du Mercure de France, 1896.)

PHOCAS, avec une couverture et 3 vignettes. Paris, Collection de l'Ymagier et se "vend au Mercure de France," 1895.

LA POÉSIE POPULAIRE. Paris, Collection de l'Ymagier et se "vend au Mercure de France," 1896.

LE MIRACLE DE THÉOPHILE, de Rutebeuf, texte du XIIIe siècle modernisé, publié avec préface. Paris, tiré de l'Ymagier et "se vend par le Mercure de France," 1896.

AUCASSIN ET NICOLETTE, chantefable du XIIIe siècle, trad. de Lacurne de Sainte-Palaye, revue et complétée d'après un texte original. Paris, L'Ymagier (1896).

L'YMAGIER. Ouvrage publié en 8 fascicules trimestriels, de 64 pages, d'octobre 1894 à juillet 1896, contenant environ 300 gravures, reproductions d'anciens bois des XVe et

XVIe siècles, grandes images coloriées, pages de vieux livres, miniatures, lithographies, bois, dessins, etc., de M.-N. Whistler, Paul Gauguin, Filiger, G. d'Espagnat, A. Seguin, O'Connor, L. Roy, etc. Paris, 1896.

ALMANACH DE L'YMAGIER, 1897, *zodiacal, astrologique, magique, cabalistique, artistique, littéraire et prophétique.* Orné de 25 bois dessinés et gravés par Georges d'Espagnat. Vignettes en rouge et en noir. Couverture en 4 couleurs. Paris, s. d.

LE PÈLERIN DU SILENCE (*Phénissa. Le Fantôme. Le Château Singulier. Le Livre des Litanies. Théâtre Muet. Le Pèlerin du Silence*). Frontispice d'Armand Seguin. Paris, Société du Mercure de France, 1896.

LE LIVRE DES MASQUES, *Portraits Symbolistes, Gloses et Documents sur les Écrivains d'Hier et d'Aujourd'hui.* Paris, Société du Mercure de France, 1896.

LES CHEVAUX DE DIOMÈDE, roman. Paris, Société du Mercure de France, 1897.

LE VIEUX ROI, tragédie nouvelle. Paris, Société du Mercure de France, 1897.

D'UN PAYS LOINTAIN, contes. Paris, Société du Mercure de France, 1898.

LE IIe LIVRE DES MASQUES. Paris, Société du Mercure de France, 1898.

LES SAINTES DU PARADIS. Dix-neuf petits poèmes, ornés de XIX bois originaux dessinés et taillés par Georges d'Espagnat. Paris, "se vend à la librairie du Mercure de France" (1898). (Réimpr. dans *Divertissements*. Paris, Société du Mercure de France, 1914.)

ESTHÉTIQUE DE LA LANGUE FRANÇAISE (*La Déformation. La Métaphore. Le Cliché. Le Vers Libre. Le Vers Populaire*). Paris, Société du Mercure de France, 1899.

LE SONGE D'UNE FEMME, roman familier. Paris, Société du Mercure de France, 1899.

La Culture des Idées (*Du Style ou de l'Écriture. La Création Subconsciente. La Dissociation des Idées. Stéphane Mallarmé et l'Idée de Décadence. Le Paganisme Éternel. La Morale de l'Amour. Ironies et Paradoxes*). Paris, Société du Mercure de France, 1900.

Oraisons Mauvaises, poèmes. Ornés par Georges d'Espagnat de vignettes en deux tons. Paris, Société du Mercure de France, 1900. (Réimpr. dans *Divertissements*. Paris, Société du Mercure de France, 1914.)

Simone, *Poème Champêtre* (1892). Paris, Société du Mercure de France, 1901. (Tirage à petit nombre sur papier verge, couverture en papier peint.) (Réimpr. dans *Divertissements*. Paris, Société du Mercure de France, 1914.)

Le Chemin de Velours, *Nouvelles Dissociations d'Idées*. Paris, Société du Mercure de France, 1902.

Le Problème du Style. *Questions d'Art, de Littérature et de Grammaire*, avec une préface et un index des noms cités. Paris, Société du Mercure de France, 1902.

Épilogues. *Réflexions sur la Vie (1895-1898)*. Paris, Société du Mercure de France, 1903.

Physique de L'Amour. *Essai sur l'Instinct Sexuel*. Paris, Société du Mercure de France, 1903.

Épilogues. *Réflexions sur la Vie, 2ᵉ série (1899-1901)*. Paris, Société du Mercure de France, 1904.

Judith Gautier, biographie illustrée de portrait frontispice de John Sargent, et d'autogr. etc. Paris, Biblioth., internat. d'édit., 1904.

Promenades Littéraires. Paris, Société du Mercure de France, 1904.

Promenades Philosophiques. Paris, Société du Mercure de France, 1905.

Épilogues. *Réflexions sur la Vie, 3ᵉ série (1902-1904)*. Paris, Société du Mercure de France, 1905.

PROMENADES LITTÉRAIRES, *2ᵉ série.* Paris, Société du Mercure de France, 1906.

UNE NUIT AU LUXEMBOURG, roman. Paris, Société du Mercure de France, 1906.

UN CŒUR VIRGINAL, roman. Couverture illustrée par Georges d'Espagnat. Paris, Société du Mercure de France, 1907.

DIALOGUES DES AMATEURS SUR LES CHOSES DU TEMPS (1905–1907). (*Épilogues, 4ᵉ série.*) Paris, Société du Mercure de France, 1907.

PROMENADES PHILOSOPHIQUES, *2ᵉ série.* Paris, Société du Mercure de France, 1908.

PROMENADES LITTÉRAIRES, *3ᵉ série.* Paris, Société du Mercure de France, 1909.

NOUVEAUX DIALOGUES DES AMATEURS SUR LES CHOSES DU TEMPS (1907–1910). (*Épilogues, 5ᵉ série.*) Paris, Société du Mercure de France, 1909.

PROMENADES PHILOSOPHIQUES, *3ᵉ série.* Paris, Société du Mercure de France, 1909.

COULEURS (*Contes Nouveaux suivis de Choses Anciennes*). Paris, Société du Mercure de France, 1912.

PROMENADES LITTÉRAIRES, *4ᵉ série.* Paris, Société du Mercure de France, 1912.

DIVERTISSEMENTS (*Hiéroglyphes. Les Saintes du Paradis. Oraisons Mauvaises. Simone. Paysages Spirituels. Le Vieux Coffret. La Main*), poèmes en vers. Paris, Société du Mercure de France, 1914.

LETTRES D'UN SATYRE. Paris, G. Crès, édit.

LE CHAT DE MISÈRE. *Idées et Paysages.* (Messein, édit. Collection des Trente.)

DANTE, BEATRICE ET LA POÉSIE AMOUREUSE, critique. (Série, "Les Hommes et les Idées.") Paris, Société du Mercure de France. s. d.

LA BELGIQUE LITTÉRAIRE. Paris, G. Crès, 1915.

PENDANT L'ORAGE. Paris, Librairie Champion, 1915.

HENRI DE RÉGNIER

LENDEMAINS, poésies. Paris, Vanier, 1885. (Réimpr. dans le recueil: *Premiers Poèmes*. Paris, Société du Mercure de France, 1899.)

APAISEMENT, poésies. Paris, Vanier, 1886. (Réimpr.: *Premiers Poèmes*. Paris, Société du Mercure de France, 1899.)

SITES, poèmes. Paris, Vanier, 1887. (Réimpr.: *Premiers Poèmes*. Paris, Société du Mercure de France, 1899.)

ÉPISODES, poèmes. Paris, Vanier, 1888. (Réimpr.: *Premiers Poèmes*. Paris, Société du Mercure de France, 1899.)

POÈMES ANCIENS ET ROMANESQUES, 1887–1889. Paris, Librairie de l'Art Indépendant, 1890. (Réimpr. dans le recueil: *Poèmes, 1887–1892*. Paris, Société du Mercure de France, 1895.)

ÉPISODES, SITES ET SONNETS, poèmes. Paris, Vanier, 1891. (Réimpr.: *Premiers Poèmes*. Paris, Société du Mercure de France, 1895.)

TEL QU'EN SONGE, poèmes. Paris, Librairie de l'Art Indépendant, 1892. (Réimpr.: *Poèmes, 1887–1892*. Paris, Société du Mercure de France, 1895.)

CONTES A SOI-MÊME, prose. Paris, Librairie de l'Art Indépendant, 1894. (Réimpr.: *La Canne de Jaspe*. Paris, Société du Mercure de France, 1897.)

LE BOSQUET DE PSYCHÉ, prose. Bruxelles, Lacomblez, 1894. (Réimpr. dans l'ouvrage suivant: *Figures et Caractères*. Paris, Société du Mercure de France, 1901.)

LE TRÈFLE NOIR, prose. Paris, Société du Mercure de France, 1895. (Réimpr. dans *La Canne de Jaspe*. Paris, Société du Mercure de France, 1897.)

ARÉTHUSE, poèmes. Paris, Librairie de l'Art Indépendant, 1895. (Réimpr. dans le recueil: *Les Jeux Rustiques et Divins*. Paris, Société du Mercure de France, 1897.)

POÈMES, 1887–1892 (*Poèmes Anciens et Romanesques. Tel Qu'en Songe*). Paris, Société du Mercure de France, 1895.

LES JEUX RUSTIQUES ET DIVINS, poèmes. (*Aréthuse. Les Roseaux de la Flûte. Inscriptions pour les Treize Portes de la Ville. La Corbeille des Heures. Poèmes Divers*.) Paris, Société du Mercure de France, 1897.

LA CANNE DE JASPE, contes. (*M. d'Amercœur. Le Trèfle Noir. Contes à Soi-Même*.) Paris, Société du Mercure de France, 1897.

PREMIERS POÈMES (*Les Lendemains. Apaisement. Sites. Épisodes. Sonnets. Poésies Diverses*). Paris, Société du Mercure de France, 1899.

LE TRÈFLE BLANC, prose. Paris, Société du Mercure de France, 1899. (Réimpr. dans *Couleur du Temps*. Paris, Société du Mercure de France, 1908.)

LA DOUBLE MAÎTRESSE, roman. Paris, Société du Mercure de France, 1900,

LES MÉDAILLES D'ARGILE, poèmes. Paris, Société du Mercure de France, 1900.

FIGURES ET CARACTÈRES (*Michelet. Alfred de Vigny. Hugo. Stéphane Mallarmé. Le Bosquet de Psyché*, etc., etc.). Paris, Société du Mercure de France, 1901.

LES AMANTS SINGULIERS, nouvelles. (*La Femme de Marbre. Le Rival. La Courte Vie de Balthasar Aldramin, Vénitien*.) Paris, Société du Mercure de France, 1901.

LE BON PLAISIR, roman. Paris, Société du Mercure de France, 1902.

LA CITÉ DES EAUX, poèmes. Paris, Société du Mercure de France, 1902.

LE MARIAGE DE MINUIT, roman contemporain. Paris, Société du Mercure de France, 1903.

LES VACANCES D'UN JEUNE HOMME SAGE, roman. Paris, Société du Mercure de France, 1903.

LES RENCONTRES DE M. DE BRÉOT, roman. Paris, Société du
Mercure de France, 1904.

LE PASSÉ VIVANT, roman moderne. Paris, Société du Mercure
de France, 1905.

LA SANDALE AILÉE (1903–1905), poèmes. Paris, Société du
Mercure de France, 1906.

SUJETS ET PAYSAGES, critique. Paris, Société du Mercure de
France, 1906.

ESQUISSES VÉNITIENNES, illustr. de Maxime Dethomas. Paris,
Collection de "L'Art Décoratif," 1906.

L'AMOUR ET LE PLAISIR, histoire galante. Paris, Barnéoud,
1906. (Réimpr. dans *Couleur du Temps*. Paris, Société
du Mercure de France, 1908.)

LA PEUR DE L'AMOUR, roman. Paris, Société du Mercure de
France, 1907.

TROIS CONTES A SOI-MÊME. (*Le Sixième Mariage de Barbe-
Bleue. Le Récit de la Dame des Sept Miroirs. Le Hertoir
Vivant.*) Miniatures de Maurice Ray. Paris, pour les
Cent Bibliophiles, 1907.

LES SCRUPULES DE SGANARELLE, comédie en trois actes et en
prose. Paris, Société du Mercure de France, 1908.

COULEUR DU TEMPS, contes. (*Le Trèfle Blanc. L'Amour et le
Plaisir. Tiburce et Ses Amis. Contes pour les Treize.*)
Paris, Société du Mercure de France, 1908.

LA FLAMBÉE, roman. Paris, Société du Mercure de France,
1909.

LE MIROIR DES HEURES (1906–1910), poèmes. Paris, Société
du Mercure de France, 1911.

L'AMPHISBÈNE, roman moderne. Paris, Société du Mercure
de France, 1912.

LE PLATEAU DE LAQUE, contes. Paris, Société du Mercure
de France, 1913.

PORTRAITS ET SOUVENIRS, critique. Paris, Société du Mercure
de France, 1913.

ROMAINE MIRMAULT, roman. Paris, Société du Mercure de France, 1914.

FRANCIS JAMMES

SIX SONNETS. Orthez, Typographie J. Goude-Dumesnil, 1891.

VERS. Orthez, Typographie J. Goude-Dumesnil, 1892.

VERS. Orthez, Typographie J. Goude-Dumesnil, 1893.

VERS. Paris, Ollendorff, 1894.

UN JOUR, poème dialogué. Paris, Société du Mercure de France, 1896.

LA NAISSANCE DU POÈTE, poème. Bruxelles, édition du "Coq Rouge," 1897.

DE L'ANGÉLUS DE L'AUBE A L'ANGÉLUS DU SOIR, 1888–1897, poésies. (*De l'Angélus de l'Aube à l'Angélus du Soir. La Naissance du Poète. Un Jour. La Mort du Poète.*) Paris, Société du Mercure de France, 1898.

QUATORZE PRIÈRES. Orthez, Imprimerie E. Faget, 1898.

LA JEUNE FILLE NUE, poème. Paris, Petite Collection de "l'Ermitage," 1899.

CLARA D'ELLÉBEUSE OU L'HISTOIRE D'UNE ANCIENNE JEUNE FILLE, roman. Paris, Société du Mercure de France, 1899. (Réimpr. à la suite du *Roman du Lièvre*. Paris, Société du Mercure de France, 1903.)

LE POÈTE ET L'OISEAU, poésies. Paris, Petite Collection de "l'Ermitage," 1899.

LE DEUIL DES PRIMEVÈRES, poèmes, 1898–1900. (*Élégies. La Jeune Fille Nue. Le Poète et l'Oiseau. Poésies Diverses. Quatorze Prières.*) Paris, Société du Mercure de France, 1901.

ALMAÏDE D'ETREMONT OU L'HISTOIRE D'UNE JEUNE FILLE PASSIONNÉE, roman. Paris, Société du Mercure de France, 1901. (Réimpr. à la suite du *Roman du Lièvre*. Paris, Société du Mercure de France, 1903.)

Le Triomphe de la Vie, poèmes, 1900–1901. (*Jean de Noarrieu.*
Existences.) Paris, Société du Mercure de France, 1902.

Le Roman du Lièvre. (*Clara d'Ellébeuse. Almaïde d'Etremont.*
Les Choses. Contes. Notes sur des Oasis. Sur J.-J. Rousseau.)
Paris, Société du Mercure de France, 1903.

Pomme d'Anis ou L'Histoire d'une Jeune Fille Infirme,
roman. Paris, Société du Mercure de France, 1904.
(Réimpr. dans *Feuilles dans le Vent.* Paris, Société du Mercure de France, 1913.)

(Cahier de Vers), vingt-cinq petits poèmes, publiés sans
titre, sans date, sans indication de lieu et sans nom d'éditeur.
Orthez, Imprimerie E. Faget (1905).

Pensée des Jardins, prose et vers. Paris, Société du Mercure
de France, 1906.

L'Église Habillée de Feuilles, poésies. Paris, Société du
Mercure de France, 1906.

Clairières dans le Ciel, poèmes, 1902–1906. (*En Dieu.*
Tristesses. Le Poète et sa Femme. Poésies Diverses. L'Église
Habillée de Feuilles.) Paris, Société du Mercure de France,
1906.

Poèmes Mesurés. Paris, Société du Mercure de France, 1908.
(A small, privately-printed edition only.)

Ma Fille Bernadette, prose. Paris, Société du Mercure de
France, 1908.

Les Géorgiques Chrétiennes, poème. Paris, Société du
Mercure de France, 1912.

Feuilles dans le Vent, prose et vers. (*Méditations. Quelque*
Hommes. Pomme d'Anis. La Brébis Égarée.) Paris,
Société du Mercure de France, 1913.

Paul Fort

La Petite Bête, comédie en un acte, en prose. Paris, Vanier,
1890.

PLUSIEURS CHOSES, poésies. Paris, Librairie de l'Art Indépendant, 1894.

PREMIÈRES LUEURS SUR LA COLLINE, poésies. Paris, Librairie de l'Art Indépendant, 1894.

MONNAIE DE FER, poésies et poèmes en prose. Paris, Librairie de l'Art Indépendant, 1894.

PRESQUE LES DOIGTS AUX CLÉS. Paris, Librairie de l'Art Indépendant, 1895.

IL Y A LÀ DES CRIS, poésies. Paris, Société du Mercure de France, 1895.

BALLADES (*Ma Légende. Mes Légendes*), poèmes en prose. Paris, Société du Mercure de France, 1896. (Réimpr. dans *Ballades Françaises, Poèmes et Ballades, 1894–1896*. Préface de Pierre Louys. Paris, Société du Mercure de France, 1897.)

BALLADES (*La Mer. Les Cloches. Les Champs*), poèmes en prose. Paris, édition du "Livre d'Art et de l'Épreuve," 1896. (Réimpr. dans *Ballades Françaises, Poèmes et Ballades, 1894–1896*. Préface de Pierre Louys. Paris, Société du Mercure de France, 1897.)

BALLADES (*Les Saisons. Aux Champs, sur la Route et devant l'Atre. Mes Légendes. L'Orage*), poèmes en prose. Paris, Société du Mercure de France, 1896. (Réimpr. dans *Ballades Françaises, Poèmes et Ballades, 1894–1896*. Préface de Pierre Louys. Paris, Société du Mercure de France, 1897.)

BALLADES (*Louis XI, Curieux Homme*), poèmes en prose. Paris, Société du Mercure de France, 1896. (Réimpr. dans *Ballades Françaises, Poèmes et Ballades, 1894–1896*. Préface de Pierre Louys. Paris, Société du Mercure de France, 1897.)

BALLADES FRANÇAISES, *première série*. Préface de Pierre Louys. Paris, Société du Mercure de France, 1897.

MONTAGNE. FORÊT. PLAINE. MER. *Ballades Françaises, IIe série*. Paris, Société du Mercure de France, 1898.

2 I

Le Roman de Louis XI, *Ballades Françaises, IIIe série.*
Paris, Société du Mercure de France, 1899.

Les Idylles Antiques, *Ballades Françaises, IVe série.* Paris,
Société du Mercure de France, 1900.

L'Amour Marin, *Ballades Françaises, V^e série.* Paris, Société
du Mercure de France, 1900.

Paris Sentimental ou le Roman de nos Vingt Ans, *Ballades
Françaises, VIe série.* Paris, Société du Mercure de France,
1902.

Les Hymnes de Feu, précédés de *Lucienne, Ballades Françaises, VIIe série.* Paris, Société du Mercure de France,
1903.

Coxcomb ou l'Homme tout Nu Tombé du Paradis, *Ballades
Françaises, VIIIe série.* Précédé de : *Le Livre des Visions
— Henri III.* Paris, Société du Mercure de France, 1906.

Ile-de-France (Paris), *Ballades Françaises, IXe série.* (Collection "Vers et Prose.") Paris, Figuière (1908).

Saint-Jean-aux-Bois. (*Coucy-le-Château et Jouv-en-Josas.*)
(Collection "Vers et Prose.") Paris, Figuière (1908). (Privately printed.)

Mortcerf, *Ballades Françaises, X^e série.* Précédé d'une
Étude sur les Ballades Françaises, par Louis Mandin. (Collection "Vers et Prose.") Paris, Figuière (1909).

La Tristresse de L'Homme, *Ballades Françaises, XIe série.*
Précédé du : *Repos de l'Ame au Bois de l'Hautil.* (Collection "Vers et Prose.") Paris, Figuière (1910).

L'Aventure Éternelle, *Ballades Françaises, XIIe série.*
Suivie de : *En Gatinais.* (Collection "Vers et Prose.")
Paris, Figuière, 1911.

Montlhéry-la-Bataille, *Ballades Françaises, XIIIe série.*
Suivie de : *L'Aventure Éternelle (Livre II).* (Collection
"Vers et Prose.") Paris, Figuière, 1912.

Vivre en Dieu, *Ballades Françaises, XIVe série.* Suivi de :
Naissance du Printemps à la Ferté-Milon, et de *L'Aventure*

Éternelle (*Livre III*). (Collection "Vers et Prose.") Paris, Figuière, 1912.

CHANSONS POUR ME CONSOLER D'ÊTRE HEUREUX, *Ballades Françaises*, *XVe série*. Suivies de: *L'Aventure Éternelle* (*Livre IV*). (Collection "Vers et Prose.") Paris, Figuière, 1913.

CHOIX DE BALLADES FRANÇAISES. (Collection "Vers et Prose.") Paris, Figuière, 1913.

LES NOCTURNES, *Ballades Françaises*, *XVIe série*. (Collection "Vers et Prose.") Paris, Figuière, 1914.

REFERENCE BOOKS

Bazalgette, Léon: ÉMILE VERHAEREN. (Opinions et une bibliographie par Ad. van Bever.) (Série, "Les Célébrités d'Aujourd'hui.") Paris, Sansot, 1907.

Bersaucourt, Albert de: CONFÉRENCE SUR ÉMILE VERHAEREN. Paris, Jouve, 1908.

Boër, Julius de: ÉMILE VERHAEREN. (Portrait par Théo van Rysselberghe et fac-simile d'autographe.) s. l. n. d. (1907). (Série, "Mannen en Vrouwen van beteekenis in onze dagen.")

Bosch, Firmin van den: IMPRESSIONS DE LITTÉRATURE CONTEMPORAINE. Bruxelles, Vromont et Cie, 1905.

Buisseret, Georges: L'ÉVOLUTION IDÉOLOGIQUE D'ÉMILE VERHAEREN. (Série "Les Hommes et les Idées.") Paris, Société du Mercure de France, 1910.

Casier, Jean: LES "MOINES" D'ÉMILE VERHAEREN. Gand, Leliaer & Siffer, 1887.

Gauchez, Maurice: ÉMILE VERHAEREN. Bruxelles, édition de "Thyrse," 1908.

Guilbeaux, Henri: ÉMILE VERHAEREN. Verviers, Wauthy, 1908.

Hauser, Otto: DIE BELGISCHE LYRIK VON 1880–1900. Grossenhain, Baumert und Rouge, 1902.

Heumann, Albert: Le Mouvement Littéraire Belge. Paris, Société du Mercure de France, 1913.

Horrent, Désiré: Écrivains Belges d'Aujourd'Hui. Bruxelles, Lacomblez, 1904.

Lemonnier, Camille: La Vie Belge. Paris, E. Fasquelle, 1905.

Mockel, Albert: Émile Verhaeren. Paris, Société du Mercure de France, 1895.

Ramaekers, Georges: Émile Verhaeren. (I. L'Homme du Nord. II. L'Homme Moderne.) Bruxelles, éditions de "La Lutte," 1900.

Rency, Georges: Physionomies Littéraires. Bruxelles, Dechenne et Cie., 1907.

Schellenberg, E. A.: Émile Verhaeren. Leipzig, Xenien-Verlag, 1911.

Schlaf, Johannes: Émile Verhaeren. Berlin & Leipzig, Schuster & Loeffler (1905).

Smet, Abbé Jos. de: Émile Verhaeren, sa Vie et ses Œuvres. Malines, 1909.

Wenguerowa, Zinaida: Portraits Littéraires. (Tome 2.) Étude reproduite en partie dans le Grand Dictionnaire Encyclopédique Russe, édition Brokaus et Efron, tome supplémentaire I. Saint Pétersbourg, 1905.

Zweig, Stefan: Émile Verhaeren. (Translated from the German into English by J. Bithell.) London, Constable; Boston & New York, Houghton Mifflin Company, 1914.

Bersaucourt, Albert de: Conférence sur A. Samain, Prononcée le 4 Décembre 1907 au Cercle des Étudiants Catholiques du Luxembourg. Paris, Bonvalot-Jouve, s.d.

Bocquet, Léon: Albert Samain, sa Vie, son Œuvre. Avec un portrait et un autogr. Préface de Francis Jammes. Paris, Société du Mercure de France, 1905.

Coppée, François: Mon Franc-Parler. (2ᵉ série.) Paris, Lemeurre, 1894.

Jarry, Alfred: SOUVENIRS. Paris, V. Lemasle, 1907.

Vallette, Alfred: ALBERT SAMAIN, notice dans *Les Portraits du Prochain Siècle*. Paris, Girard, 1894.

Delior, Paul: REMY DE GOURMONT ET SON ŒUVRE. (Série "Les Hommes et les Idées.") Paris, Société du Mercure de France, 1909.

Denise, Louis: REMY DE GOURMONT, notice publiée dans *Les Portraits du Prochain Siècle*. Paris, Girard, 1894.

Escoube, Paul: PRÉFÉRENCES. Paris, Société du Mercure de France, 1913.

Goffin, Arnold: A PROPOS DE STYLE ET D'ESTHÉTIQUE. Bruxelles, Société Belge de Librairie, 1903.

Miomandre, Francis de: VISAGES. Bruges, A. Herbert, 1907.

Poinsot, M. C.: ANTHOLOGIE DES POÈTES NORMANDS CONTEMPORAINS. Paris, Floury, 1903.

Querlon, Pierre de: REMY DE GOURMONT. (Opinions, documents et une bibliographie par Ad. van Bever.) (Série "Les Célébrités d'Aujourd'hui.") Paris, Sansot, 1903.

Vorluni, Giuseppe: REMY DE GOURMONT. Napoli, Detken & Rocholl, 1911.

Gourmont, Jean de: HENRI DE RÉGNIER ET SON ŒUVRE. Avec un portrait et un autogr. (Bibliographie par Ad. van Bever.) (Série "Les Hommes et les Idées.") Paris, Société du Mercure de France, 1908.

Léautaud, Paul: HENRI DE RÉGNIER. (Biogr. précédée d'un portr. illustr. et autogr. suivie d'opinions et d'une bibliographie par Ad. van Bever.) Paris, Sansot, 1904.

Mauclair, Camille: HENRI DE RÉGNIER. *Portraits du Prochain Siècle*. Paris, Girard, 1894.

Mockel, Albert: PROPOS DE LITTÉRATURE. Paris, Librairie de L'Art Indépendant, 1894.

Braun, Thomas: DES POÈTES SIMPLES: FRANCIS JAMMES. Bruxelles, "Fédération de Libre Esthétique," 1900.

Pilon, Edmond: FRANCIS JAMMES ET LE SENTIMENT DE LA NATURE. (Bibliographie par Ad. van Bever.) (Série,

"Les Hommes et les Idées.") Paris, Société du Mercure de France, 1908.

Hirsch, Paul-Armand: Paul Fort, notice dans *Les Portraits du Prochain Siècle*. Paris, Girard, 1894.

Mandin, Louis: Étude sur les "Ballades Françaises" de Paul Fort. (Collection "Vers et Prose.") Paris, Figuière, 1911.

Beaunier, André: La Poésie Nouvelle. Paris, Société du Mercure de France, 1902.

Bever, Ad. van, et Léautaud, Paul: Poètes d'Aujourd'hui (nouvelle édition). Paris, Société du Mercure de France, 1910.

Blum, Léon: En Lisant. *Réflexions Critiques*. Paris, Société d'Éd. Littér., 1906.

Bordeaux, Henri: Les Écrivains et les Mœurs, Essais et Figurines (1897–1900). Paris, Plon, 1900.

Brisson, Adolphe: Pointes Sèches. Paris, A. Colin, 1898.

Coulon, Marcel: Témoignages. Paris, Société du Mercure de France, 1911.

Deschamps, Gaston: La Vie et les Livres. (*3ᵉ série*.) Paris, A. Colin, 1896.

Doumic, René: Les Jeunes. Paris, Perrin, 1896.

Duhamel, Georges: Les Poètes et la Poésie (1912–1913). Paris, Société du Mercure de France, 1914.

Florian-Parmentier: Toutes les Lyres. (Anthologie Critique ornée de dessins et de portraits, *nouvelle série*.) Paris, Gastein-Serge (1911).

Fons, Pierre: L'Ame Latine. *Nos Maîtres*. Toulouse, 1903.

Fons, Pierre: Le Réveil de Pallas. Paris, Sansot, 1906.

Gilbert, Eugène: France et Belgique. Paris, Plon, Nourrit et Cie., 1905.

Gosse, Edmund: French Profiles. London, Heinemann, 1902.

Gregh, Fernand: La Fenêtre Ouverte. Paris, Fasquelle, 1901.

Hamel, A. G. Van: HET LETTERKUNDIG LEVEN VAN FRANK-
RIJK. Amsterdam, Gids, 1907.

Heumann, Albert: LE MOUVEMENT LITTÉRAIRE BELGE D'EX-
PRESSION FRANÇAISE DEPUIS 1880. Paris, Société du
Mercure de France, 1913.

Huret, Jules: ENQUÊTE SUR L'ÉVOLUTION LITTÉRAIRE. Paris,
Charpentier-Fasquelle, 1891.

Key, Ellen: SEELEN UND WERKE. Berlin, S. Fischer, 1911.

Kinon, Victor: PORTRAITS D'AUTEURS. Bruxelles, Dechenne,
1910.

Lasserre, Pierre: LE ROMANTISME FRANÇAIS. Paris, Société du
Mercure de France, 1913.

Lazare, Bernard: FIGURES CONTEMPORAINES. Paris, Perrin,
1895.

Mercereau, Alexandre: LA LITTÉRATURE ET LES IDÉES NOU-
VELLES. Paris, Figuière; London, Stephen Swift, 1912.

Nouhuys, W. G. Van: VAN OVER DE GREZEN, STUDIEN EN
CRITIEKEN. Baarn, Hollandia Drukkerij, 1906.

Oppeln-Bronikowski, F. von: DAS JUNGE FRANKREICH. Berlin,
Œsterheld & Co., 1908.

Pellissier, Georges: ÉTUDES DE LITTÉRATURE CONTEMPORAINE.
Paris, Perrin, 1898.

Pellissier, Georges: ÉTUDES DE LITTÉRATURE ET DE MORALE
CONTEMPORAINE. Paris, Perrin, 1905.

Retté, Adolphe: LE SYMBOLISME. Paris, Librairie Léon Vanier,
1903.

Rimestad, Christian: FRANSK POESI I DET NITTENDE AARHUN-
DREDE. Kopenhague, Det Schubotheske, 1906.

Souza, Robert de: LA POÉSIE POPULAIRE ET LE LYRISME
SENTIMENTAL. Paris, Société du Mercure de France, 1899.

Tellier, Jules: NOS POÈTES. Paris, Despret, 1888.

Thompson, Vance: FRENCH PORTRAITS. Boston, Richard G.
Badger & Co., 1900; New York, Mitchell Kennerley,
1915.

Velley, Charles et Le Cardonnel, Georges: LA LITTÉRATURE CONTEMPORAINE, 1905. *Opinions des Écrivains de ce Temps.* Paris, Société du Mercure de France, 1906.

Vigié-Lecoq, E.: LA POÉSIE CONTEMPORAINE (1884–1896). Paris, Société du Mercure de France, 1897.

Visan, Tancrède de: L'ATTITUDE DU LYRISME CONTEMPORAINE. Paris, Société du Mercure de France, 1911.

Wyzewa, Théodor de: NOS MAÎTRES. Paris, Perrin, 1895.

Zilliacus, Emil: DEN NYARE FRANSKA POESIN OCH ANTIKEN. Helsingfors, Aktiebolaget Handelstryckeriet, 1905.